HOW TO START A BUSINESS IN FLORIDA

with forms

Sixth Edition

Mark Warda
Attorney at Law

SPHINX® PUBLISHING
AN IMPRINT OF SOURCEBOOKS, INC.®
NAPERVILLE, ILLINOIS

Sixth Edition, 2001

Published by: **Sphinx® Publishing, An Imprint of Sourcebooks, Inc.®**

Naperville Office
P.O. Box 4410
Naperville, Illinois 60567-4410
630-961-3900
Fax: 630-961-2168
http://www.sourcebooks.com

This publication is designed to provide accurate and authoritative information in regard to the subject matter covered. It is sold with the understanding that the publisher is not engaged in rendering legal, accounting, or other professional service. If legal advice or other expert assistance is required, the services of a competent professional person should be sought.

From a Declaration of Principles Jointly Adopted by a Committee of the American Bar Association and a Committee of Publishers and Associations

This product is not a substitute for legal advice.

Disclaimer required by Texas statutes.

Library of Congress Cataloging-in-Publication Data

Warda, Mark.
     How to start a business in Florida : with forms / Mark Warda.-- 6th ed.
         p. cm. -- (Legal survival guides)
     Includes bibliographical references and index.
     ISBN 1-57248-152-8
     1. Business enterprises--Law and legislation--Florida--Popular works. 2. Business enterprises--Taxation--Law and legislation--Florida--Popular works. I. Title. II. Series.

KFF205.Z9 W37 2001
346.759'065--dc21   2001020721

Contents

Restraining Trade
Commercial Bribery
Intellectual Property Protection

Using Self-Help
Law Books

Before using a self-help law book, you should realize the advantages and disadvantages of doing your own legal work and understand the challenges and diligence that this requires.

THE GROWING TREND

Rest assured that you won't be the first or only person handling your own legal matter. For example, in some states, more than seventy-five percent of divorces and other cases have at least one party representing him or herself. Because of the high cost of legal services, this is a major trend and many courts are struggling to make it easier for people to represent themselves. However, some courts are not happy with people who do not use attorneys and refuse to help them in any way. For some, the attitude is, "Go to the law library and figure it out for yourself."

We at Sphinx write and publish self-help law books to give people an alternative to the often complicated and confusing legal books found in most law libraries. We have made the explanations of the law as simple and easy to understand as possible. Of course, unlike an attorney advising an individual client, we cannot cover every conceivable possibility.

COST/VALUE ANALYSIS

Whenever you shop for a product or service, you are faced with various levels of quality and price. In deciding what product or service to buy, you make a cost/value analysis on the basis of your willingness to pay and the quality you desire.

When buying a car, you decide whether you want transportation, comfort, status, or sex appeal. Accordingly, you decide among such choices as a Neon, a Lincoln, a Rolls Royce, or a Porsche. Before making a decision, you usually weigh the merits of each option against the cost.

When you get a headache, you can take a pain reliever (such as aspirin) or visit a medical specialist for a neurological examination. Given this choice, most people, of course, take a pain reliever, since it costs only pennies; whereas a medical examination costs hundreds of dollars and takes a lot of time. This is usually a logical choice because it is rare to need anything more than a pain reliever for a headache. But in some cases, a headache may indicate a brain tumor and failing to see a specialist right away can result in complications. Should everyone with a headache go to a specialist? Of course not, but people treating their own illnesses must realize that they are betting on the basis of their cost/value analysis of the situation. They are taking the most logical option.

The same cost/value analysis must be made when deciding to do one's own legal work. Many legal situations are very straight forward, requiring a simple form and no complicated analysis. Anyone with a little intelligence and a book of instructions can handle the matter without outside help.

But there is always the chance that complications are involved that only an attorney would notice. To simplify the law into a book like this, several legal cases often must be condensed into a single sentence or paragraph. Otherwise, the book would be several hundred pages long and too complicated for most people. However, this simplification necessarily leaves out many details and nuances that would apply to special or unusual situations. Also, there are many ways to interpret most legal questions. Your case may come before a judge who disagrees with the analysis of our authors.

Therefore, in deciding to use a self-help law book and to do your own legal work, you must realize that you are making a cost/value analysis. You have decided that the money you will save in doing it yourself outweighs the chance that your case will not turn out to your satisfaction. Most people handling their own simple legal matters never have a problem, but occasionally people find that it ended up costing them more to have an attorney straighten out the situation than it would have if they had hired an attorney in the beginning. Keep this in mind if you decide to handle your own case, and be sure to consult an attorney if you feel you might need further guidance.

LOCAL RULES

The next thing to remember is that a book which covers the law for the entire nation, or even for an entire state, cannot possibly include every procedural difference of every county court. Whenever possible, we provide the exact form needed; however, in some areas, each county, or even each judge, may require unique forms and procedures. In our *state* books, our forms usually cover the majority of counties in the state, or provide examples of the type of form that will be required. In our *national* books, our forms are sometimes even more general in nature but are designed to give a good idea of the type of form that will be needed in most locations. Nonetheless, keep in mind that your *state*, county, or judge may have a requirement, or use a form, that is not included in this book.

You should not necessarily expect to be able to get all of the information and resources you need solely from within the pages of this book. This book will serve as your guide, giving you specific information whenever possible and helping you to find out what else you will need to know. This is just like if you decided to build your own backyard deck. You might purchase a book on how to build decks. However, such a book would not include the building codes and permit requirements of every city, town, county, and township in the nation; nor would it include the lumber, nails, saws, hammers, and other materials and tools you would need to actually build the deck. You would use the book as your guide, and then do some work and research involving such matters as whether you need a permit of some kind, what type and grade of wood are available in your area, whether to use hand tools or power tools, and how to use those tools.

Before using the forms in a book like this, you should check with your court clerk to see if there are any local rules of which you should be aware, or local forms you will need to use. Often, such forms will require the same information as the forms in the book but are merely laid out differently, use slightly different language, or use different color paper so the clerks can easily find them. They will sometimes require additional information.

CHANGES IN THE LAW

Besides being subject to local rules and practices, the law is subject to change at any time. The courts and the legislatures of all fifty states are constantly revising the laws. It is possible that while you are reading this book, some aspect of the law is being changed.

In most cases, the change will be of minimal significance. A form will be redesigned, additional information will be required, or a waiting period will be extended. As a result, you might need to revise a form, file an extra form, or wait out a longer time period; these types of changes will not usually affect the outcome of your case. On the other hand, sometimes a major part of the law is changed, the entire law in a particular area is rewritten, or a case that was the basis of a central legal point is overruled. In such instances, your entire ability to pursue your case may be impaired.

Again, you should weigh the value of your case against the cost of an attorney and make a decision as to what you believe is in your best interest.

INTRODUCTION

Each year about a hundred thousand new corporations are registered in Florida and thousands more partnerships and proprietorships open for business. Florida is booming! Nearly 1,000 people move to the state each day and the demand for new products and services keeps growing. Some have said Florida is now what California was to the '60s—a thriving, trend-setting center of activity where little shops can bloom into expansive enterprises.

The best way to take part in this boom is to run your own business. Be your own boss and be as successful as you dare to be.

But if you do not follow the laws of the state, your progress can be slowed or stopped by government fines, civil judgments or even criminal penalties.

This book is intended to give you the framework for legally opening a business in Florida. It also includes information on where to find special rules for each type of business. If you have problems that are not covered by this book, you should seek out an attorney who can be available for your ongoing needs.

In order to cover all of the aspects of any business you are thinking of starting, you should read through this entire book, rather than skipping to the parts that look most interesting. There are many laws that may not sound like they apply to you but which do have provisions which will affect your business.

In recent years the government bureaucracies have been amending and lengthening their forms regularly. The forms included in this book were the most recent available at the time of publication. It is possible that some may be revised at the time you read this book, but in most cases previous versions of the forms will still be accepted.

DECIDING TO START A BUSINESS

1

If you are reading this book, then you have probably made a serious decision to take the plunge and start your own business. Hundreds of thousands of people make the same decision each year and many of them become very successful. Some barely make a living, others become billionaires. A lot of them also fail. Knowledge can only help your chances of success. You need to know why some succeed while others fail. Some of what follows may seem obvious, but to someone wrapped up in a new business idea, some of this information is occasionally overlooked.

KNOW YOUR STRENGTHS

The last thing a budding entrepreneur wants to hear is that he is not cut out for running his own business. Those "do you have what it takes" quizzes are ignored with the fear that the answer might be one the entrepreneur does not want to hear. But even if you lack some skills you can be successful if you know where to get them.

You should consider all of the skills and knowledge that running a successful business means and decide whether you have what it takes. If you do not, it does not necessarily mean you are doomed to be an employee all your life. Perhaps you just need a partner who has the skills you lack. Perhaps you can hire someone with the skills you need, or you can structure your business to avoid areas where you are weak. If those do not work, maybe you can learn the skills.

For example, if you are not good at dealing with employees (either you are too passive and get taken advantage of, or too tough and scare them off) you can:

- handle product development yourself and have a partner or - manager deal with employees;

- take seminars in employee management; or

- structure your business so that you don't need employees. Either use independent contractors or set yourself up as an independent contractor.

Here are some of the factors to consider when planning your business:

- If it takes months or years before your business turns a profit do you have the resources to hold out? Businesses have gone under or have been sold just before they were about to take off, and staying power is an important ingredient to success.

- Are you willing to put in a lot of overtime to make your business a success? Owners of businesses do not set their own hours; the business sets them for the owner. Many business owners work long hours seven days a week, but they enjoy running their business more than family picnics or fishing.

- Are you willing to do the dirtiest or most unpleasant work of the business? Emergencies come up and employees are not always dependable. You might need to mop up a flooded room, spend a weekend stuffing 10,000 envelopes or work Christmas if someone calls in sick.

- Do you know enough about the product or service? Are you aware of the trends in the industry and what changes new technology might bring? Think of the people who started typesetting or printing businesses just before type was replaced by laser printers.

- Do you know enough about accounting and inventory to manage the business? Do you have a good "head for business?" Some people naturally know how to save money and do things profitably. Others are in the habit of buying the best and the most expensive of everything. The latter can be fatal to a struggling new business.

- Are you good at managing employees?

- Do you know how to sell your product or service? You can have the best product on the market but people do not know about it. If you are a wholesaler, shelf space in major stores is hard to get, especially for a new company without a record, a large line of products, or a large advertising budget.

- Do you know enough about getting publicity? The media receive thousands of press releases and announcements each day and most are thrown away. Do not count on free publicity to put your name in front of the public.

Know Your Business

Not only do you need to know the concept of a business, but you need the experience of working in a business. Maybe you always dreamed of running a bed and breakfast or having your own pizza place. Have you ever worked in such a business? If not, you may have no idea of the day-to-day headaches and problems of the business. For example, do you really know how much to allow for theft, spoilage, and unhappy customers.

You might feel silly taking an entry level job at a pizza place when you would rather start your own, but it might be the most valuable preparation you could have. A few weeks of seeing how a business operates could mean the difference between success and failure.

Working in a business as an employee is one of the best ways to be a success at running such a business. New people with new ideas who work in old stodgy industries have been known to revolutionize them with obvious improvements that no one before dared to try.

DO THE MATH

Conventional wisdom says you need a business plan before committing yourself to a new venture, but lots of businesses are started successfully without the owner even knowing what a business plan is. They have a great concept, put it on the market and it takes off. But you at least need to do some basic calculations to see if the business can make a profit. Here are some examples:

- If you want to start a retail shop, figure out how many people are close enough to become customers, and how many other stores will be competing for those customers. Visit some of those other shops and see how busy they are. Without giving away your plans to compete, ask some general questions like "how's business?" and maybe they'll share their frustrations or successes.

- Whether you sell a good or a service, do the math to find out how much profit is in it. For example: if you plan to start a house painting company, find out what you will have to pay to hire painters; what it will cost you for all of the insurance; what bonding and licensing you will need; and what the advertising will cost you. Figure out how many jobs you can do per month and what other painters are charging. In some industries in different areas of the country there may be a large margin of profit or there may be almost no profit.

- Find out if there is a demand for your product or service. Suppose you have designed a beautiful new kind of candle and your friends all say you should open a shop because "everyone will want them." Before making a hundred of them and renting a store, bring a few to craft shows or flea markets and see what happens.

- Figure out what the income and expenses would be for a typical month of your new business. List monthly expenses such as rent, salaries, utilities, insurance, taxes, supplies, advertising, services, and other overhead. Then figure out how much profit you will average from each sale. Next, figure out how many sales you will need to cover your overhead and divide by the number of business days in the month. Can you reasonably expect that many sales? How will you get those sales?

Most types of businesses have trade associations, which often have figures on how profitable its members are. Some even have start-up kits for people wanting to start businesses. One good source of information on such organizations is the *Encyclopedia of Associations* published by Gale Research Inc. and available in many library reference sections. Producers of products to the trade often give assistance to small companies getting started to win their loyalty. Contact the largest suppliers of the products your business will be using and see if they can be of help.

SOURCES FOR FURTHER GUIDANCE

The following offices offer free or low-cost guidance for new businesses:

SCORE

Service Corps of Retired Executives. Florida is a haven for retired people and many of them are glad to give free guidance to new businesses.

Pinellas County (Clearwater)	Suncoast/Pinellas SCORE	727-532-6800
Palm Beach County (Delray Beach)	South Palm Beach SCORE	561-278-7752
Broward County	Ft. Lauderdale SCORE	954-356-7263
Lee County (Ft. Myers)	Southwest Florida SCORE	941-489-2935
St. Lucie County (Ft. Pierce)	Treasure Coast SCORE	561-489-0548
Alachua County	Gainesville SCORE	352-375-8278
Volusia/Flagler County (Holly Hills)	Volusia/Flagler SCORE	904-255-6889
South Broward County (Hollywood)	South Broward SCORE	954-966-8415
Duval County	Jacksonville SCORE	904-443-1911
Bay County (Lynn Haven)	Bay County SCORE	850-271-1108
Polk County (Lakeland)	Central Florida SCORE	863-687-5783
Citrus County (Lecanto)	Citrus County SCORE	352-621-0775
Brevard County (Melbourne)	Space Coast SCORE	407-254-2288
Dade County (Miami)	Dade SCORE	305-371-6889
Collier County (Naples)	Naples SCORE	941-254-9440
Pasco County (New Port Richey)	Pasco County SCORE	727-842-4638
Marion County (Ocala)	Ocala SCORE	352-629-5959

Orange County (Orlando)	Orlando SCORE	407-648-6476
Charlotte County (Punta Gorda)	Charlotte County SCORE	941-575-1818
Sarasota County	Manasota SCORE	941-955-1029
Leon County	Tallahassee SCORE	850-487-2665
Hillsborough County (Tampa)	Hillsborough SCORE	813-870-0125
Lake County (Tavares)	Lake-Sumter SCORE	352-365-3556
Palm Beach County	Palm Beach SCORE	561-833-1672

SMALL BUSINESS DEVELOPMENT CENTERS

Educational programs for small businesses are offered through the Small Business Development Centers at many Florida colleges and universities. You should see if they have any that could help you in any areas in which you are weak.

Alachua (Gainesville)	The University of North Florida	850-470-4980
	The University of West Florida	850-470-4980
Bay (Lynn Haven)	Gulf Coast Community College	850-271-1108
Brevard (Melbourne)	Brevard Community College	407-632-1111
Broward (Dania)	Florida International University	954-987-0100
Broward (Ft. Lauderdale)	Florida Atlantic University	954-771-6520
Dade (Miami)	Florida International University	305-348-2272
	Florida International Univ. (North)	305-919-5790
	Miami Dade Community College	305-237-1906
Duval (Jacksonville)	The University of North Florida	904-620-2476
Escambia (Pensacola)	The University of West Florida	850-595-5480
Hillsborough (Tampa)	The University of South Florida	813-905-5800
Indian River (Ft. Pierce)	Indian River Community College	561-462-4756
Lee (Fort Myers)	Florida Gulf Coast University	941-590-7316
Leon (Tallahassee)	Florida A & M University	850-599-3407
Marion (Ocala)	The University of North Florida	352-622-8763
Okaloosa (Ft. Walton Bch)	The University of West Florida	850-863-6543
Orange (Orlando)	The University of Central Florida	407-823-5554
Palm Beach (Boca Raton)	Florida Atlantic University	561-362-5620
Polk (Bartow)	The University of South Florida	941-534-4370
Seminole (Sanford)	Seminole Community College	407-328-4722
Volusia (Daytona Beach)	Daytona Beach Community College	904-947-5463

COUNTY ECONOMIC DEVELOPMENT ORGANIZATIONS

While not all counties have SCORE offices or Small Business Development Centers, every county has an organization that is involved with economic development. Some will be more helpful than others, but you should at least see what your local office has to offer.

Alachua	Gainesville Council for Economic Outreach	352-378-7300
Baker	Baker County Chamber of Commerce	904-259-6433
Bay	Bay County Chamber of Commerce	850-785-5206
Bradford	Bradford County Chamber of Commerce	904-964-5278
Brevard	Economic Development Commission	321-638-2000
Broward	Broward Economic Development Council	954-524-3113
Calhoun	Calhoun County Chamber of Commerce	850-674-4519
Charlotte	Economic Dev. Council of Charlotte County	941-627-3023
Citrus	Economic Dev. Assn. of Citrus County, Inc.	352-795-2000
Clay	Clay County Development Authority	904-264-7373
Collier	Economic Dev. Council of Collier County	941-263-8989
Columbia	Lake City Chamber of Commerce	904-752-3690
Dade	The Beacon Council	305-579-1300
DeSoto	Economic Development Director	863-993-4800
Dixie	Dixie County Development Committee	352-498-5454
Duval	Cornerstone—Partners in Progress	904-366-6652
Escambia	Committee of 100	850-438-4081
Flagler	Flagler County Committee of 100	904-447-9020
Franklin	Apalachicola Bay Chamber of Commerce	850-653-9419
Gadsden	Gadsden County Chamber of Commerce	850-627-9231
Gilchrist	Gilchrist County Industrial Dev. Association	352-463-2571
Glades	Glades County Chamber of Commerce	863-946-0061
Gulf	Port St. Joe-Gulf County Chamber	850-227-1223
Hamilton	Hamilton County Chamber of Commerce	904-792-1300
Hardee	Hardee County Chamber of Commerce	863-773-3030
Hendry	Hendry County Development Authority	863-675-6007
Hernando	Economic Dev. Comm. of Hernando Co.	352-799-7275
Highlands	Highlands County EDC-IDA	863-385-1025
Hillsborough	Greater Tampa Chamber of Commerce	813-276-9410
Holmes	Holmes County Development Commission	850-547-4682
Indian River	Indian River County Chamber of Commerce	561-567-3491
Jackson	Jackson County Development Council	850-526-4005
Jefferson	Jefferson County Chamber of Commerce	850-997-6559
Lafayette	Lafayette County Development Authority	904-294-1805
Lake	Economic Dev.t Commission of Mid-Florida, Inc.	407-422-7159
Lee	Lee County Economic Development Office	941-338-3161
Leon	Tallahassee Economic Development Council	850-224-8116
Levy	Nature Coast Business Development Authority	352-486-5470
Liberty	Liberty County Chamber of Commerce	850-643-2359
Madison	Greater Madison County Chamber	850-973-2788
Manatee	Economic Dev. Council, Manatee Ch. of Comm.	941-748-4842

Marion	Ocala-Marion County Economic Dev.Council	352-629-2757
Martin	Business Development Board of Martin County	561-221-1380
Monroe	Marathon Chamber of Commerce	305-743-5417
Nassau	Nassau County Economic Development Board	904-225-8878
Okaloosa	Economic Dev. Council of Okaloosa County, Inc.	850-651-7374
Okeechobee	Okeechobee Development Authority	941-467-5505
Orange	Economic Dev. Commission of Mid-Florida, Inc.	407-422-7159
Osceola	Economic Dev. Commission of Mid-Florida, Inc.	407-422-7159
Palm Beach	Business Dev. Bd. of Palm Beach County, Inc.	561-835-1008
Pasco	Pasco County Committee of 100, Incorporated	813-996-4075
Pinellas	Department of Economic Development	727-464-8114
Polk	Lakeland Economic Development Council	863-687-3788
Putnam	Putnam County Chamber of Commerce	904-328-5401
Santa Rosa	Santa Rosa County Council of Economic Activity	850-623-0174
Sarasota	Sarasota County Committee of 100	941-955-2508 x232
Seminole	Economic Dev. Commission of Mid-Florida, Inc.	407-422-7159
St. John	St. Augustine - St. Johns County Ch. of Comm.	904-829-6478
St. Lucie	St. Lucie County Chamber of Commerce	561-595-9999
Sumpter	Sumter County Development Council, Inc.	352-793-3003
Suwannee	Suwannee County Chamber of Commerce	904-362-3071
Taylor	Taylor County Chamber of Commerce	850-584-5366
Union	Union County Chamber of Commerce	904-964-5278
Volusia	Volusia County Business Development Corp.	904-274-3800
Wakulla	Wakulla County Chamber of Commerce	850-926-1848
Walton	Walton County Economic Dev. Council, Inc.	850-892-0555
Washington	Washington County Chamber of Commerce	850-638-4157

SMALL BUSINESS
ADMINISTRATION
OFFICES

The federal Small Business Administration has two offices in Florida.

NORTH FLORIDA DISTRICT OFFICE
7825 Baymeadows Way, Suite 100B
Jacksonville, Florida 32256
Phone: (904) 443-1900
Fax: (904) 443-1980
TDD: (904) 443-1909
http://www.sba.gov/fl/north/

SOUTH FLORIDA DISTRICT OFFICE
100 S. Biscayne Blvd. - 7th Fl.
Miami, FL 33131
(305)536-5521
Fax (305)536-5058
http://www.sba.gov/fl/south/

Choosing the Form of Your Business 2

Basic Forms of Doing Business

The four most common forms for a business in Florida are proprietorship, partnership, corporation and limited partnership. Laws have been passed in recent years that allowed creation of a new type of enterprise: *limited liability companies*. These offer new benefits for certain kinds of businesses. The characteristics, advantages and disadvantages of each are as follows:

PROPRIETORSHIP **Characteristics.** A proprietorship is one person doing business in his or her own name or under a fictitious name.

Advantages. Simplicity is just one advantage. There is also no organizational expense, and no extra tax forms or reports.

Disadvantages. The proprietor is personally liable for all debts and obligations. There is also no continuation of the business after death. All profits are directly taxable, which is certainly a disadvantage for the proprietor, and business affairs are easily mixed with personal affairs.

GENERAL **Characteristics.** This involves two or more people carrying on a
PARTNERSHIP business together and sharing the profits and losses.

Advantages. Partners can combine expertise and assets. A general partnership allows liability to be spread among more persons. Also, the business can be continued after the death of a partner if bought out by a surviving partner.

Disadvantages. Each partner is liable for acts of other partners within the scope of the business. This means that if your partner harms a customer or signs a million-dollar credit line in the partnership name, you can be personally liable. Even if left in the business, all profits are taxable. Two more disadvantages: control is shared by all parties and the death of a partner may result in liquidation. In a general partnership, it is often hard to get rid of a bad partner.

CORPORATION

Characteristics. A *corporation* is an artificial legal "person" that carries on business through its officers for its shareholders. (In Florida, one person may form a corporation and be the sole shareholder and officer.) Laws covering corporations are contained in the Florida Statutes (Fla. Stat.) Chapter (Ch.) 607. This legal person carries on business in its own name and shareholders are not necessarily liable for its acts.

An *S corporation* is a corporation that has filed Internal Revenue Service (IRS) Form 2553 choosing to have all profits taxed to the shareholders, rather than to the corporation. An S corporation files a tax return but pays no federal or state tax. The profit shown on the S corporation tax return is reported on the owners' tax returns.

A C *corporation* is any corporation that has not elected to be taxed as an S corporation. A C corporation pays income tax on its profits. The effect of this is that when dividends are paid to shareholders they are taxed twice, once for the corporation and once when they are paid to the shareholders. In Florida, a C corporation must also pay corporate income tax.

A *professional service corporation* is a corporation formed by a professional such as a doctor or accountant. Florida has special rules for professional service corporations that differ slightly from those of other corporations. These rules are included in Florida Statutes, Chapter 621. There are also special tax rules for professional service corporations.

A *nonprofit corporation* is usually used for organizations such as churches and condominium associations. However, with careful planning, some types of businesses can be set up as nonprofit corporations and save a lot in taxes. While a nonprofit corporation cannot pay dividends, it can pay its officers and employees fair salaries. Some of the major American nonprofit organizations pay their officers well over $100,000 a year. Florida's special rules for nonprofit corporations are included in Florida Statutes, Chapter 617.

Advantages. If properly organized, shareholders have no liability for corporate debts and lawsuits; and officers usually have no personal liability for their corporate act. The existence of a corporation may be perpetual. There are tax advantages allowed only to corporations. There is prestige in owning a corporation. Two excellent advantages: capital may be raised by issuing stock, and it is easy to transfer ownership upon death. A small corporation can be set up as an S corporation to avoid corporate taxes but still retain corporate advantages. Some types of businesses can be set up as nonprofit corporations that provide significant tax savings.

Disadvantages. The start-up costs for forming a corporation are certainly a disadvantage; plus there are certain formalities such as annual meetings, separate bank accounts and tax forms. Unless a corporation registers as an S corporation, it must pay federal income tax separate from the tax paid by the owners, and must pay Florida income tax. Over the years, there have occasionally been proposals to tax S corporations with an exemption for small operations, but none of these have passed the legislature.

LIMITED PARTNERSHIP

Characteristics. A limited partnership has characteristics similar to both a corporation and a partnership. There are *general partners* who have the control and personal liability, and there are *limited partners* who only put up money and whose liability is limited to what they paid for their share of the partnership (like corporate stock). A new type of limited partnership, a limited liability limited partnership, allows all partners to avoid liability.

Advantages. Capital can be contributed by limited partners who have no control of the business or liability for its debts.

Disadvantages. A great disadvantage is high start-up costs. Also, an extensive partnership agreement is required because general partners are personally liable for partnership debts and for the acts of each other. (One solution to this problem is to use a corporation as the general partner.)

Limited Liability Company

Characteristics. Florida was the second state in the United States to allow a limited liability company (LLC). This new invention is like a limited partnership without general partners. It has characteristics of both a corporation and a partnership: none of the partners have liability and all can have some control. Few people have used LLCs in Florida because they were subject to the corporate income tax. But as of 1998, LLCs are exempt from Florida corporate income tax. Florida's LLC law also allows Professional Limited Liability Companies, which are used for such businesses as doctors and lawyers. Florida no longer has limited liability partnerships.

Advantages. The limited liability company offers the tax benefits of a partnership with the protection from liability of a corporation. While both a corporation and an LLC offer a business owner protection from business debts, the LLC also offers protection of the company's assets from the debts of an owner. It offers more tax benefits than an S corporation because it may pass through more depreciation and deductions, have different classes of ownership, have an unlimited number of members, and have aliens as members. It is similar to a Latin-American "Limitada" or a German "GmbH & Co. K.G." and is expected to attract foreign investment to Florida.

Disadvantages. LLCs pay social security tax on all profits (up to a limit); whereas S corporation profits are exempt from social security tax. Because a limited liability company is a new invention, there are not a lot of answers to legal questions which may arise. (However the courts will probably rely on corporation and limited partnership law.)

START-UP PROCEDURES

PROPRIETORSHIP

In a proprietorship, all accounts, property and licenses are taken in the name of the owner. See Chapter 3 for using a fictitious name.

PARTNERSHIP

To form a partnership, a written agreement should be prepared to spell out rights and obligations of the parties. It may be registered with the Secretary of State, but this is not required. Most accounts, property and licenses can be in either the partnership name or that of the partners. For more information, see the references to other books at the end of this book.

CORPORATION

To form a corporation, *articles of incorporation* must be filed with the Secretary of State in Tallahassee along with $70 in filing fees and taxes. An organizational meeting is then held. At the meeting, officers are elected, stock issued and other formalities are complied with in order to avoid the corporate entity being set aside later and treated as though it never was formed. Licenses and accounts are titled in the name of the corporation. One person or more may form a for-profit corporation, but at least three persons are needed to form a nonprofit corporation. The references at the end of this book have more information.

LIMITED PARTNERSHIP

A written limited partnership agreement must be drawn up and registered with the Secretary of State in Tallahassee, and a lengthy disclosure document given to all prospective limited partners. Because of the complexity of securities laws and the criminal penalties for violation, it is advantageous to have an attorney organize a limited partnership.

LIMITED LIABILITY COMPANY

One or more persons may form a limited liability company by filing articles of organization with the Secretary of State in Tallahassee. Licenses and accounts are in the name of the company. For more information, please see the references in the back of this book.

FOREIGN NATIONALS

Persons who are not citizens nor legal permanent residents of the United States are free to start any type of business organization in Florida. The type that would be most advantageous would be the LLC because it allows foreign owners (unlike an S corporation) and it avoids corporate taxation (unlike a C corporation).

Two legal issues that foreign persons should be concerned with when starting a business in Florida are their immigration status and the proper reporting of the business's foreign owners.

IMMIGRATION STATUS
The ownership of a U.S. business does not automatically confer rights to enter or remain in the United States. Different types of visas are available to investors and business owners and each of these has strict requirements.

A visa to enter the United States may be permanent or temporary. *Permanent visas* for business owners usually require investments of from $500,000 to $1,000,000 that result in the creation of new jobs. However, there are ways to obtain visas for smaller investments if structured right. For more information on this area you should consult an immigration specialist or a book on immigration.

Temporary visas may be used by business owners to enter the U.S., however, these are hard to get because in most cases the foreign person must prove that there are no U.S. residents qualified to take the job.

REPORTING
U.S. businesses that own real property and are controlled by foreigners are required to file certain federal reports under the International Investment Survey Act, the Agricultural Foreign Investment Disclosure Act, and the Foreign Investment in Real Property Tax Act (FIRPTA). If these laws apply to your business you should consult an attorney who specializes in foreign ownership of U.S. businesses.

Business Comparison Chart

	Sole Proprietorship	General Partnership	Limited Partnership	Limited Liability Co.	Corporation C or S	Nonprofit Corporation
Liability Protection	No	No	For limited partners	For all members	For all shareholders	For all members
Taxes	Pass through	Pass through	Pass through	Pass through	S corps. pass through C corps. pay tax	None on Employees pay on wages
Minimum # of members	1	2	2	1	1	3
Startup fee	None	$50 optional	$35 plus $7 per $1000 Min. $87.50	$125	$70	$70
Annual fee	None	$25 optional	$103.75 plus $7 per $1000 Min. $156.25	$50	$150	$61.25
Diff. classes of ownership	No	Yes	Yes	Yes	S corps. No C corps. Yes	No ownership Diff. classes of membership
Survives after Death	No	No	Yes	Yes	Yes	Yes
Best for	1 person low-risk business or no assets	low-risk business	low-risk business with silent partners	All types of businesses	All types of businesses	Educational

BUSINESS START-UP CHECKLIST

- ❏ Make your plan
    - ❏ Obtain and read all relevant publications on your type of business
    - ❏ Obtain and read all laws and regulations affecting your business
    - ❏ Calculate whether your plan will produce a profit
    - ❏ Plan your sources of capital
    - ❏ Plan your sources of goods or services
    - ❏ Plan your marketing efforts
- ❏ Choose your business name
    - ❏ Check other business names and trademarks
    - ❏ Register your name, trademark, etc.
- ❏ Choose the business form
    - ❏ Prepare and file organizational papers
    - ❏ Prepare and file fictitious name if necessary
- ❏ Choose the location
    - ❏ Check competitors
    - ❏ Check zoning
- ❏ Obtain necessary licenses
    - ❏ City?   ❏ State?
    - ❏ County?   ❏ Federal?
- ❏ Choose a bank
    - ❏ Checking
    - ❏ Credit card processing
    - ❏ Loans
- ❏ Obtain necessary insurance
    - ❏ Worker's Comp   ❏ Automobile
    - ❏ Liability   ❏ Health
    - ❏ Hazard   ❏ Life/disability
- ❏ File necessary federal tax registrations
- ❏ File necessary state tax registrations
- ❏ Set up a bookkeeping system
- ❏ Plan your hiring
    - ❏ Obtain required posters
    - ❏ Obtain or prepare employment application
    - ❏ Obtain new hire tax forms
    - ❏ Prepare employment policies
    - ❏ Determine compliance with health and safety laws
- ❏ Plan your opening
    - ❏ Obtain all necessary equipment and supplies
    - ❏ Obtain all necessary inventory
    - ❏ Do all necessary marketing and publicity
    - ❏ Obtain all necessary forms and agreements
    - ❏ Prepare your company policies on refunds, exchanges, returns

Naming Your Business 3

Preliminary Considerations

Before deciding upon a name for your business, you should be sure that it is not already being used by someone else. Many business owners have spent thousands of dollars on publicity and printing, only to throw it all away because another company owned the name. A company that owns a name can take you to court and force you to stop using that name. It can also sue you for damages if it thinks your use of the name cost it a financial loss.

If you will be running a small local shop with no plans for expansion, you should at least check out whether the name has been trademarked. If someone else is using the same name anywhere in the country and has registered it as a federal trademark, they can sue you if you use it. If you plan to expand or to deal nationally, then you should do a thorough search of the name.

The first places to look are the local phone books and official records of your county. Next, you should check with the Secretary of State's office in Tallahassee to see if someone has registered a fictitious or corporate name the same as, or confusingly similar to, the one you have chosen. This can be done either by calling them or by visiting their Internet site:

http://ccfcorp.dos.state.fl.us/index.html

To do a national search, you should check trade directories and phone books of major cities. These can be found at many libraries and are usually reference books that cannot be checked out. The *Trade Names Directory* is a two volume set of names compiled from many sources published by Gale Research Co.

If you have a computer with Internet access, you can use it to search all of the yellow page listings in the U.S. at a number of sites at no charge. One website, **http://www.infoseek.com**, offers free searches of yellow pages for all states at once.

To be sure that your use of the name does not violate someone else's trademark rights you should have a trademark search done of the mark in the United States Patent and Trademark Office (USPTO). In the past, this required a visit to their offices or the hiring of a search form for over a hundred dollars. But in 1999, the USPTO put its trademark records online and you can now search them at: **http://www.uspto.gov/tmdb/index.html**. If you do not have access to the Internet you might be able to search at a public library or have one of their employees order an online search for you for a small fee. If this is not available to you, you can have the search done through a firm. One such firm is Government Liaison Services, Inc., P. O. Box 10648, Arlington, VA 22210. Tel. 703-524-8200. They also offer searches of 100 trade directories and 4800 phone books.

No matter how thorough your search is, there is no guarantee that there is not a local user somewhere with rights to the mark. If, for example, you register a name for a new chain of restaurants and later find out that someone in Tucumcari, New Mexico, has been using the name longer than you; that person will still have the right to use the name, but just in his local area. If you do not want his restaurant to cause confusion with your chain, you can try to buy him out. Similarly, if you are operating a small business under a unique name and a law firm in New York writes and offers to buy the right to your name, you can assume that some large corporation wants to start a major expansion under that name.

The best way to make sure a name you are using is not already owned by someone else is to make up a name. Names such as Xerox, Kodak and Exxon were made up and did not have any meaning prior to their use. Remember that there are millions of businesses and even something you make up may already be in use. Do a search anyway.

FICTITIOUS NAMES

In Florida, as in most states, unless you do business in your own legal name you must register the name you are using, called a *fictitious name*. When you use a fictitious name you are "doing business as" (d/b/a) whatever name you are using. The name must be registered with the Secretary of State's office in Tallahassee. Previously, registrations of fictitious names were handled by each county. Businesses that had been registered with their county were supposed to reregister with the Secretary of State between January 1, 1991 and December 31, 1992. Because some did not do so, but may still be in business, you should be sure to check the county records as well as the state.

A fictitious name registration is good for five years and expires on December 31st of the fifth year. It can be renewed for additional five year periods.

It is a misdemeanor to fail to register a fictitious name, and you may not sue anyone unless you are registered. If someone sues you and you are not registered, you may have to pay their attorney's fees and court costs.

If your name is *John Doe* and you are operating a masonry business, you may operate your business as *John Doe, Mason* without registering it. But any other use of a name should be registered, such as:

Doe Masonry   Doe Masonry Company
Doe Company   Florida Sunshine Masonry

Example: Legally, you would use the full name "John Doe d/b/a Doe Masonry."

You cannot use the words, "corporation," "incorporated," "corp.," or "inc." unless you are a corporation. However, corporations do not have to register the name they are using unless it is different from their registered corporate name.

Attorneys and professionals licensed by the Department of Professional Regulation do not have to register the names under which they practice their profession.

To register a fictitious name you must first place an ad announcing your intent to use the name. Situate the ad in a newspaper of general circulation for the county in which you will be maintaining your principal place of business. The ad only has to be run once. The ad would typically be placed in the classified section under "Legal Notices" and could be worded as follows:

FICTITIOUS NAME NOTICE

Notice is hereby given that the undersigned, desiring to engage in business under the name of DOE COMPANY intends to register the name with the Clerk of the Circuit Court of Liberty County, Florida

| JOHN DOE | 75% Owner |
| JIM DOE | 25% Owner |

John Doe, 123 Main Street, Libertyville, FL 32101

You should compare ad rates before placing the ad. Many counties have weekly newspapers that specialize in legal ads and charge a third of what the large newspapers charge. Check the news stands, especially around the courthouse.

After the ad has appeared, you must file an APPLICATION FOR REGISTRATION OF FICTITIOUS NAME with the Secretary of State. (see form 2, p.202.) Unlike corporate names and trademarks which are carefully screened by the Secretary of State to avoid duplication, fictitious name registrations are accepted without regard to who else is using the name. If you apply for registration of a trademark or corporate name, the Secretary of State will check all other registrations and refuse registration if the name or a similar name is already registered. But the registration of a fictitious name does not bestow any rights to the name upon the registrant; it merely notifies the world which persons are behind the business. So the Secretary of State will allow anyone to register any name, even if 100 others have already registered that name.

As discussed previously, you should do some research to see if the name you intend to use is already being used by anyone else. Even persons who have not registered a name can acquire some legal rights to the name through mere use.

Some businesses have special requirements for registration of their fictitious names. For example, prior to obtaining its license from the state, a private investigative agency must obtain permission from the Department of Business and Professional Regulation for the use of its proposed name. Other businesses may have similar requirements. See Chapter 3 for a list of state regulated professions with references to the laws that apply to them.

Appendix A has a sample filled-in APPLICATION FOR REGISTRATION OF FICTITIOUS NAME. A blank form and instructions are included in Appendix B. (see form 2, p.202.)

CORPORATE NAMES

A corporation does not have to register a fictitious name because it already has a legal name. The name of a corporation must contain one of the following words:

Incorporated	Inc.
Company	Co.
Corporation	Corp.

It is not advisable to use only the word "Company" or "Co." because unincorporated businesses also use these words; therefore, a person dealing with you might not realize you are incorporated. If this happens, you might end up with personal liability for corporate debts. You may use a combination of two of the words, such as ABC Co., Inc.

If the name of the corporation does not contain one of the above words it will be rejected by the Secretary of State. It will also be rejected if the name used by it is already taken or is similar to the name of another corporation, or if it uses a forbidden word such as "Bank" or "Trust." To check on a name, you may call the corporate name information number in Tallahassee: 850-487-6052. Keep trying, they are often busy. You can also check their website listed on page 17.

If a name you pick is taken by another company, you may be able to change it slightly and have it accepted. For example, if there is already a Tri-City Upholstery, Inc., and it is in a different county, you may be allowed to use Tri-City Upholstery of Liberty County, Inc. *But*, even if this is approved by the Secretary of State, you might get sued by the other company if your business is close to theirs or there is a likelihood of confusion.

Also, do not have anything printed until your corporate papers are returned to you. Sometimes a name is approved over the phone and rejected when submitted. Once you have chosen a corporate name and know it is available, you should immediately register your corporation.

If a corporation wants to do business under a name other than its corporate name, it can register a fictitious name such as "Doe Corporation d/b/a Doe Industries." But if the name used leads people to believe that the business is not a corporation, the right to limited liability may be lost. If you use such a name, it should always be accompanied by the corporate name.

PROFESSIONAL ASSOCIATIONS

Professionals such as attorneys, doctors, dentists, life insurance agents, and architects can form corporations or limited liability companies in which to practice. These are better than general partnerships because they protect the professional from the malpractice of his or her co-workers.

These professional corporations and professional limited liability companies are covered by Florida Statutes, Chapter 621.

Under Florida law, a professional corporation cannot use the usual corporate designations: Inc., Corp., or Co.; but must use the words *Professional Association*, the abbreviation, *P.A.*, or the word *Chartered*. Other states use abbreviations such as *P.C.* (professional corporation) or *P.S.C.* (professional service corporation) but neither of these are legal in Florida.

A professional LLC can use the word *chartered*, the words *professional limited company*, or the abbreviations *P.L.* or *L.C.*

The Word "Limited"

The words *Limited* or *Ltd.* should not be used unless the entity is a limited partnership, limited liability company, or a limited liability partnership. If a corporation wishes to use the word limited in its name, it must still use one of the corporate words or abbreviations such as *incorporated* or *corp.*

Domain Names

With the Internet changing so rapidly, all of the rules for Internet names have not yet been worked out. Originally, the first person to reserve a name owned it, and enterprising souls bought up the names of most of the fortune 500 corporations. Then a few of the corporations went to court and the rule was developed that if a company had a trademark for a name, that company could stop someone else from using it if the other person did not have a trademark. More recently, Congress made it illegal for "cybersquatters" to register the names of famous persons and companies.

You cannot yet get a trademark merely for using a domain name. Trademarks are granted for the use of a name in commerce. Once you have a valid trademark, you will be safe using it for your domain name.

In 2001 several new top level domains (TLDs) will be introduced. These are the last letters of the URL (uniform resource locator), such as ".com" and ".net." At the time of this publication the new TLDs and the registration procedures had not been announced.

If you wish to protect your domain name, the best thing to do at this point is to get a trademark for it. To do this, you would have to use it on your goods or services. The following section gives some basic information about trademarks. To find out if a domain name is available, go to:

http://www.whois.net

TRADEMARKS

As your business builds goodwill, its name will become more valuable and you will want to protect it from others who may wish to copy it. To protect a name used to describe your goods or services, you can register it as a trademark (for goods) or a service mark (for services) with either the Secretary of State of the state of Florida or with the United States Patent and Trademark Office.

You cannot obtain a trademark for the name of your business, but you can trademark the name you use on your goods and services. In most cases, you use your company name on your goods as your trademark. In effect, it protects your company name. Another way to protect your company name is to incorporate. A particular corporate name can only be registered by one company in Florida.

STATE REGISTRATION
State registration would be useful if you only expect to use your trademark within the state of Florida. Federal registration would protect your mark anywhere in the country. The registration of a mark gives you exclu-

sive use of the mark for the types of goods for which you register it. The only exception is persons who have already been using the mark. You cannot stop people who have been using the mark prior to your registration.

The procedure for state registration is simple and the cost is $87.50. First, you should check the availability of the name with the Secretary of State's office. This can be done by writing the Division of Corporations—Secretary of State, Trademark Section, P.O. Box 6327, Tallahassee, FL 32314, calling them at 850-487-6051 or checking their website:

http://ccfcorp.dos.state.fl.us/index.html

Before a mark can be registered, it must be used in Florida. For goods, this means it must be used on the goods themselves, or on containers, tags, labels, or displays of the goods. For services, it must be used in the sale or advertising of the services. The use must be in an actual transaction with a customer. A sample mailed to a friend is not an acceptable use.

The $87.50 fee will register the mark in only one "class of goods." If the mark is used on more than one class of goods, a separate registration must be filed. The registration is good for ten years. Six months prior to its expiration, it must be renewed. The renewal fee is $87.50 for each class of goods.

In Appendix A there is a sample filled-in APPLICATION FOR THE REGISTRATION OF A TRADEMARK OR SERVICE MARK. A blank form and instructions are in Appendix B of this book. (see form 3, p.203.) For questions about filing the application, call 850-488-9000.

FEDERAL
REGISTRATION

For federal registration the procedure is a little more complicated. There are two types of applications depending upon whether you have already made actual use of the mark or whether you merely have an intention to use the mark in the future. For a trademark that has been in use, you must file an application form along with specimens showing actual use and a drawing of the mark that complies with all of the rules of the United States Patent and Trademark Office. For an *intent to use* application you must file two separate forms—one when you make the initial application and the other after you have made actual use of the mark—as well as the specimens and drawing. Before a mark can be entitled to federal registration the use of the mark must be in *interstate commerce* or in commerce with another state. The fee for registration is $245, but if you file an *intent to use* application there is a second fee of $100 for the filing after actual use. For more information on how to register a federal trademark, see For Further Reference section beginning on page 173.

FINANCING YOUR BUSINESS 4

The way to finance your business is determined by how fast you want your business to grow and how much risk of failure you are able to handle. Letting the business grow with its own income is the slowest but safest way to grow. Taking out a personal loan against your house to expand quickly is the fastest but riskiest way to grow.

GROWING WITH PROFITS

Many successful businesses have started out with little money and used the profits to grow bigger and bigger. If you have another source of income to live on (such as a job or a spouse) you can plow all the income of your fledgling business into growth.

Some businesses start as hobbies or part-time ventures on the weekend while the entrepreneur holds down a full time job. Many types of goods or service businesses can start this way. Even some multi-million dollar corporations, such as Apple Computer, started out this way.

This allows you to test your idea with little risk. If you find you are not good at running that type of business, or the time or location was not right for your idea, all you are out is the time you spent and your start-up capital.

However, a business can only grow so big from its own income. In many cases, as a business grows, it gets to a point where the orders are so big that money must be borrowed to produce the product to fill them. With this kind of order, there is the risk that if the customer cannot pay or goes bankrupt, the business will also go under. At such a point, a business owner should investigate the credit worthiness of the customer and weigh the risks. Some businesses have grown rapidly, some have gone under, and others have decided not to take the risk and stayed small. You can worry about that down the road.

USING YOUR SAVINGS

If you have savings you can tap to get your business started, that is the best source. You will not have to pay high interest rates and you will not have to worry about paying someone back.

HOME EQUITY | If you have owned your home for several years, it is possible that the equity has grown substantially and you can get a second mortgage to finance your business. If you have been in the home for many years and have a good record of paying your bills, some lenders will make second mortgages that exceed the equity. Just remember, if your business fails, you may lose your house.

RETIREMENT ACCOUNTS | Be careful about borrowing from your retirement savings. There are tax penalties for borrowing from or against certain types of retirement accounts. Also, your future financial security may be lost if your business does not succeed.

HAVING TOO MUCH MONEY | It probably does not seem possible to have too much money with which to start a business, but many businesses have failed for that reason. With plenty of start-up capital available, a business owner does not need to watch expenses and can become wasteful. Employees get used to lavish spending. Once the money runs out and the business must run on its own earnings, it fails.

Starting with the bare minimum forces a business to watch its expenses and be frugal. It necessitates finding the least expensive solutions to problems that crop up and creative ways to be productive.

BORROWING MONEY

It is extremely tempting to look to others to get the money to start a business. The risk of failure is less worrisome and the pressure is lower, but that is a problem with borrowing. If it is others' money, you do not have quite the same incentive to succeed as if everything you own is on the line.

Actually, you should be even more concerned when using the money of others. Your reputation should be more valuable than the money itself, which can always be replaced. Yet that is not always the case. How many people borrow again and again from their parents for failed business ventures?

FAMILY   Depending on how much money your family can spare, it may be the most comfortable or most uncomfortable source of funds for you. If you have been assured a large inheritance and your parents have more funds than they need to live on, you may be able to borrow against your inheritance without worry. It will be your money anyway and you need it much more now than you will ten or twenty or more years from now. If you lose it all, it's your own loss.

However, if you are borrowing your widowed mother's source of income, asking her to cash in a CD she lives on to finance your get-rich-quick scheme, you should have second thoughts about it. Stop and consider all the real reasons your business might not take off and what your mother would do without the income.

FRIENDS   Borrowing from friends is like borrowing from family members. If you know they have the funds available and could survive a loss, you may want to risk it, but if they would be loaning you their only resources, do not chance it.

Financial problems can be the worst thing for a relationship, whether it is a casual friendship or a long term romantic involvement. Before you borrow from a friend, try to imagine what would happen if you could not pay it back and how you would feel if it caused the end of your relationship.

The ideal situation is if your friend were a co-venturer in your business and the burden would not be totally on you to see how the funds were spent. Still, realize that such a venture will put extra strain on the relationship.

BANKS   In a way, a bank can be a more comfortable party from which to borrow because you do not have a personal relationship with them as you do with a friend or family member. If you fail, they will write your loan off rather than disown you. But a bank can also be the least comfortable party to borrow from because they will demand realistic projections and be on top of you to perform. If you do not meet their expectations, they may call your loan just when you need it most.

The best thing about a bank loan is that they will require you to do your homework: you must have plans that make sense to a banker. If they approve your loan, you know that your plans are at least reasonable.

Bank loans are not cheap or easy. You will be paying a good interest rate, and you will have to put up collateral. If your business does not have equipment or receivables, they may require you to put up your house and other personal property to guarantee the loan.

Banks are a little easier to deal with when you get a Small Business Administration (SBA) loan. That is because the SBA guarantees that it will pay the bank if you default on the loan. SBA loans are obtained through local bank branches.

CREDIT CARDS

Borrowing against a credit card is one of the fastest growing ways of financing a business, but it can be one of the most expensive ways. The rates can go higher than twenty percent, but many cards offer lower rates and some people are able to get numerous cards. Some successful businesses have used the partners' credit cards to get off the ground or to weather through a cash crunch, but if the business does not begin to generate the cash to make the payments, you could soon end up in bankruptcy. A good strategy is only to use credit cards for a long-term asset like a computer or for something that will quickly generate cash, like buying inventory to fill an order. Do not use credit cards to pay expenses that are not generating revenue.

GETTING A RICH PARTNER

One of the best business combinations is a young entrepreneur with ideas and ambition and a retired investor with business experience and money. Together they can supply everything the business needs.

How to find such a partner? Be creative. You should have investigated the business you are starting and know others who have been in such businesses. Have any of them had partners retire over the last few years? Are any of them planning to phase out of the business?

SELLING SHARES OF YOUR BUSINESS

Silent investors are the best source of capital for your business. You retain full control of the business and if it happens to fail you have no obligation to them. Unfortunately, few silent investors are interested in a new business. It is only after you have proven your concept to be successful and built up a rather large enterprise, that you will be able to attract such investors.

The most common way to obtain money from investors is to issue stock to them. For this the best type of business entity is the corporation. It gives you almost unlimited flexibility in the number and kinds of shares of stock you can issue.

The Florida Venture Capital Finance Directory is a 174 page book that includes over 270 listings of sources of capital. It is available for $15.85 including shipping and tax from:

> Enterprise Florida Capital Development
> 390 N. Orange Ave. #1300
> Orlando, FL 32801
> 407-316-4692
> wjones@Floridabusiness.com

UNDERSTANDING SECURITIES LAWS

There is one major problem with selling stock in your business and that is all of the federal and state regulations with which you must comply. Both the state and federal governments have long and complicated laws dealing with the sales of "securities." There are also hundreds of court cases attempting to explain what these laws mean. A thorough explanation of this area of law is obviously beyond the scope of this book.

Basically, securities have been held to exist in any case in which a person provides money to someone with the expectation that he will get a profit through the efforts of that person. This can apply to any situation where someone buys stock in, or makes a loan to your business. What the laws require is disclosure of the risks involved, and in some cases, registration of the securities with the government. There are some exemptions, such as for small amounts of money and for limited numbers of investors.

Penalties for violation of securities laws are severe, including triple damages and prison terms. You should consult a specialist in securities laws before issuing any security. You can often get an introductory consultation at a reasonable rate to learn your options.

USING THE INTERNET TO FIND CAPITAL

In 1995, the owners of Wit Beer made headlines in all the business magazines by successfully raising $1.6 million for their business on the Internet. It seemed so easy, every business wanted to try. What was not made clear in most of the stories was that the owner was a corporate securities lawyer and that he did all of the necessary legal work to prepare a prospectus and properly register the stock, something that would have cost anyone else over $100,000 in legal fees. Also, most of the interest in the stock came from the articles, not from the Internet promotion. Today, a similar effort would probably not be nearly as successful.

Before attempting to market your company's shares on the Internet, be sure to get an opinion from a securities lawyer or do some serious research into securities laws. The lawyer who marketed Wit Beer's shares on the Internet has started a business to advise others on raising capital. It is Wit SoundView Corporation located at 826 Broadway, 7th Floor, New York, NY 10003.

http://www.witcapital.com/home/index.jsp

The Internet does have some sources of capital listed. The following sites may be helpful.

America's Business Funding Directory:
   http://www.businessfinance.com

Angel Capital Electronic Network (SBA): http://www.sba.gov

Inc. Magazine: http://mothra.inc.com/finance

NVST: http://www.nvst.com

The Capital Network: http://www.thecapitalnetwork.com

LOCATING YOUR BUSINESS 5

The right location for your business will be determined by what type of business it is, and how fast you expect to grow. For some types of businesses, the location will not be important to your success or failure; in others it will be crucial.

WORKING OUT OF YOUR HOME

Many small businesses get started out of the home. Chapter 6 discusses the legalities of home businesses. This section discusses the practicalities.

Starting a business out of your home can save you the rent, electricity, insurance, and other costs of setting up at another location. For some people this is ideal, and they can combine their home and work duties easily and efficiently. For other people it is a disaster. A spouse, children, neighbors, television, and household chores can be so distracting that no other work gets done.

Since residential rates are usually lower than business lines, many people use their residential telephone line to conduct business or add a second residential line. However, if you wish to be listed in the yellow pages, you will need to have a business line in your home. If you are running two or more types of businesses, you can probably add their names as additional listings on the original number and avoid paying for another business line.

You also should consider whether the type of business you are starting is compatible with a home office. For example, if your business mostly consists of making phone calls or calling clients, then the home may be an ideal place to run it. If your clients need to visit you or you will need daily pickups and deliveries by truck, then the home may not be a good location. This is discussed in more detail in the next chapter.

CHOOSING A RETAIL SITE

For most types of retail stores the location is of prime importance. Such things to consider are how close it is to your potential customers, how visible it is to the public, and how easily accessible it is to both autos and pedestrians. The attractiveness and safety should also be considered.

Location would be less important for a business that was the only one of its kind in the area. For example, if there was only one moped parts dealer or Armenian restaurant in a metropolitan area, people would have to come to wherever you are if they want your products or services. However, even with such businesses, keep in mind that there is competition. People who want moped parts can order them by mail and restaurant customers can choose another type of cuisine.

You should look up all the businesses like the one you plan to run in the phone book and mark them on a map. For some businesses, like a cleaners, you would want to be far from the others. But for other businesses, like antique stores, you would want to be near the others. (Antique stores usually do not carry the same things, they do not compete, and people like to go to an "antique district" and visit all the shops.)

Choosing Office, Manufacturing, or Warehouse Space

If your business will be the type where customers will not come to you, then locating it near customers is not as much of a concern and you can probably save money by locating away from the high traffic, central business districts. However, you should consider the convenience for employees and not locate in an area that would be unattractive to them, or too far from where they would likely live.

For manufacturing or warehouse operations, you should consider your proximity to a post office, trucking company or rail line. Where several sites are available you might consider which one has the earliest or most convenient pick-up schedule for the carriers you plan to use.

Leasing a Site

A lease of space can be one of the biggest expenses of a small business so you should do a lot of homework before signing one. There are a lot of terms in a commercial lease that can make or break your business. These are the most critical:

ZONING   Before signing a lease, you should be sure that everything that your business will need to do is allowed by the zoning of the property.

RESTRICTIONS   In some shopping centers, existing tenants have guarantees that other tenants do not compete with them. For example, if you plan to open a restaurant and bakery you may be forbidden to sell carry out baked goods if the supermarket has a bakery and a noncompete clause.

SIGNS   Business signs are regulated by zoning laws, sign laws and property restrictions. If you rent a hidden location with no possibility for adequate signage, your business will have a lot smaller chance of success than with a more visible site or much larger sign.

ADA COMPLIANCE	The Americans with Disabilities Act (ADA) requires that reasonable accommodations be made to make businesses accessible to the handicapped. When a business is remodeled many more changes are required than if no remodeling is done. When renting space you should be sure that it complies with the law, or that the landlord will be responsible for compliance. Be aware of the full costs you will bear.
EXPANSION	As your business grows, you may need to expand your space. The time to find out about your options is before you sign the lease. Perhaps you you can take over adjoining units when those leases expire.
RENEWAL	Location is a key to success for some businesses. If you spend five years building up a clientele, you do not want someone to take over your locale at the end of your lease. Therefore, you should have a renewal clause on your lease. Usually this allows an increase in rent based on inflation.
GUARANTY	Most landlords of commercial space will not rent to a small corporation without a personal guaranty of the lease. This is a very risky thing for a new business owner to do. The lifetime rent on a long term commercial lease can be hundreds of thousands of dollars and if your business fails the last thing you want to do is be personally responsible for five years of rent.
	Where space is scarce or a location is hot, a landlord can get the guarantees he demands and there is nothing you can do about it (except perhaps set up an asset protection plan ahead of time). But where several units are vacant or the commercial rental market is soft, often you can negotiate out of the personal guaranty. If the lease is five years, maybe you can get away with a guaranty of just the first year. Give it a try.
DUTY TO OPEN	Some shopping centers have rules requiring all shops to be open certain hours. If you cannot afford to staff it the whole time required or if you have religious or other reasons that make this a problem, you should negotiate it out of the lease or find another location.
SUBLEASE	At some point you may decide to sell your business, and in many cases the location is the most valuable aspect of it. For this reason you should

be sure that you have the right to either assign your lease or to sublease the property. If this is impossible, one way around a prohibition is to incorporate your business before signing the lease and then when you sell the business, sell the stock. But some lease clauses prohibit transfer of "any interest" in the business, so read the lease carefully.

BUYING A SITE

If you are experienced with owning rental property you will probably be more inclined to buy a site for your business. If you have no experience with real estate, you should probably rent and not take on the extra cost and responsibility of property ownership.

One reason to buy your site is that you can build up equity. Rather than pay rent to a landlord you can pay off a mortgage and eventually own the property.

SEPARATING THE OWNERSHIP

One risk in buying a business site is that if the business gets into financial trouble the creditors may go after the building as well. For this reason most people who buy a site for their business keep the ownership out of the business. For example, the business will be a corporation and the real estate will be owned personally by the owner or by a trust unrelated to the business.

EXPANSION

Before buying a site you should consider the growth potential of your business. If it grows quickly will you be able to expand at that site or will you have to move? Might the property next door be available for sale in the future if you need it? Can you get an option on it?

If the site is a good investment whether or not you have your business then by all means buy it. But if its main use is for your business, think twice.

ZONING

Some of the concerns when buying a site are the same as when renting. You will want to make sure that the zoning permits the type of business you wish to start, or that you can get a variance without a large expense or delay. Be aware that just because a business is now using the site does not mean that you can expand or remodel the business at that site. Check with the zoning department and find out exactly what is allowed.

SIGNS

Signs are another concern. Some cities have regulated signs and do not allow new or larger ones. Some businesses have used these laws to get publicity. A car dealer who was told to take down a large number of American flags on his lot filed a federal lawsuit and rallied the community behind him.

ADA
COMPLIANCE

ADA compliance is another concern when buying a commercial building. Find out from the building department if the building is in compliance or what needs to be done to put it in compliance. If you remodel, the requirements may be more strict.

NOTE: *When dealing with public officials, keep in mind that they do not always know what the law is, or do not accurately explain it. They often try to intimidate people into doing things that are not required by law. Read the requirements yourself and question the officials if they seem to be interpreting it wrong. Seek legal advice if officials refuse to reexamine the law, or move away from an erroneous position.*

NOTE: *Also consider that keeping them happy may be worth the price. If you are already doing something they have overlooked, do not make a big deal over a little thing they want changed, or they may subject you to a full inspection or audit.*

CHECKING GOVERNMENTAL REGULATIONS

When looking for a site for your business, you should investigate the different governmental regulations in your area. For example, a location just outside the city or county limits might have a lower licensing fee, a lower sales tax rate, and less strict sign requirements.

LICENSING YOUR BUSINESS 6

OCCUPATIONAL LICENSES AND ZONING

Some Florida counties and cities require you to obtain an occupational license. If you are in a city you may need both a city and a county license. Businesses that do work in several cities, such as builders, must obtain a license from each city in which they do work. This does not have to be done until you actually begin a job in a particular city.

County occupational licenses can be obtained from the tax collector in the county courthouse. City licenses are usually available at city hall. Be sure to find out if zoning allows your type of business before buying or leasing property. The licensing departments will check the zoning before issuing your license.

If you will be preparing or serving food, you will need to check with the local health department to be sure that the premises complies with their regulations. In some areas, if food has been served on the premises in the past, there is no problem getting a license. If food has never been served on the premises, then the property must comply with all the newest regulations. This can be very costly.

HOME BUSINESSES

Problems occasionally arise when persons attempt to start a business in their home. Small new businesses cannot afford to pay rent for commercial space and cities often try to forbid business in residential areas. Getting a county occupational license or advertising a fictitious name often gives notice to the city that a business is being conducted in a residential area.

Some people avoid the problem by starting their businesses without occupational licenses, figuring that the penalties for not having a license (if they are caught) are less expensive than the cost of office space. Others get the county license and ignore the city rules. If a person regularly parks commercial trucks and equipment on his property, or has delivery trucks coming and going, or employee cars parked along the street, there will probably be complaints from neighbors and the city will probably take legal action. But if a person's business consists merely of making phone calls out of the home and keeping supplies there, the problem may never become an issue.

If a problem does arise regarding a home business that does not disturb the neighbors, a good argument can be made that the zoning law that prohibits the business is unconstitutional. When zoning laws were first instituted, they were not meant to stop people from doing things in a residence that had historically been part of the life in a residence. Consider an artist. Should a zoning law prohibit a person from sitting in his home and painting pictures? If he sells them for a living is there a difference? Can the government force him to rent commercial space just because he decides to sell the paintings he paints?

Similar arguments can be made for many home businesses. For hundreds of years people performed income-producing activities in their homes. (The author is waiting for his city fathers to tell him to stop writing books in his home office.) But court battles with a city are expensive and probably not worth the effort for a small business. The best course of action is to keep a low profile. Using a post office box for the business is sometimes helpful in diverting attention away from the residence.

STATE-REGULATED PROFESSIONS

Many professionals require special state licenses. You will probably be called upon to produce such a license when applying for an - occupational license.

If you are in a regulated profession you should be aware of the laws that apply to your profession. The following pages contain a list of professions, the state statutes and administrative code covering them, and the phone number of the regulating division of government. You can make copies of these laws at your local public library or county law library. If you do not think your profession is regulated, you should read through the list anyway. Some of those included may surprise you.

	Phone	Fla. Stats.	F.A.C.
Accountancy	352-333-2500	455 & 473	61H1
Acupuncture	850-245-4161	457	61F1
Alcoholic Beverages	850-488-8288	210, 561-569	61A
Architecture	850-488-6685	481	61G1
Asbestos Consultants	850-921-6765	469	61E1
Athlete Agents	850-488-7587	468	61-24
Athlete Trainers	850-488-0595	468	61-25
Attorneys	850-561-5600	454	
Auctioneers	850-488-5189	468	61G2
Barbering	850-488-6888	476	61G3
Chiropractic	850-488-0595	460	61F2
Clinical Social Workers	850-488-0595	491	61F4
Construction Contracting	904-727-6530	489	61G4
Cosmetology	850-488-5702	477	61G5
Dentistry	850-488-0595	466	61F5
Electrical Contracting	850-488-3109	489	61G6
Employee Leasing	850-921-6347	468	61G7

Engineering	850-521-0500	471	61G15
Fire Equipment	850-922-3172	633	
Fishing, Freshwater	850-488-4066	372	
Fishing, Saltwater	850-487-3122	370	
Funeral Directing.	850-488-8690	470	61G8
			61E-5
Geologists	850-487-7990	492	61G16
Health Testing Services	850-488-0595	483	
Hearing Aid Sales	850-487-1813	468	61G9
Hotels	850-922-5335	509	61C
Hypnotists	850-488-0595	456	
Interior Designers	850-488-6685	481	61G1
Land Sales	850-488-1122	475, 498	61B
Land Surveying	850-413-7480	472, 177	61G17
Landscape Architects	850-488-6685	481	61G10
Massage Practice	850-488-0595	480	61G11
Medical Doctors	850-488-0595	458	61F6
Midwifery	850-488-0595	467	61E8
Mobile Home parks	800-700-2013	723	61B
Mortgage Brokers	407-245-0800	494	
Naturopathy	850-488-0595	462	
Nursing	850-488-0595	464	61F7
Nursing Homes	850-488-0595	400, 468	61G12
Opticians	850-488-0595	484	61G13
Optometry	850-488-0595	463	61F8
Osteopathy	850-488-0595	459	61F9
Pharmacy	850-488-0595	465	61F10
Pilot Commissioners	850-488-3387	310	61G14
Plumbing	904-727-6530	469	

Podiatry	850-488-0595	461	61F12
Private Investigators	850-487-0482	493	
Physical Therapy	850-488-0595	486	61F11
Psychological Services	850-488-0595	490	61E9, 61F13
Radiologic Technologists	850-488-0595	468	
Real Estate Appraisal	407-245-0800	475	61J1
Real Estate Brokerage	407-245-0800	475	61J2
Restaurants	850-488-1113	509	61C
Second hand Dealers	800-352-3671	538	
Septic Tank Contracting	904-727-6530	489	
Speech Pathology & Audiology	850-488-0595	468	61F14
Surveyors and Mappers	850-413-7480	455, 472	61G17
Talent Agencies	850-488-7587	468	61-19
Timeshares	850-487-2753	721	61B
Veterinary Medicine	850-487-1820	474	61G18

FEDERAL LICENSES

So far there are few businesses that require federal registration. If you are in any of the types of businesses listed below, you should check with the federal agency beside it.

Radio or television stations or manufacturers of equipment emitting radio waves:

Federal Communications Commission
1919 M Street, NW
Washington, DC 20550
http://www.fcc.gov

Manufacturers of alcohol, tobacco or fire arms:

> Bureau of Alcohol, Tobacco and Firearms,
> Treasury Department
> 1200 Pennsylvania Ave., NW
> Washington, DC 20226
> http://www.atf.treas.gov

Securities brokers and providers of investment advice:

> Securities and Exchange Commission
> 450 - 5th Street NW
> Washington, DC 20549
> http://www.sec.gov

Manufacturers of drugs and processors of meat:

> Food and Drug Administration
> 5600 Fishers Lane
> Rockville, MD 28057
> http://www.fda.gov

Interstate carriers:

> Surface Transportation Board
> 12th St. & Constitution Ave.
> Washington, DC 20423
> http://www.stb.dot.gov

Exporting:

> Bureau of Export Administration
> Department of Commerce
> 14th St. & Constitution Ave., NW
> Washington, DC 20220
> http://www.bxa.doc.gov

CONTRACT LAWS 7

As a business owner, you will need to know the basics of forming a simple contract for your transactions with both customers and vendors. There is a lot of misunderstanding about what the law is and people may give you erroneous information. Relying on it can cost you money. This chapter will give you a quick overview of the principles that apply to your transactions and the pitfalls to avoid. If you face more complicated contract questions, you should consult a law library or an attorney familiar with small business law.

TRADITIONAL CONTRACT LAW

One of the first things taught in law school is that a contract is not legal unless three elements are present: offer, acceptance, and consideration. The rest of the semester dissects exactly what may be a valid offer, acceptance, and consideration. For your purposes, the important things to remember are:

- If you make an offer to someone, it may result in a binding contract, even if you change your mind or find out it was a bad deal for you.

- Unless an offer is accepted and both parties agree to the same terms, there is no contract.

- A contract does not always have to be in writing. Some laws require certain contracts to be in writing, but as a general rule an oral contract is legal. The problem is in proving that the contract existed.

- Without consideration (the exchange of something of value or mutual promises) there is not a valid contract.

As mentioned above, an entire semester is spent analyzing each of the three elements of a contract. The most important rules for the business owner are:

- An advertisement is not an offer. Suppose you put an ad in the newspaper offering "New IBM computers only $1995!" but there is a typo in the ad and it says $19.95? Can people come in and say "I accept, here's my $19.95" creating a legal contract? Fortunately, no. Courts have ruled that the ad is not an offer that a person can accept. It is an invitation to come in and make offers, which the business can accept or reject.

- The same rule applies to the price tag on an item. If someone switches price tags on your merchandise, or if you accidentally put the wrong price on it, you are not required by law to sell it at that price. If you intentionally put the wrong price, you may be liable under the "bait and switch" law. And many merchants honor a mistaken price just because refusing to would constitute bad will and probably lose a customer.

- When a person makes an offer, several things may happen. It may be accepted, creating a legal contract. It may be rejected. It may expire before it has been accepted. Or, it may be withdrawn before acceptance. A contract may expire either by a date made in the offer ("This offer remains open until noon on January 29, 2000") or after a reasonable amount of time. What is *reasonable* is a legal question that a court must decide. If someone makes you an offer to sell goods, clearly you cannot come back five years later and accept. Can you accept a week later or a month later and create a legal contract? That depends on the type of goods and the circumstances.

- A person accepting an offer cannot add any terms to it. If you offer to sell a car for $1,000, and the other party says they accept as long as you put new tires on it, there is no contract. An acceptance with changed terms is considered a rejection and a counteroffer.

- When someone rejects your offer and makes a counteroffer, a contract can be created by your acceptance of the counteroffer.

These rules can affect your business on a daily basis. Suppose you offer to sell something to one customer over the phone and five minutes later another customer walks in and offers you more for it. To protect yourself, you should call the first customer and withdraw your offer before accepting the offer of the second customer. If the first customer accepts before you have withdrawn your offer, you may be sued if you have sold the item to the second customer.

There are a few exceptions to the basic rules of contracts, these are:

- Consent to a contract must be voluntary. If it is made under a threat, the contract is not valid. If a business refuses to give a person's car back unless they pay $200 for changing the oil, the customer could probably sue and get the $200 back.

- Contracts to do illegal acts or acts "against public policy" are not enforceable. If an electrician signs a contract to put some wiring in a house that is not legal, the customer could probably not force him to do it because the court would refuse to require an illegal act.

- If either party to an offer dies, then the offer expires and cannot be accepted by the heirs. If a painter is hired to paint a portrait, and dies before completing it, his wife cannot finish it and require payment. However, a corporation does not die, even if its owners die. If a corporation is hired to build a house and the owner dies, his heirs may take over the corporation and finish the job and require payment.

- Contracts made under misrepresentation are not enforceable. For example, if someone tells you a car has 35,000 miles on it and you later discover it has 135,000 miles, you may be able to rescind the contract for fraud and misrepresentation.

- If there was a mutual mistake a contract may be rescinded. For example, if both you and the seller thought the car had 35,000 miles on it and both relied on that assumption, the contract could be rescinded. However, if the seller knew the car has 135, 000 miles on it, but you assumed it had 35,000 but did not ask, you probably could not rescind the contract.

Statutory Contract Law

The previous section discussed the basics of contract law. These are not usually stated in the statutes, but are the legal principles decided by judges over the past hundreds of years. In recent times the legislatures have made numerous exceptions to these principles. In most cases, these laws have been passed when the legislature felt that traditional law was not fair. The important laws that affect contracts are the following:

Statutes of Frauds

Statutes of frauds state when a contract must be in writing to be valid. Some people believe a contract is not valid unless it is in writing, but that is not so. Only those types of contracts mentioned in the statutes of frauds must be in writing. Of course an oral contract is much harder to prove in court than one that is in writing.

In Florida, some of the contracts that must be in writing, and the applicable statute sections are as follows:

- sales of any interest in real estate (Fla. Stat., Sec. 689.01 and 725.01.);

- leases of real estate over one year (Fla. Stat., Sec. 725.01.);

- guarantees of debts of another person (Fla. Stat., Sec. 725.01.);

- subscriptions to newspapers and periodicals (Fla. Stat., Sec. 725.01.);

- sales of goods of over $500 (Fla. Stat., Sec. 672.201.);

- sales of personal property of over $5,000 (Fla. Stat., Sec. 671.206.);

- agreements that take over one year to complete (Fla. Stat., Sec. 725.01.);

- sales of securities (Fla. Stat., Sec. 678.319.); and

- guarantees by doctors, dentists, and chiropractors for certain results (Fla. Stat., Sec. 725.01.)

Due to the alleged unfair practices by some types of businesses, laws have been passed controlling the types of contracts they may use. Most notable among these are health clubs and door-to-door solicitations. The laws covering these businesses usually give the consumer a certain time to cancel the contract. These laws are described in Chapter 12 on advertising and promotion laws.

Preparing Your Contracts

Consumer Protection Law

Before you open your business, you should obtain or prepare the contracts or policies you will use in your business. In some businesses, such as a restaurant, you will not need much. Perhaps you will want a sign near the entrance stating "shirt and shoes required" or "diners must be seated by 10:30 p.m."

However, if you are a building contractor or a similar business, you will need detailed contracts to use with your customers. If you do not clearly spell out your rights and obligations, you may end up in court and lose thousands of dollars in profits.

Of course, the best way to have an effective contract is to have an - attorney, who is experienced in the subject, prepare one to meet the needs of your business. However, since this may be too expensive for your new operation, you may want to go elsewhere. Three sources for the contracts you will need are other businesses like yours, trade associations and legal form books. You should obtain as many different contracts as possible, compare them, and decide which terms are most comfortable for you.

INSURANCE 8

There are few laws requiring you to have insurance, but if you do not have insurance you may face liability that may ruin your business. You should be aware of the types of insurance available and weigh the risks of a loss against the cost of a policy.

Be aware that there can be a wide range of prices and coverage in insurance policies. You should get at least three quotes from different insurance agents and ask each one to explain the benefits of his or her policy.

WORKERS' COMPENSATION

If you have four or more employees, or if you are in the construction industry and have one or more employees, you are required by law to carry workers' compensation insurance.

The term, *employee*, is specifically defined in Florida Statutes, Chapter 440. You should read this law carefully if you think you need to comply with this law. For example, part-time employees, students, aliens, or illegal workers count as employees. However, under certain conditions, volunteers, real estate agents, musical performers, taxi cab or limo drivers, officers of a corporation, casual workers, and persons who transport property by vehicle, are not considered employees.

Independent contractors as defined in Florida Statutes, Chapter 440 are also not considered employees.

To protect yourself from litigation, you may wish to carry workers' compensation insurance even if you are not required to have it.

This insurance can be obtained from most insurance companies and, at least for low-risk occupations, is not expensive. If you have such coverage, you are protected against potentially ruinous claims by employees or their heirs in case of accident or death.

For high-risk occupations, such as roofing, it can be very expensive, sometimes thirty to fifty cents for each dollar of payroll. For this reason, construction companies try all types of ways to become exempt, such as hiring independent contractors or only having a few employees who are also officers of the business. However, the requirements for the exemptions are strict. Anyone intending to obtain an exemption should first check with an attorney specializing in workers' compensation to be sure to do it right.

Failure to provide workers' compensation insurance when required is considered serious. It could result in a fine of up to $500, up to a year in prison, and an injunction against employing anyone. Failure to obtain the insurance within ninety-six hours of written notification can result in a fine of $100 per day. If a person is injured on a job, even if another employee caused it or the injured person contributed to his own injury, you may be required to pay for all resulting losses.

There are other requirements of the workers' compensation law, such as reporting any on-the-job deaths of workers within twenty-four hours. Also, it is a misdemeanor to deduct the amount of the premiums from the employee's wages.

Those who are exempt from the law are supposed to file an affidavit each year with the state stating that they are exempt. Also, a notice must be posted in the workplace stating that employees are not entitled to workers' compensation benefits.

This law has been subject to frequent change lately so you should check with the Division of Workers' Compensation for the latest requirements. Ask for the booklet, *Employers Rights and Responsibilities*, or their latest publication. Call 800-342-1741 or write:

>Bureau of Compliance
>Division of Workers' Compensation
>2012 Capital Cir. S.E.
>Suite 209, Hartman Bldg
>Tallahassee, FL 32399-2161
>Tel. 850-487-2536
>http://www2.myflorida.com/les/wcl

LIABILITY INSURANCE

In most cases, you are not required to carry liability insurance. A notable exception is for physicians who must carry $200,000 in liability coverage. (Fla. Stat., Sec. 458.320.)

Liability insurance can be divided into two main areas: coverage for injuries on your premises and by your employees; and coverage for injuries caused by your products or services.

Coverage for the first type of injury is usually very reasonably priced. Injuries in your business or by your employees (such as in an auto accident) are covered by standard premises or auto policies. But coverage for injuries by products may be harder to find and more expensive. In the current liability crisis, juries have awarded ridiculously high judgments for accidents involving products that had little if any impact on the accident. The situation has become so bad that some entire industries have gone out of business or moved overseas.

ASSET PROTECTION

Hopefully, laws will soon be passed to protect businesses from these unfair awards. For now, if insurance is unavailable or unaffordable, you can go without and use a corporation and other asset protection devices to protect yourself from liability.

The best way to find out if insurance is available for your type of business is to check with other businesses. If there is a trade group for your industry their newsletter or magazine may contain ads for insurers.

UMBRELLA
POLICY

As a business owner you will be a more visible target for lawsuits even if there is little merit to them. Lawyers know that a *nuisance suit* is often settled for thousands of dollars. Because of your greater exposure you should consider getting a personal umbrella policy. This is a policy that covers you for claims of up to a million—or even two or five million—dollars and is very reasonably priced.

HAZARD INSURANCE

One of the worst things that can happen to your business is a fire, flood, or other disaster. With lost customer lists, inventory, and equipment, many businesses have been forced to close after such a disaster.

The premium for such insurance is usually reasonable and could protect you from loss of your business. You can even get business interruption insurance, which will cover your losses while your business is getting back on its feet.

HOME BUSINESS INSURANCE

There is a special insurance problem for home businesses. Most homeowner and tenant insurance policies do not cover business activities. In fact, under some policies you may be denied coverage if you used your home for a business.

If you merely use your home to make business phone calls and send letters, you will probably not have a problem and not need extra coverage. But if you own equipment, or have dedicated a portion of your home exclusively to the business, you could have a problem. Check with your insurance agent for the options that are available to you.

If your business is a sole proprietorship, and you have, say, a computer that you use both personally and for your business, it would probably be covered under your homeowners' policy. But if you incorporate your business and bought the computer in the name of the corporation, coverage might be denied. If a computer is your main business asset you could get a special insurance policy in the company name covering just the computer. One company that offers such a policy is Safeware at 800-723-9273 or 800-800-1492.

AUTOMOBILE INSURANCE

If you or any of your employees will be using an automobile for business purposes, be sure that such use is covered. Sometimes a policy may include an exclusion for business use. Check to be sure your liability policy covers you if one of your employees causes an accident while running a business errand.

HEALTH INSURANCE

While new businesses can rarely afford health insurance for their employees, the sooner they can obtain it, the better chance they will have to find and keep good employees. Those starting a business usually need insurance for themselves (unless they have a working spouse who can cover the family) and they can sometimes get a better rate if they get a small business package.

Florida has a nonprofit organization, Community Health Purchasing Alliance, that helps businesses with under fifty employees locate affordable health insurance plans. They can be reached at 800-469-2472.

SALES TAX BONDS

For some businesses the Florida Department of Revenue will require a bond to guarantee payment of sales taxes. This can be obtained from your insurance agent.

EMPLOYEE THEFT

If you fear employees may be able to steal from your business, you may want to have them *bonded*. This means that you pay an insurance company a premium to guarantee employees' honesty and if they cheat you the insurance company pays you damages. This can cover all existing and new employees.

Your Business and the Internet 9

The Internet has opened up a world of opportunities for businesses. A few years ago getting national visibility cost a fortune. Today a business can set up a Web page for a few hundred dollars and, with some clever publicity and a little luck, millions of people around the world will see it.

But this new world has new legal issues and new liabilities. Not all of them have been addressed by laws or by the courts. Before you begin doing business on the Internet, you should know the existing rules and the areas where legal issues exist.

Domain Names

A *domain name* is the address of your website. For example, www.apple.com is the domain name of Apple Computer Company. The last part of the domain name, the ".com" (or "dot com") is the *top level domain,* or TLD. Dot com is the most popular, but others are currently available in the United States, including .net and .org. (Originally .net was only available to network service providers and .org only to nonprofit organizations, but regulations have eliminated those requirements.)

It may seem like most words have been taken as a dot-com name, but if you combine two or three short words or abbreviations, a nearly unlimited number of possibilities are available. For example, if you have a business dealing with automobiles, most likely someone has already registered automobile.com and auto.com. But you can come up with all kinds of variations, using adjectives or your name, depending on your type of business:

autos4u.com	joesauto.com	autobob.com
myauto.com	yourauto.com	onlyautos.com
greatauto.com	autosfirst.com	usautos.com
greatautos.com	firstautoworld.com	4autos.com

When the Internet first began, some individuals realized that major corporations would soon want to register their names. Since the registration was easy and cheap, people registered names they thought would ultimately be used by someone else.

At first, some companies paid high fees to buy their names from the registrants. But one company, Intermatic, filed a lawsuit instead of paying. The owner of the mark they wanted had registered numerous trademarks, such as britishairways.com and ussteel.com. The court ruled that since Intermatic owned a trademark on the name, the registration of their name by someone else violated that trademark and that Intermatic was entitled to it.

Since then people have registered names that are not trademarks, such as CalRipkin.com, and have attempted to charge the individuals with those names to buy their domain. In 1998, Congress stepped in and passed the Anti-Cybersquatting Consumer Protection Act. This law makes it illegal to register a domain with no legitimate need to use it.

This law helped a lot of companies protect their names, but then some companies started abusing it and tried to stop legitimate users of similar names. This is especially likely against small companies. Two organizations have been set up to help small companies protect their domains: the Domain Defense Advocate and the Domain Name Rights Coalition. Their websites are:

www.ajax.org/dda

www.domain-name.org

Registering a domain name for your own business is a simple process. There are many companies that offer registration services. For a list of those companies, visit the site of the Internet Corporation for Assigned Names and Numbers (ICANN) at **http://www.icann.org**. You can link directly to any member's site and compare the costs and registration procedures required for the different top-level domains.

WEB PAGES

There are many new companies eager to help you set up a website. Some offer turnkey sites for a low flat rate. Custom sites can cost tens of thousands of dollars. If you have plenty of capital you may want to have your site handled by one of these professionals. However, setting up a website is a fairly simple process, and once you learn the basics you can handle most of it in-house.

If you are new to the Web, you may want to look at the following sites, which will familiarize you with the Internet jargon and give you a basic introduction to the Web:

http://www.learnthenet.com   http://www.webopedia.com

SITE SETUP   There are seven steps to setting up a website: site purpose, design, content, structure, programming, testing, and publicity. Whether you do it yourself, hire a professional site designer, or use a college student, the steps toward creating an effective site are the same.

Before beginning your own site you should look at other sites, including those of major corporations and of small businesses. Look at the sites of all the companies that compete with you. Look at hundreds of sites and click through them to see how they work (or don't work!)

Site purpose. To know what to include on your site you must decide what its purpose will be. Do you want to take orders for your products or services, attract new employees, give away samples, or show off your company headquarters? You might want to do several of these things.

Site design. After looking at other sites you can see that there are numerous ways to design a site. It can be crowded, or open and airy; it can have several windows (frames) open at once or just one, and it can allow long scrolling or just click-throughs.

You will have to decide whether the site will have text only; text plus photographs and graphics; or text plus photos, graphics, and other design elements such as animation or Java script. Additionally, you will begin to make decisions about colors, fonts, and the basic graphic appearance of the site.

Site content. You must create the content for your site. For this, you can use your existing promotional materials, you can write new material just for the Web site, or you can use a combination of the two. Whatever you choose, remember that the written material should be concise, free of errors, and easy for your target audience to read. Any graphics, including photographs, and written materials not created by you require permission. You should obtain such permission from the lawful copyright holder in order to use any copyrighted material. Once you know your site's purpose, look, and content, you can begin to piece the site together.

Site structure. You must decide how the content (text plus photographs, graphics, animation, etc.) will be structured–what content will be on which page, and how a user will link from one part of the site to another. For example, your first page may have the business name and then choices to click on, such as "about us," "opportunities," "product catalog," etc. Have those choices connect to another page containing the detailed information so that a user will see the catalog when they click on "product catalog." Or your site could have a choice to click on a link to another website related to yours.

Site programming and setup. When you know nothing about setting up a website, it can seem like a daunting task that will require an expert. However, "programming" here means merely putting a site together. There are inexpensive computer programs available that make it very simple.

Commercial programs such as Microsoft FrontPage, Dreamweaver, Pagemaker, Photoshop, MS Publisher, and PageMill allow you to set up

Web pages as easily as laying out a print publication. These programs will convert the text and graphics you create into HTML, the programming language of the Web. Before you choose Web design software and design your site, you should determine which Web hosting service you will use. Make sure that the design software you use is compatible with the host server's system. The Web host will be the provider who will give you space on their server and who may provide other services to you, such as secure order processing and analysis of your site to see who is visiting and linking to it.

If you have an America Online account, you can download design software and a tutorial for free. AOL has recently collaborated with a Web hosting service at **http://www.verioprimehost.com** and offers a number of different hosting packages for the consumer and e-business. You do not have to use AOL's design software in order to use this service. You are eligible to use this site whether you design your own pages, have someone else do the design work for you, or use AOL's templates. This service allows you to use your own domain name and choose the package that is appropriate for your business.

If you have used a page layout program, you can usually get a simple Web page up and running within a day or two. If you don't have much experience with a computer, you might consider hiring a college student to set up a Web page for you.

Site testing. Some of the website setup programs allow you to thoroughly check your new site to see if all the pictures are included and all the links are proper. There are also websites you can go to that will check out your site. Some even allow you to improve your site, such as by reducing the size of your graphics so they download faster. Use a major search engine listed on page 62 to look for companies that can test your site before you launch it on the Web.

Site publicity. Once you set up your website, you will want to get people to look at it. *Publicity* means getting your site noticed as much as possible by drawing people to it.

The first thing to do to get noticed is to be sure your site is registered with as many *search engines* as possible. These are pages that people use to find things on the Internet, such as Yahoo and Excite. They do not automatically know about you just because you created a website. You must tell them about your site, and they must examine and catalog it.

For a fee, there are services that will register your site with numerous search engines. If you are starting out on a shoestring, you can easily do it yourself. While there are hundreds of search engines, most people use a dozen or so of the bigger ones. If your site is in a niche area, such as geneology services, then you would want to be listed on any specific geneology search engines. Most businesses should be mainly concerned with getting on the biggest ones. The biggest search engines at this time are:

www.altavista.com	www.lycos.com
www.dejanews.com	www.magellan.com
www.excite.com	www.metacrawler.com
www.fastsearch	www.northernlight.com
www.goto.com	www.webcrawler.com
www.hotbot.com	www.yahoo.com
www.infoseek.com	

Most of these sites have a place to click to "add your site" to their system. There are sites that rate the search engines, help you list on the search engines, or check to see if you are listed. One site is:

http://www.searchiq.com

A *meta tag* is an invisible subject word added to your site that can be found by a search engine. For example, if you are a pest control company, you may want to list all of the scientific names of the pests you control and all of the treatments you have available; but you may not need them to be part of the visual design of your site. List these words as meta tags when you set up your page so people searching for those words will find your site.

Some companies thought that a clever way to get viewers would be to use commonly searched names, or names of major competitors, as meta tags to attract people looking for those big companies. For example, a small delivery service that has nothing to do with UPS or Federal Express might use those company names as meta tags so people looking for them would find the smaller company. While it may sound like a good idea, it has been declared illegal trademark infringement. Today many companies have computer programs scanning the Internet for improper use of their trademarks.

Once you have made sure that your site is passively listed in all the search engines, you may want to actively promote your site. However, self-promotion is seen as a bad thing on the Internet, especially if its purpose is to make money.

Newsgroups are places on the Internet where people interested in a specific topic can exchange information. For example, expectant mothers have a group where they can trade advice and experiences. If you have a product that would be great for expectant mothers, that would be a good place for it to be discussed. However, if you log into the group and merely announce your product, suggesting people order it from your Web site, you will probably be *flamed* (sent a lot of hate mail).

If you join the group, however, and become a regular, and in answer to someone's problem, mention that you "saw this product that might help," your information will be better received. It may seem unethical to plug your product without disclosing your interest, but this is a procedure used by many large companies. They hire people to plug their product (or rock star) all over the Internet. So, perhaps it has become an acceptable marketing method and consumers know to take plugs with a grain of salt. Let your conscience be your guide.

Keep in mind that Internet publicity works both ways. If you have a great product and people love it, you will get a lot of business. If you sell a shoddy product, give poor service, and don't keep your customers happy, bad publicity on the Internet can kill your business. Besides being an equalizer between large and small companies, the Internet can be a filtering mechanism between good and bad products.

There is no worse breach of Internet etiquette ("netiquette") than to send advertising by e-mail to strangers. It is called *spamming*, and doing it can have serious consequences. There is anti-spamming legislation currently pending at the federal level. Many states, including California, Colorado, Connecticut, Delaware, Idaho, Illinois, Iowa, Louisiana, Missouri, Nevada, North Carolina, Oklahoma, Pennsylvania, Rhode Island, Tennessee, Virginia, Washington, and West Virginia, have enacted anti-spamming legislation. This legislation sets specific requirements for unsolicited bulk e-mail and makes certain practices illegal. You should check with an attorney to see if your business practices fall within the legal limits of these laws. Additionally, many Internet Service Providers (ISPs) have restrictions on unsolicited bulk e-mail (spam); you should check with your ISP to make sure you do not violate its policies.

ADVERTISING

Banner ads are the small rectangular ads on many Web pages which usually blink or move. Although most computer users seem to have become immune to them, there is still a big market in the sale and exchange of them.

If your site gets enough viewers, people may pay you to place their ads there. Another possibility is to trade ads with another site. In fact there are companies that broker ad trades among Web sites. Such trades used to be taxable transactions, but after January 5, 2000, such trades were no longer taxable under IRS Notice 2000-6.

LEGAL ISSUES

Before you set up a Web page, you should consider the legal issues described below.

JURISDICTION

Jurisdiction is the power of a court in a particular location to decide a particular case. Usually you have to have been physically present in a jurisdiction or have done business there before you can be sued there. Since the Internet extends your business's ability to reach people in far-away places, there may be instances when you could be subject to legal jurisdiction far from your own state (or country). There are a number of cases that have been decided in this country regarding the Internet and jurisdiction, but very few cases have been decided on this issue outside of the United States.

In most instances, U.S. courts use the pre-Internet test–whether you have been present in another jurisdiction or have had enough contact with someone in the other jurisdiction. The fact that the Internet itself is not a "place" will not shield you from being sued in another state when you have shipped you company's product there, have entered into a contract with a resident of that state, or have defamed a foreign resident with content on your website.

According to the Court, there is a spectrum of contact required between you, your website, and consumers, or audiences. (*Zippo Manufacturing Co. v. Zippo Dot Com, Inc.*, 952 F. Supp. 1119 (W.D. Pa 1997)) It is *clear* that the one end of the spectrum includes the shipping, contracting, and defamation mentioned above as sufficient to establish jurisdiction. The more interactive your site is with consumers, the more you target an audience for your goods in a particular location, and the farther you reach to send your goods out into the world, the more it becomes possible for someone to sue you outside of your own jurisdiction–possibly even in another country.

The law is not even remotely final on these issues. The American Bar Association, among other groups, is studying this topic in detail. At present, no final, global solution or agreement about jurisdictional issues exists.

One way to protect yourself from the possibility of being sued in a faraway jurisdiction would be to have a statement on your website stating that those using the site or doing business with you agree that "jurisdiction for any actions regarding this site" or your company will be in your home county.

For extra protection you can have a preliminary page that must be clicked before entering your website. However, this may be overkill for a small business with little risk of lawsuits. If you are in any business for which you could have serious liability, you should review some competitors' sites and see how they handle the liability issue. They often have a place to click for "legal notice" or "disclaimer" on their first page.

You may want to consult with an attorney to discuss the specific disclaimer you will use on your website, where it should appear, and whether you will have users of your site actively "agree" to this disclaimer or just "passively" read it. However, these disclaimers are not enforceable everywhere in the world. Until there is global agreement on jurisdictional issues, this may remain an area of uncertainty for some time to come.

LIBEL

Libel is any publication that injures the reputation of another. This can occur in print, writing, pictures, or signs. All that is required for *publication* is that you transmit the material to at least one other person. When putting together your website you must keep in mind that it is visible to millions of people all over the planet and that if you libel a person or company you may have to pay damages. Many countries do not have the freedom of speech that we do and a statement that is not libel in the United States may be libelous elsewhere.

COPYRIGHT
INFRINGEMENT

It is so easy to copy and "borrow" information on the Internet that it is easy to infringe copyrights without even knowing it. A *copyright* exists for a work as soon as the creator creates it. There is no need to register the copyright or to put a copyright notice on it. So, practically everything on the Internet belongs to someone. Some people freely give their works away. For example, many people have created web artwork (*gifs* and *animated gifs*) that they freely allow people to copy. There are numerous sites that provide hundreds or thousands of free gifs that you can add to your Web pages. Some require you to acknowledge the source; some don't.

You should always be sure that the works are free for the taking before using them.

LINKING AND
FRAMING

One way to violate copyright laws is to improperly link other sites to yours either directly or with framing. *Linking* is when you provide a place on your site to click, which takes someone to another site. *Framing* occurs when you set up your site so that when you link to another site, your site is still viewable as a frame around the linked-to site.

While many sites are glad to be linked to others, some, especially providers of valuable information, object. Courts have ruled that linking and framing can be a copyright violation. One rule that has developed is that it is usually okay to link to the first page of a site, but not to link to some valuable information deeper within the site. The rationale for this is that the owner of the site wants visitors to go through the various levels of their site (viewing all the ads) before getting the information. By linking to the information you are giving away their product without the ads.

The problem with linking to the first page of a site is that it may be a tedious or difficult task to find the needed page from there. Many sites are poorly designed and make it nearly impossible to find anything.

The best solution, if you wish to link to another page, is to ask permission. Email the Webmaster or other person in charge of the site, if one is given, and explain what you want to do. If they grant permission, be sure to print out a copy of their e-mail for your records.

PRIVACY   Since the Internet is such an easy way to share information, there are many concerns that it will cause a loss of individual privacy. The two main concerns arise when you post information that others consider private, and when you gather information from customers and use it in a way that violates their privacy.

While public actions of politicians and celebrities are fair game, details about their private lives are sometimes protected by law, and details about persons who are not public figures are often protected. The laws in each state are different, and what might be allowable in one state could be illegal in another. If your site will provide any personal information about individuals, you should discuss the possibility of liability with an attorney.

Several well-known companies have been in the news lately for violations of their customers' privacy. They either shared what the customer was buying or downloading, or looked for additional information on the customer's computer. To let customers know that you do not violate certain standards of privacy, you can subscribe to one of the privacy codes that have been promulgated for the Internet. These allow you to put a symbol on your site guaranteeing to your customers that you follow the code.

The websites of three of the organizations that offer this service, and their fees at the time of this publication, are:

www.privacybot.com	$30
www.bbbonline.com	$150 to $3,000
www.trustee.com	$299 to $4,999

PROTECTING YOURSELF

The easiest way to protect yourself personally from the various possible types of liability is to set up a corporation or limited liability company to own the website. This is not foolproof protection since, in some cases, you could be sued personally as well, but it is one level of protection.

COPPA

If your website is aimed at children under the age of thirteen, or if it attracts children of that age, then you are covered by the federal Children Online Privacy Protection Act of 1998 (COPPA). This law requires such Web sites to:

- give notice on the site of what information is being collected;

- obtain verifiable parental consent to collect the information;

- allow the parent to review the information collected;

- allow the parent to delete the child's information or to refuse to allow the use of the information;

- limit the information collected to only that necessary to participate on the site; and

- protect the security and confidentiality of the information.

FINANCIAL TRANSACTIONS

In the future, there will be easy ways to exchange money on the Internet. Some companies have already been started that promote their own kinds of electronic money. Whether any of these become universal is yet to be seen.

For now, the easiest way to exchange money on the Internet is through traditional credit cards. Because of concerns that email can be abducted in transit and read by others, most companies use a "secure" site in which customers are guaranteed that their card data is encrypted before being sent.

When setting up your website, you should ask the provider if you can be set up with a secure site for transmitting credit card data. If they cannot provide it, you will need to contract with another software provider. Use a major search engine listed on page 62 to look for companies that provide credit card services to businesses on the web.

As a practical matter, there is very little to worry about when sending credit card data by email. If you do not have a secure site, another option is to allow purchasers to fax or phone in their credit card data. However, keep in mind that this extra step will lose some business unless your products are unique and your buyers are very motivated.

The least effective option is to provide an order form on the site, which can be printed out and mailed in with a check. Again, your customers must be really motivated or they will lose interest after finding out this extra work is involved.

FTC RULES

Because the Internet is an instrument of interstate commerce, it is a legitimate subject for federal regulation. The Federal Trade Commission (FTC) first said that all of its consumer protection rules applied to the

Internet, but lately it has been adding specific rules and issuing publications. The following publications are available from the FTC website at **http://www.ftc.gov/bcp/menu-internet.htm** or by mail from Consumer Response Center, Federal Trade Commission, 600 Pennsylvania, NW, Room H-130, Washington, DC 20580-0001.

- *Advertising and Marketing on the Internet: The Rules of the Road*

- *BBB-Online: Code of Online Business Practices*

- *Electronic Commerce: Selling Internationally. A Guide for Business Alert*

- *How to Comply With The Children's Online Privacy Protection Rule*

- *Internet Auctions: A Guide for Buyer and Sellers*

- *Selling on the Internet: Prompt Delivery Rules Alert*

- *Website Woes: Avoiding Web Service Scams Alert*

FRAUD

Because the Internet is somewhat anonymous, it is a tempting place for those with fraudulent schemes to look for victims. As a business consumer, you should exercise caution when dealing with unknown or anonymous parties on the Internet.

Recently, the U.S. Department of Justice, the FBI, and the National White Collar Crime Center launched the Internet Fraud Complaint Center (IFCC). If you suspect that you are the victim of fraud online, whether as a consumer or a business, you can report incidents to the IFCC on their website, **http://www.ifccfbi.gov**. The IFCC is currently staffed by FBI agents and representatives of the National White Collar Crime Center and will work with state and local law enforcement officials to prevent, investigate, and prosecute high-tech and economic crime online.

HEALTH AND SAFETY LAWS 10

FEDERAL LAWS

OSHA   The Occupational Safety and Health Administration (OSHA) is a good example of government regulation so severe it strangles businesses out of existence. Robert D. Moran, a former chairman of the committee that hears appeals from OSHA rulings once said that "there isn't a person on earth who can be certain he is in full compliance with the requirements of this standard at any point in time." The point of the law is to place the duty on the employer to keep the workplace free from recognized hazards that are likely to cause death or serious bodily injury to workers.

For example, OSHA decided to analyze repetitive-strain injuries, or "RSI," such as carpal tunnel syndrome. The Bureau of Labor Statistics estimated that 7% of workplace illnesses are RSI and the National Safety Council estimated 4%. OSHA, however, determined that 60% is a more accurate figure and came out with a 600 page list of proposed regulations, guidelines, and suggestions. These regulations would have affected over one-half of all businesses in America and cost billions of dollars. Fortunately, these regulations were shot down by Congress in 1995, after an outcry from businesses. Shortly thereafter, OSHA officials ignored Congress' sentiment and promised to launch a new effort.

Fortunately, for small businesses the regulations are not as cumbersome as for larger enterprises. If you have ten or fewer employees or if you are in certain types of businesses, you do not have to keep a record of illnesses, injuries, and exposure to hazardous substances of employees. If you have eleven or more employees, you do have to keep this record, which is called *Log 200*. All employers are required to display a poster that you can get from OSHA.

Within forty-eight hours of an on-the-job death of an employee or injury of five or more employees on the job, the area director of OSHA must be contacted.

For more information, you should write or call an OSHA office:

> OSHA Regional Office
> 61 Forsyth St. S.W.
> Atlanta, GA 30303
> 404-562-2300
> 404-562-2295 (fax)
> Jacksonville: 904-232-2895
> Fort Lauderdale: 954-424-0242
> Tampa: 813-626-1177

or visit their website: **http://www.osha.gov** and obtain copies of their publications, *OSHA Handbook for Small Business* (OSHA 2209), and *OSHA Publications and Audiovisual Programs Catalog* (OSHA 2019). They also have a poster that is required to be posted in the workplace. Find it at:

> http://www.osha.gov/oshpubs/poster.html

The Hazard Communication Standard requires that employees be made aware of the hazards in the workplace. (Code of Federal Regulations (C.F.R., Title 29, Section (Sec.) 1910.1200.) It is especially applicable to those working with chemicals but this can even include offices that use copy machines. Businesses using hazardous chemicals must have a comprehensive program for informing employees of the hazards and for protecting them from contamination.

For more information, you can contact OSHA at the previously-mentioned addresses, phone numbers, or websites. They can supply a copy of the regulation and a booklet called *OSHA 3084*, which explains the law.

EPA The Worker Protection Standard for Agricultural Pesticides requires safety training, decontamination sites and, of course, posters. The Environmental Protection Agency will provide information on compliance with this law. They can be reached at 800-490-9198, or their website at:

> http://www.epa.gov

They can be reached by mail at:

> Environmental Protection Agency
> 1200 Pennsylvania Ave. N.W.
> Washington, DC 20460

FDA
The Pure Food and Drug Act of 1906 prohibits the misbranding or adulteration of food and drugs. It also created the Food and Drug Administration (FDA), which has promulgated tons of regulations and which must give permission before a new drug can be introduced into the market. If you will be dealing with any food or drugs you should keep abreast of their policies. Their website is: **http://www.fda.gov**, their small business site is: **http://www.fda.gov/ora/fed_state/small_business/ sb_guide/default.htm** and their local small business representative is:

> FDA, Southeast Region
> Small Business Representative, Barbara Ward-Groves
> 60 Eight St. NE
> Atlanta, GA 30309
> Phone 404-347-4001 Ext 5256
> Fax 404-347-4349

HAZARDOUS MATERIALS TRANSPORTATION
There are regulations that control the shipping and packing of hazardous materials. For more information contact:

> Office of Hazardous Materials Transportation
> 400 Seventh St.
> S.W., Washington, DC 20590
> 202-366-8553.
> http://hazmat.dot.gov

CPSC
The Consumer Product Safety Commission has a set of rules that cover the safety of products. The commission feels that because its rules cover products, rather than people or companies, they apply to everyone producing such products. However, federal laws do not apply to small businesses that do not affect interstate commerce. Whether a small business would fall under a CPSC rule would depend on the size and nature of your business.

The CPSC rules are contained in the Code of Federal Regulations, Title 16 in the following parts. These can be found at most law libraries, some public libraries, and on the Internet at: **http://www.access.gpo.gov/nara/ cfr/cfr-table-search.html**. The CPSC's site is: **http://cpsc.gov/index.html**.

PRODUCT	PART
Antennas, CB and TV	1402
Architectural Glazing Material	1201
Articles Hazardous to Children Under 3	1501
Baby Cribs-Full Size	1508
Baby Cribs-Non-Full Size	1509
Bicycle Helmets	1203
Bicycles	1512
Carpets and Rugs	1630, 1631
Cellulose Insulation	1209, 1404
Cigarette Lighters	1210
Citizens Band Base Station Antennas	1204
Coal and Wood Burning Appliances	1406
Consumer Products Containing Chlorofluorocarbons	1401
Electrically Operated Toys	1505
Emberizing Materials Containing Asbestos (banned)	1305
Extremely Flammable Contact Adhesives (banned)	1302
Fireworks	1507
Garage Door Openers	1211
Hazardous Lawn Darts (banned)	1306
Hazardous Substances	1500
Human Subjects	1028
Lawn Mowers, Walk-Behind	1205
Lead-Containing Paint (banned)	1303
Matchbooks	1202
Mattresses	1632
Pacifiers	1511
Patching Compounds Containing Asbestos (banned)	1304
Poisons	1700
Rattles	1510
Self-Pressurized Consumer Products	1401
Sleepwear-Childrens	1615, 1616
Swimming Pool Slides	1207
Toys, Electrical	1505
Unstable Refuse Bins (banned)	1301

ADDITIONAL
REGULATIONS

Every day there are proposals for new laws and regulations. It would be impossible to include every conceivable one in this book. To be up to date on the laws that affect your type of business, you should belong to a trade association for your industry and subscribe to newsletters that cover your industry. Attending industry conventions is a good way to learn more and to discover new ways to increase your profits.

FLORIDA LAWS

HAZARDOUS
OCCUPATIONS

Under Florida Statutes, Chapter 769, railroading, operating street railways, generating and selling electricity; telegraph and telephone business; express business; blasting and dynamiting; operating automobiles for public use; and boating when the boat is powered by steam, gas, or electricity are considered hazardous occupations. The owners of such enterprises are liable for injuries or death of their employees because there is a presumption that they did not use reasonable care. They must be able to rebut this presumption in order to be found not liable. In cases where the employee is at fault, the damages are apportioned, or divided according to fault. Employers may not contract with employees to avoid the liability of this law.

SMOKING

The Florida Clean Indoor Air Act passed in 1985 contains the following rules regarding smoking in "public places" and at "public meetings." (Fla. Stat., Sections 386.201-.212.)

- Public places are defined as the following areas used by the general public: government buildings, public transportation facilities and terminals (unless covered by federal smoking laws), elevators, hospitals, nursing homes, educational facilities, public school buses, libraries, courtrooms, jury waiting and deliberation rooms, museums, theaters, auditoriums, arenas, recreational facilities, restaurants which seat more than fifty persons (except restaurants which designate smoking areas according to customer demand), retail stores (except tobacco stores), grocery stores, places of employment, health care facilities, day care centers, and common areas of retirement homes and condominiums.

- Public meetings are all those open to the public (including homeowner, condominium, or renter associations) except those held in private homes.

- No person may smoke in a public place or at a public meeting except in designated smoking areas and except in private social functions where the seating is controlled by the sponsor.

- Smoking areas may be designated. Smoke in adjacent non-smoking areas must be minimized but no physical modification of the area is required.

- There may not be smoking areas in elevators, school buses, public transportation facilities, rest rooms, hospitals, doctors' or dentists' waiting rooms, jury deliberation rooms, county public health units, day care centers, schools or other educational facilities or common areas.

- Patients' rooms in hospitals, nursing homes or health care facilities may not be designated as smoking areas unless all patients agree and it is ordered by the attending physician.

- No more than half the rooms in a health care facility may be designated as smoking areas.

- No more than half the square footage of an enclosed area used for common purposes in a public place shall be designated for smoking except restaurants that cannot have more than sixty-five percent of their dining room seats located in a designated smoking area.

- Designated smoking areas must be conspicuously posted with letters of reasonable size that can be easily read. "No smoking except in designated areas" signs may also be posted when appropriate.

- Employers of smoking and non-smoking employees are required to institute and post policies regarding designation of smoking and non-smoking areas.

- Exemptions from the law may be requested from the Department of Health and Rehabilitative Services or from the Division of Hotels and Motels of the Department of Business and Professional Regulation.

- Businesses that fail to comply with the law can receive a warning, then a $100 fine, a $500 fine and a court order to comply. Individuals who violate the smoking law can be fined up to $100 for the first violation and up to $500 for subsequent violations.

EMPLOYMENT AND LABOR LAWS 11

HIRING AND FIRING LAWS

For small businesses, there are not many rules regarding who you may hire or fire. Fortunately, the ancient law that an employee can be fired at any time (or may quit at any time) still prevails for small businesses. But in certain situations, and as you grow, you will come under a number of laws that affect your hiring and firing practices.

One of the most important things to consider when hiring someone is that if you fire them they may be entitled to unemployment compensation. If so, your unemployment compensation tax rate will go up and it can cost you a lot of money. Therefore, you should only hire people you are sure you will keep and you should avoid situations where your former employees can make claims against your company.

One way this can be done is by hiring only part-time employees. The drawback to this is that you may not be able to attract the best - employees. When hiring dishwashers or busboys this may not be an issue, but when hiring someone to develop a software product, you do not want them to leave halfway through the development.

A better solution is to screen applicants to begin with and only hire those who you feel certain will work out. Of course this is easier said than done. Some people interview well but then turn out to be incompetent at the job.

The best record to look for is someone who has stayed a long time at each of their previous jobs. Next best is someone who has not stayed as long (for good reasons) but has always been employed. The worst type of hire would be someone who is or has been collecting unemployment compensation.

The reason those who have collected compensation are a bad risk is that if they collect in the future, even if it is not your fault, your employment of them could make you chargeable for their claim. For example, you hire someone who has been on unemployment compensation and they work out well for a year, but then they quit to take another job, and are fired after a few weeks. In this situation, you would be chargeable for most of their claim because their last five quarters of work are analyzed. Look for a steady job history.

In the author's experience, the intelligence of an employee is more important than his or her experience. An employee with years of typing experience may be fast, but unable to figure out how to use your new computer. Whereas an intelligent employee can learn the equipment quickly and eventually gain speed. Of course, common sense is important in all situations.

The bottom line is that you cannot know if an employee will be able to fill your needs from a resume and interview. Once you have found someone who you think will work out, offer them a job with a ninety day probationary period. If you are not completely satisfied with them after the ninety days, offer to extend the probationary period for ninety additional days rather than end the relationship immediately. Of course, all of this should be in writing.

BACKGROUND CHECKS

Checking references is important, but beware that a former boss may be a good friend, or even a relative. It has always been considered acceptable to exaggerate on resumes, but in recent years, some applicants have been found to be completely fabricating sections of their education and experience.

POLYGRAPH TESTS

Under the federal Employee Polygraph Protection Act you cannot require an employee or prospective employee to take a polygraph test unless you are in the armored car, guard, or pharmaceutical business.

DRUG TESTS   Under the ADA drug testing can only be required of applicants who have been offered jobs conditioned upon passing the drug test. Under Florida law employers are allowed to test employees before and after they are hired. (Fla. Stat., Sec. 440.102.) They can obtain discounts on drug tests if they qualify under the drug-free workplace program. (Fla. Stat., Sec. 627.0915.) Employers can also deny medical and indemnity benefits for failure to pass a test.

FIRING

In most cases, unless you have a contract with an employee for a set time period, you can fire him or her at any time. This is only fair since the employee can quit at any time. The exceptions to this are: if you fired someone based on illegal discrimination (see page 84), for filing some sort of health or safety complaint (see page 71), or for refusing your sexual advances (see page 88).

NEW HIRE REPORTING

In order to track down parents who do not pay child support, a federal law was passed in 1996 that requires the reporting of new hires. The Personal Responsibility and Work Opportunity Reconciliation Act of 1996 (PRWORA) provides that such information must be reported by employers to their state government.

Within twenty days of hiring a new employee, an employer must provide the state with information about the employee including the name, social security number and address. This information can be submitted in several ways including mail, fax, magnetic tape or over the Internet. There is a special form that can be used for this reporting; however, an employer can use the EMPLOYEE'S WITHHOLDING ALLOWANCE CERTIFICATE (IRS FORM W-4) for this purpose. (see form 7, p.219.) Since this form must be filled out for all employees anyway, it would be pointless to use a separate form for the new hire reporting. A copy of the **IRS FORM W-4** is included in Appendix B and this may be faxed to the Florida toll-free number, 800-688-2680 or mailed to:

> Florida New Hire Reporting Program
> P. O. Box 6500
> Tallahassee, FL 32314-6500

For more information about the program you can call them at 800-979-9014, write to them at the above address, or visit their website:

> http://www.fl-newhire.com

EMPLOYMENT AGREEMENTS

To avoid misunderstanding with employees you should use an employment agreement or an employee handbook. These can spell out in detail the policies of your company and the rights of your employees. They can protect your trade secrets and spell out clearly that employment can be terminated at any time by either party.

While it may be difficult or awkward to ask an existing employee to sign such an agreement, an applicant hoping you will hire them will usually sign whatever is necessary to obtain the job. However, because of the unequal bargaining position, you should not use an agreement that would make you look bad if the matter ever went to court.

If having an employee sign an agreement is awkward, you can usually obtain the same rights by putting the company policies in an employee manual. Each existing and new employee should be given a copy along with a letter stating that the rules apply to all employees and that by accepting or continuing employment at your company they agree to abide by the rules. Having an employee sign a receipt for the letter and manual is proof that they received it.

One danger of an employment agreement or handbook is that it may be interpreted to create a long term employment contract. To avoid this be sure that you clearly state in the agreement or handbook that the employment is "at will" and can be terminated at any time by either party.

Some other things to consider in an employment agreement or handbook are:

- what the salary and other compensation will be;

- what the hours of employment will be;

- what the probationary period will be;

- that the employee cannot sign any contracts binding the employer; and

- that the employee agrees to arbitration rather than filing a lawsuit.

INDEPENDENT CONTRACTORS

One way to avoid problems with employees and taxes at the same time is to have all of your work done through independent contractors. This can relieve you of most of the burdens of employment laws and the obligation to pay social security and medicare taxes for the workers.

An independent contractor is, in effect, a separate business that you pay to do a job. You pay them just as you pay any company from which you buy products or services. At the end of the year if the amount paid exceeds $600, you will issue a 1099 form instead of the W-2 that you issue to employees.

This may seem too good to be true; and in some situations it is. The IRS does not like independent contractor arrangements because it is too easy for the independent contractors to cheat on their taxes. To limit the use of independent contractors, the IRS has strict regulations on who may and may not be classified as an independent contractor. Also, companies who do not appear to pay enough in wages for their field of business are audited.

The highest at-risk jobs are those that are not traditionally done by independent contractors. For example, you could not get away with hiring a secretary as an independent contractor. One of the most important factors considered in determining if a worker can be an independent contractor is the amount of control the company has over his or her work. If you need someone to paint your building and you agree to pay them a certain price to do it according to their own methods and schedule, you can pay them as an independent contractor. But if you tell them when to work, how to do the job and provide them with the tools and materials, they will be classified as an employee.

If you just need some typing done and you take it to a typing service and pick it up when it is ready, you will be safe in treating them as independent contractors. But, if you need someone to come into your office to type on your machine at your schedule, you will probably be required to treat that person as an employee for tax purposes.

The IRS has a form you can use in determining if a person is an employee or an independent contractor called DETERMINATION OF EMPLOYEE WORK STATUS (IRS FORM SS-8). It is included in Appendix B of this book along with instructions. (see form 6, p.215.)

INDEPENDENT CONTRACTORS V. EMPLOYEES

In deciding whether to make use of independent contractors or - employees, you should weigh the following advantages and disadvantages.

Advantages.

- Lower taxes. You do not have to pay social security, medicare, unemployment, or other employee taxes.

- Less paperwork. You do not have to handle federal withholding deposits or the monthly employer returns to the state or federal government.

- Less insurance. You do not have to pay workers' compensation insurance and since the workers are not your employees you do not have to insure against their possible liabilities.

- More flexibility. You can use independent contractors when you need them and not pay them when business is slow.

Disadvantages.

- The IRS and state tax offices are strict about when workers can may be qualified as independent contractors. They will audit companies whose use of independent contractors does not appear to be legitimate.

- If your use of independent contractors is found to be improper you may have to pay back taxes and penalties and have problems with your pension plan.

- While employees usually cannot sue you for their injuries (if you have covered them with workers' compensation) independent contractors can sue you if their injuries were your fault.

- If you are paying someone to produce a creative work (writing, photography, artwork) you receive less rights to the work of an independent contractor.

- You have less control over the work of an independent contractor and less flexibility in terminating them if you are not satisfied that the job is being done the way you require.

- You have less loyalty from an independent contractor who works sporadically for you and possibly others than from your own full time employees.

For some businesses, the advantages outweigh the disadvantages. For others they do not. Consider your business plans and the consequences from each type of arrangement. Keep in mind that it will be easier to start with independent contractors and switch to employees than to hire employees and have to fire them to hire independent contractors.

Temporary Workers

Another way to avoid the hassles of hiring employees is to get workers from a temporary agency. In this arrangement you may pay a higher amount per hour for the work but the agency will take care of all of the tax and insurance requirements. Since these can be expensive and time-consuming, the extra cost may be well worth it.

Whether or not temporary workers will work for you depends upon the type of business you are in and tasks you need performed. For such jobs as sales management, you would probably want someone who will stay with you long term and develop relationships with the buyers, but for order fulfillment, temporary workers might work out well.

Another advantage of temporary workers is that you can easily stop using those who do not work out well for you, but if you find one who is ideal, you may be able to hire him or her on a full time basis.

In recent years a new wrinkle has developed in the temporary worker area. Many large companies are beginning to use them because they are so much cheaper than paying the benefits demanded by full-time employees. For example, Microsoft Corp. has had as many as 6,000 temporary workers, some of whom work for them for years. Some of the temporary workers recently won a lawsuit declaring that they are really employees and are entitled to the same benefits of other employees (such as pension plans).

The law is not yet settled in this area as to what arrangements will result in a temporary worker being declared an employee. That will take several more court cases, some of which have already been filed. A few things you can do to protect yourself are:

- Be sure that any of your benefit plans make it clear that they do not apply to workers obtained through temporary agencies.

- Do not keep the same temporary workers for longer than a year.

- Do not list temporary workers in any employee directories or hold them out to the public as your employees.

- Do not allow them to use your business cards or stationery.

DISCRIMINATION LAWS

FEDERAL LAW   There are numerous federal laws forbidding discrimination based upon race, sex, pregnancy, color, religion, national origin, age, or disability. The laws apply to both hiring and firing, and to employment practices such as salaries, promotions and benefits. Most of these laws only apply to an employer who has fifteen or more employees for twenty weeks of a calendar year or has federal contracts or subcontracts. Therefore, you most likely will not be required to comply with the law immediately upon opening your business. However, there are similar state laws that may apply to your business.

One exception is the Equal Pay Act, which applies to employers with two or more employees and requires that women be paid the same as men in the same type of job.

Employers with fifteen or more employees are required to display a poster regarding discrimination. This poster is available from the Equal Employment Opportunity Commission, 2401 E. Street, N.W., Washington, DC 20506. Employers with 100 or more employees are required to file an annual report with the EEOC.

When hiring employees, some questions are illegal or inadvisable to ask. The following questions should not be included on your employment application, or in your interviews, unless the information is somehow directly tied to the duties of the job:

- Do not ask about an applicant's citizenship or place of birth. But after hiring an employee you must ask about his or her right to work in this country.

- Do not ask a female applicant her maiden name. You can ask if she has been known by any other name in order to do a background check.

- Do not ask if applicants have children, plan to have them, or have child care. You can ask if an applicant will be able to work the required hours.

- Do not ask if the applicant has religious objections for working Saturday or Sunday. You can mention if the job requires such hours and ask whether the applicant can meet this job requirement.

- Do not ask an applicant's age. You can ask if an applicant is eighteen or over, or for a liquor-related job if they are twenty-one or over.

- Do not ask an applicant's weight.

- Do not ask if an applicant has AIDS or is HIV positive.

- Do not ask if the applicant has filed a workers' compensation claim.

- Do not ask about the applicant's previous health problems.

- Do not ask if the applicant is married or whether their spouse would object to the job, hours, or duties.

- Do not ask if the applicant owns a home, furniture, car, as it is considered racially-discriminatory.

- Do not ask if the applicant was ever arrested. You can ask if the applicant was ever convicted of a crime.

The most recent, and perhaps most onerous, law is the Americans with Disabilities Act (ADA) of 1990. Under this law employers who do not make "reasonable accommodations for disabled employees" will face fines of up to $100,000, as well as other civil penalties and civil damage awards.

While the goal of creating more opportunities for people with disabilities is a good one, the result of this law is to place all of the costs of achieving this goal on businesses that are faced with disabled applicants. For example, it has been suggested that the requirement of "reasonable accommodation" will require some companies to hire blind applicants for jobs that require reading and then to hire second employees to read to the blind employees. We will only know the extent to which this law can be applied after some unlucky employers have been taken to court.

A study released by two MIT economists in late 1998 indicated that since the ADA was passed employers have hired less rather than more disabled people. It is theorized that this may be due to the expense of the "reasonable accommodations" or the fear of lawsuits by disabled employees.

The ADA currently applies to employers with fifteen or more employees. Employers who need more than fifteen employees might want to consider contracting with independent contractors to avoid problems with this law, particularly if the number of employees is only slightly larger than fifteen.

To find out how this law affects your business, you might want to pay the government $25 for their *ADA Technical Assistance Manual.* You can order it from The Superintendent of Documents, P. O. Box 371954, Pittsburgh, PA 15250-7954, or you can fax your credit card order to 202-512-2233.

Tax benefits. There are three types of tax credits to help small business with the burden of these laws.

- Businesses can deduct up to $15,000 a year for making their premises accessible to the disabled and can depreciate the rest. (Internal Revenue Code (IRC), Section 190.)

- Small businesses (under $1,000,000 in revenue and under thirty employees) can get a tax credit each year for 50% of the cost of making their premises accessible to the disabled, but this only applies to the amount between $250 and $10,500.

- Small businesses can get a credit of up to 40% of the first $6,000 of wages paid to certain new employees who qualify through the PRE-SCREENING NOTICE AND CERTIFICATION REQUEST (IRS FORM 8850). The form and instructions are in Appendix B. (see form 13, p.240.)

Records. To protect against potential claims of discrimination, all employers should keep detailed records showing reasons for hiring or not hiring applicants and for firing employees.

FLORIDA LAW

Discrimination. Florida has its own laws regarding discrimination in employment practices. The Florida Civil Rights Act of 1992, prohibits discrimination or classification based upon race, color, religion, sex, national origin, age, handicap or marital status. An employer who violates this law can be sued and be required to pay back pay, damages and punitive damages. (Fla. Stat., Sec. 760.10.)

Equal pay. Florida Statutes, Section 448.07 is Florida's counterpart to the federal law providing for equal pay to both sexes for the same job. This state statute is meant to fill the gap of workers not covered by federal law. Therefore, it does not apply to workers who are covered by the Fair Labor Standards Act, which is the federal wage and hour law discussed on page 91.

Sickle-cell anemia. Florida Statutes, Sections 448.075 and 448.076 prohibit discrimination based upon the sickle-cell trait and prohibit a requirement of screening for sickle-cell trait as a basis for employment.

AIDS. Florida Statutes, Section 760.50 forbids the refusal to hire, fire, or segregate people on the basis of a person being HIV positive or having taken an HIV test. However, the employer has the burden of proving that being HIV-free is a necessary condition of the job. A person unknowingly violating this law is subject to a minimum $1,000 fine plus attorney fees and a person who knowingly violates it is subject to a minimum $5,000 fine plus attorney fees.

SEXUAL HARASSMENT

FEDERAL LAW

What began as protection for employees who were fired or not promoted for failing to succumb to sexual advances of their superiors has been expanded to outlaw nearly any sexual comments or references in the workplace. One university was even forced to take down a painting by Goya depicting a nude because a teacher felt sexually harassed by its presence.

In the 1980s, the Equal Employment Opportunity Commission interpreted the Title VII of the Civil Rights Act of 1964 to forbid sexual harassment. After that, the courts took over and reviewed all types of conduct in the workplace. The numerous lawsuits that followed began a trend toward expanding the definition of sexual harassment and favoring employees.

The EEOC has held the following in sexual harassment cases:

- The victim as well as the harasser may be a woman or a man.

- The victim does not have to be of the opposite sex.

- The harasser can be the victim's supervisor, an agent of the employer, a supervisor in another area, a co-worker, or a non-employee.

- The victim does not have to be the person harassed but could be anyone affected by the offensive conduct.

- Unlawful sexual harassment may occur without economic injury to or discharge of the victim.

- The harasser's conduct must be unwelcome.

Some of the actions that have been considered harassment are:

- displaying sexually explicit posters in the workplace;

- requiring female employees to wear revealing uniforms;

- rating of sexual attractiveness of female employees as they passed male employees' desks;

- continued sexual jokes and innuendos.;

- demands for sexual favors from subordinates;

- unwelcomed sexual propositions or flirtation;

- unwelcomed physical contact; and

- whistling or leering at members of the opposite sex.

In 1993, the United States Supreme Court ruled that an employee can make a claim for sexual harassment even without proof of a specific injury. However, lower federal courts in more recent cases (such as the Paula Jones case against President Clinton) have dismissed cases where no specific injury was shown (although these cases may be overruled by a higher court). These new cases may indicate that the pendulum has stopped moving toward expanded rights for the employee.

On the other hand, another recent case ruled that an employer can be liable for the harassment of an employee by a supervisor, even if the employer was unaware of the supervisor's conduct, if the employer did not have a system in place to allow complaints against harassment. This area of law is still developing and to avoid a possible lawsuit you should be aware of the things that could potentially cause liability and avoid them.

Some things a business can do to protect against claims of sexual harassment are:

- Distribute a written policy against all kinds of sexual harassment to all employees.

- Encourage employees to report all incidents of sexual harassment.

- Insure there is no retaliation against those who complain.

- Make clear that your policy is "zero tolerance."

- Explain that sexual harassment includes both requests for sexual favors and a work environment that some employees may consider hostile.

- Allow employees to report harassment to someone other than their immediate supervisor in case that person is involved in the harassment.

- Promise as much confidentiality as possible to complainants.

FLORIDA LAW   Florida's Civil Rights Act also prohibits sexual harassment. (Fla. Stat., Ch. 760.) It applies to employers with fifteen or more employees for each working day in each of twenty or more calendar weeks in the current or preceding calendar year.

The law requires employers to post notices as required by the Florida Commission on Human Relations and allows victims to either file complaints with the commission or to sue in civil court for damages including punitive damages.

COMMON LAW   Although both the federal and Florida civil rights laws only apply to businesses with fifteen or more employees, it is possible for an employee to sue for sexual harassment in civil court. However, this is difficult and expensive and would only be worthwhile where there were substantial damages.

WAGE AND HOUR LAWS

FEDERAL LAW

Businesses covered. The Fair Labor Standards Act (FLSA) applies to all employers who are engaged in *interstate commerce* or in the production of goods for interstate commerce (anything which will cross the state line) and all employees of hospitals, schools, residential facilities for the disabled or aged, or public agencies. It also applies to all employees of enterprises that gross $500,000 or more per year.

While many small businesses might not think they are engaged in interstate commerce, the laws have been interpreted so broadly that nearly any use of the mails, interstate telephone service, or other interstate services, however minor, is enough to bring a business under the law. The authors of our Constitution clearly intended for most rights to be reserved to the states, but the *commerce clause* has been used to expand federal control to many unintended areas.

Minimum wage. The federal wage and hour laws are contained in the Federal Fair Labor Standards Act. In 1996, Congress passed and President Clinton signed legislation raising the minimum wage to $5.15 an hour beginning September 1, 1997.

In certain circumstances a wage of $3.62 may be paid to employees under twenty years of age for a ninety-day training period.

For employees who regularly receive more than $30 a month in tips, the minimum wage is $2.13 per hour. But if the employee's tips do not bring him up to the full $5.15 minimum wage, then the employer must make up the difference.

Overtime. Workers who work over forty hours in a week must be paid time-and-a-half for the time worked over forty hours.

Exempt employees. While nearly all businesses are covered, certain employees are exempt from the FLSA. Exempt employees include employees that are considered executives, administrative and managerial, professionals, computer professionals, and outside salespeople.

Whether or not one of these exceptions applies to a particular employee is a complicated legal question. Thousands of court cases have been decided on this issue but they have given no clear answers. In one case a person could be determined to be exempt because of his duties, but in another, a person with the same duties could be found not exempt.

One thing that is clear is that the determination is made on the employee's function, and not just the job title. You cannot make a secretary exempt by calling her a manager if most of her duties are clerical. For more information contact:

> Wage and Hour Division
> U. S. Department of Labor
> 200 Constitution Ave., N.W. Room S-3325
> Washington, DC 20210
> http://www.dol.gov/dol/esa/public/whd_org.htm

Or call a local office:

> Ft. Lauderdale 954-256-6896
> Jacksonville 904-232-2489
> Miami 305-598-6607
> Orlando 407-648-6471
> Tampa 813-288-1242

On the Internet you can obtain information on the Department of Labor's *Small Business Handbook* at:

> http://www.dol.gov/dol/asp/public/programs/handbook/main.htm

FLORIDA LAW

Florida's only law regarding wages or hours is one regarding a day's work. (Fla. Stat., Sec. 448.01.) Unless provided otherwise in a written agreement, ten hours a day is a legal day's work. An employee is entitled to "extra pay" for all work in excess of ten hours. However, this law would only affect those few businesses to which the above federal laws do not apply.

PENSION AND BENEFIT LAWS

There are no laws requiring small businesses to provide any types of special benefits to employees. Such benefits are given to attract and keep good employees. With pension plans the main concern is if you do start one it must comply with federal tax laws.

HOLIDAYS
There are no federal or Florida laws that require that employees be given holidays off. You can require them to work Thanksgiving and Christmas and dock their pay or fire them for failing to show up. Of course you will not have much luck keeping employees with such a policy.

Most companies give full time employees a certain number of paid holidays, such as: New Year's Day (January 1); Memorial Day (last Monday in May); Fourth of July; Labor Day (first Monday in September); Thanksgiving (fourth Thursday in November) and Christmas (December 25). Some, but not many, employers include other holidays such as Martin Luther King, Jr.'s birthday (January 15); President's Day; and Columbus Day. If one of the holidays falls on a Saturday or Sunday, many employers give the preceding Friday or following Monday off.

Florida law says that legal holidays include all of those in the previous paragraph (except President's Day) as well as the following:

Robert E. Lee's birthday (January 19)

Abraham Lincoln's birthday (February 12)

Susan B. Anthony's birthday (February 15)

George Washington's birthday (February 22)

Good Friday (varies)

Pascua Florida Day (April 2)

Confederate Memorial Day (April 26)

Jefferson Davis' birthday (June 3)

Flag Day (June 14)

Columbus Day and Farmers' Day (second Monday in October)

Veterans' Day (November 11)

General Election Day (varies)

However, the fact that these are designated state holidays does not mean anything. In fact, not even the state government is closed on all of these days.

SICK DAYS

There is no federal or Florida law mandating that an employee be paid for time that he or she is home sick. The situation seems to be that the larger the company, the more paid sick leave is allowed. Part-time workers rarely get sick leave and small business sick leave is usually limited for the simple reason that they cannot afford to pay for time that employees do not work.

Some small companies have an official policy of no paid sick leave, but when an important employee misses a day because he or she is clearly sick, it is paid.

BREAKS

There are no federal or Florida laws requiring coffee breaks or lunch breaks. However, it is common sense that employees will be more productive if they have reasonable breaks for nourishment or to use the toilet facilities.

PENSION PLANS AND RETIREMENT ACCOUNTS

Few small new businesses can afford to provide pension plans for their employees. The first concern of a small business is usually how the owner can shelter income in a pension plan without having to set up a pension plan for an employee. Under most pension plans this is not allowed.

IRA. Anyone with $2,000 of earnings can put up to that amount in an Individual Retirement Account (IRA). Unless the person or his or her spouse are covered by a company pension plan and have income over a certain amount, the amount put into the account is fully tax deductible.

ROTH IRA. Contributions to a Roth IRA are not tax deductible but then when the money is taken out it is not taxable. People who expect to still have taxable income when they withdraw from their IRA can benefit from these.

SEP IRA, SAR-SEP IRA, SIMPLE IRA. With these types of retirement accounts, a person can put a much greater amount into a retirement plan and deduct it from their taxable income. Employees must also be covered by such plans, but certain employees are exempt so it is sometimes possible to use these for the owners alone. The best source for more information is a mutual fund company (such as Vanguard, Fidelity, Dreyfus, etc.) or a local bank, which can set up the plan and provide you with all of the rules.

These have an advantage over qualified plans (discussed below) since they do not have the high annual fees. One Internet site that contains some useful information on these accounts is:

http://www.retirement-information.com/iraaccts.htm

Qualified Retirement Plans. Qualified retirement plans are 401(k) plans, Keogh plans, and corporate retirement plans. These are covered by ERISA, the Employee Retirement Income Security Act, which is a complicated law meant to protect employee pension plans. Congress did not want employees who contributed to pension plans all their lives ending up with nothing when the plan goes bankrupt. The law is so complicated and the penalties so severe that some companies are cancelling their pension plans, and applications for new plans are a fraction of what they were previously. However, many banks and mutual funds have created "canned plans" which can be used instead of drafting one from scratch. Still the fees for administering them are steep. Check with a bank or mutual fund for details.

FAMILY AND MEDICAL LEAVE LAW

FEDERAL LAW

To assist business owners in deciding what type of leave to offer their employees, Congress passed the Family and Medical Leave Act of 1993 (FMLA). This law requires an employee to be given up to twelve weeks of unpaid leave when:

- the employee or employee's spouse has a child;

- the employee adopts a child or takes in a foster child;

- the employee needs to care for an ill spouse, child, or parent; or

- the employee becomes seriously ill.

Fortunately, the law only applies to employers with fifty or more employees. Also, the top ten percent of an employer's salaried employees can be denied this leave because of the disruption in business their loss could cause.

FLORIDA LAW

There is no Florida law requiring family or medical leave.

CHILD LABOR LAWS

FEDERAL LAW The Federal Fair Labor Standards Act also contains rules regarding the hiring of children. The basic rules are that children under sixteen years old may not be hired at all except in a few jobs, such as acting and newspaper delivery, and those under eighteen may not be hired for dangerous jobs. Children may not work more than three hours a day/eighteen hours a week in a school week, or more than eight hours a day/forty hours a week in a non-school week. If you plan to hire children, you should check the Federal Fair Labor Standards Act, which is in United States Code (U.S.C.), Title 29 and also the related regulations, which are in Code of Federal Regulations (C.F.R.), Title 29.

FLORIDA LAW Florida also has a set of child labor laws as follows:

Child labor (Fla. Stat., Sec. 450.021.) The following rules apply to child labor in Florida in addition to federal laws:

- Minors of any age may work as pages in the legislature, in the entertainment industry, and in domestic or farm work for their parents. Children working for their parents may not do so during school hours.

- No child ten years of age or younger may engage in the sale and distribution of newspapers or the street trades.

- No child under fourteen years of age may be employed in any gainful occupation at any time except as described above.

- No person under eighteen years of age may work where alcoholic beverages are sold at retail unless excepted by Florida's Division of Alcoholic Beverages and Tobacco. (Fla. Stat., Sec. 562.13.)

Hazardous occupations (Fla. Stat., Sec. 450.061.) No child under sixteen years of age may work in the following occupations, or use the following equipment:

- power-driven machinery (except mowers with blades of forty inches or less);

- oiling or cleaning machines;

- work in freezers or meat coolers;

- use meat or vegetable slicers;

- power-driven laundry or dry cleaning machinery;

- door-to-door sales of subscriptions or products except for merchandise of nonprofit organizations;

- spray painting;

- operating a motor vehicle;

- any manufacturing using industrial machines;

- manufacturing or transportation of explosive or flammable materials;

- logging; and

- alligator wrestling.

No person under the age of eighteen may work in the following occupations or use this equipment:

- in or around explosives;

- logging or sawmilling;

- in or around toxic substances, corrosives and pesticides;

- firefighting;

- slaughtering, meat packing, processing or rendering;

- electrical work;

- operating or assisting to operate tractors over twenty PTO horse-power, forklifts, earth-moving equipment, any harvesting, planting, or plowing machinery or any moving machinery;

- on any scaffolding, roofs or ladders above six feet;

- wrecking, demolition, or excavation;

- mining occupations;

- operation of power-driven bakery, metalforming, woodworking, paper products, printing, or hoisting machines; and

- manufacturing of brick, tile, or similar materials.

Poster (Fla. Stat., Sec. 450.045(2)). Anyone employing a minor must display a poster explaining the Florida and federal child labor laws. (This is a good source of information for employers as well.) It is available at no charge from:

> Florida Dept. of Labor and Employment Security
> Child Labor Section
> P. O. Box 1698
> Tallahassee, FL 32302-1698

Proof of child's age (Fla. Stat., Sec. 450.045). A person who employs a child must keep on file proof of the child's age, such as a photocopy of a birth certificate, driver's license, school age certificate, passport or visa.

Children's hours (Fla. Stat., Sec. 450.081). In addition to the requirements above, no child seventeen years of age or younger may work more than six consecutive days in one week. Such children must have a meal break of at least thirty minutes after four hours of work. No child sixteen or seventeen years of age may work more than thirty hours in a week or more than eight hours in a day when the following day is a school day. No such child may work before 6:30 a.m. or after 11 p.m. No such child may work during school hours except in a vocational educational program.

No child fifteen years of age or younger may work before 7:00 A.M. or after 7:00 P.M. when school is scheduled the next day. No such child shall work more than fifteen hours a week or more than three hours in a day prior to a school day except in a vocational education program.

However, these rules do not apply during holiday and summer vacations, or to sixteen or seventeen-year-old graduates, students with school authorized exemptions, students with economic hardships, children in domestic work in private homes, children working for their parents, or to pages working for the legislature.

Child labor law waivers. The Division of Labor, Employment, and Training of the Department of Labor and Employment Security may grant a waiver of the child labor law.

IMMIGRATION LAWS

FEDERAL LAW

Documentation requirement. In 1986, a law was passed by Congress that imposes strict penalties for any business that hires aliens who are not eligible to work. Under this law you must verify both the identity and the employment eligibility of anyone you hire by using the EMPLOYMENT ELIGIBILITY VERIFICATION (IRS FORM I-9). (see form 4, p.209.) Both you and the employee must fill out the form and you must check an employee's identification cards or papers. Fines for hiring illegal aliens range from $250 to $2,000 for the first offense and up to $10,000 for the third offense. Failure to maintain the proper paperwork may result in a fine of up to $1,000. The law does not apply to independent contractors with whom you may contract and it does not penalize you if the employee used fake identification.

There are also penalties that apply to employers of four or more persons for discriminating against eligible applicants because they appear foreign or because of their national origin or citizenship status.

In Appendix A there is a sample filled-in **IRS FORM I-9**. Appendix B has a list of acceptable documentation, a blank form, and instructions. (see form 4, p.209.) The blank form can also be downloaded from the following website:

http://www.ins.usdoj.gov/forms/download/i-9.htm

For more information call 202-514-2000. For the *Handbook for Employers and Instructions for Completing Form I-9*, check the INS website **http://www.ins.usdoj.gov** or write to the following address:

U. S. Department of Justice
Immigration and Naturalization Service
425 I Street, NW
Washington, DC 20536

The Illegal Immigration Reform and Immigrant Responsibility Act of 1996 (IIRIRA) required changes in the rules but as of early 1999 the INS had not yet promulgated final versions of the rules. The interim rule made the following changes to the requirements:

- remove documents 2, 3, 8 and 9 from column A;

- allow document 4 only for aliens authorized to work for a specific employer; and

- new rules for employees who do not have their original documents.

However, no new forms or instructions have been made available and employers are not yet being prosecuted for violations of these changes. Employers can receive updates to these laws by fax. To receive them, send your name address and fax number to 202-305-2523.

Foreign employees. If you wish to hire employees who are foreign citizens and are not able to provide the documentation explained above, they must first obtain a work visa from the Immigration and Naturalization Service (INS) of the United States Department of Justice.

Work visas for foreigners are not easy to get. Millions of people around the globe would like to come to the U.S. to work and the laws are designed to keep most of them out to protect the jobs of American citizens.

Whether or not a person can get a work visa depends on whether there is a shortage of U.S. workers available to fill the job. For jobs requiring few or no skills, it is practically impossible to get a visa. For highly skilled jobs, such as nurses, physical therapists, and for those of exceptional ability, such as Nobel Prize winners and Olympic medalists, obtaining a visa is fairly easy.

There are several types of visas and different rules for different countries. For example, NAFTA has made it easier for some types of workers to enter the U.S. from Canada and Mexico. For some positions the shortage of workers is assumed by the INS. For others, a business must first advertise a position available in the U.S. Only after no qualified persons apply, can it hire someone from another country.

The visa system is complicated and subject to regular change. (In late 2000 a new law expanded the number of certain worker visas from 115,000 to 195,000.) If you wish to hire a foreign worker you should consult with an immigration specialist or a book on the subject.

FLORIDA LAW   Florida Statutes, Sections 448.09 makes it illegal to hire aliens who are not legally authorized to work.

HIRING "OFF THE BOOKS"

Because of the taxes, insurance, and red tape involved with hiring employees, some new businesses hire people "off the books." They pay them in cash and never admit they are employees. While the cash paid in wages would not be deductible, they consider this a smaller cost than compliance. Some even use "off the books" receipts to cover it.

Except when your spouse or child is giving you some temporary help this is a terrible idea. Hiring people off the books can result in civil fines, loss of insurance coverage, and even criminal penalties. When engaged in dangerous work like roofing or using power tools, you are risking millions of dollars in potential liability if a worker is killed or seriously injured.

It may be more costly and time consuming to comply with the employment laws, but if you are concerned with long term growth with less risk, it is the wiser way to go.

FEDERAL CONTRACTS

Companies that do work for the federal government are subject to several laws.

The Davis-Bacon Act requires contractors engaged in U.S. government construction projects to pay wages and benefits that are equal to or better than the prevailing wages in the area.

The McNamara-O'Hara Service Contract Act sets wages and other labor standards for contractors furnishing services to agencies of the U.S. government.

The Walsh-Healey Public Contracts Act requires the Department of Labor to settle disputes regarding manufacturers supplying products to the U.S. government.

Miscellaneous Laws

FEDERAL LAW

Affirmative action. In most cases, the federal government does not yet tell employers who they must hire. This would be especially true for new small businesses. The only situation where a small business would need to comply with affirmative action requirements would be if it accepted federal contracts or subcontracts. These requirements could include the hiring of minorities or of Vietnam veterans.

Layoffs. Companies with 100 or more full-time employees at one location are subject to the Worker Adjustment and Retraining Notification Act. This law requires a sixty-day notification prior to certain lay-offs and has other strict provisions.

Unions. The National Labor Relations Act of 1935 gives employees the right to organize a union or to join one. (U.S.C., Title 29, beginning with Sec. 151.) There are things employers can do to protect themselves, but you should consult a labor attorney or a book on the subject before taking action that might be illegal and result in fines.

Poster laws. Yes, there are laws regarding what posters you may or may not display in the workplace. A previous edition of this book stated that nothing forbids Playboy or Playgirl-type posters, but a "politically correct" federal judge in 1991, ruled that Playboy posters in a workplace were sexual harassment. However, there are other poster laws that require certain posters to be displayed to inform employees of their rights. Not all businesses are required to display all posters, but the following list should be of help.

- All employers must display the wage and hour poster available from:

  > U. S. Department of Labor
  > 200 Constitution Ave., NW
  > Washington, DC 20210

- Employers with fifteen or more employees for twenty weeks of the year must display the sex, race, religion, and ethnic discrimination poster and the age discrimination poster available from:

  > EEOC
  > 2401 E Street NW
  > Washington, DC 20506

- Employers with federal contracts or subcontracts of $10,000 or more must display the sex, race, etc. discrimination poster mentioned above plus a poster regarding Vietnam Era Veterans available from the local federal contracting office.

- Employers with government contracts subject to the Service Contract Act or the Public Contracts Act must display a notice to employees working on government contracts available from:

  > Employment Standards Division
  > U. S. Department of Labor
  > 200 Constitution Ave., NW
  > Washington, DC 20210

FLORIDA LAW

Threat of discharge for failing to trade with particular firm. (Fla. Stat., Sec. 448.03.) It is a misdemeanor for an employer to require an employee to deal with or not to deal with any particular firm or person (in his personal affairs) or to discharge or threaten to discharge an employee for such a reason.

Wrongful combination against workers. (Fla. Stat., Sec. 448.045.) It is a first degree criminal misdemeanor for two or more persons to conspire to deny a person work, cause the discharge of a person in a firm, or threaten to injure the life, property, or business of any person for this purpose.

Seats. (Fla. Stat., Sec. 448.05.) It is a second degree misdemeanor to fail to provide a seat for an employee or to fail to allow an employee to make reasonable use of the seat when such use will not interfere with the requirements of the employment.

Devices used as payment for labor. (Fla Stat., Ch. 532.) If any person issues coupons, tokens or other devices for payment of labor, he is liable for payment in cash of the full face value on or before the thirtieth day after issuance no matter what other restrictions are printed on the device. Anyone violating this rule will be liable for the full value, interest and ten percent attorney's fees.

Checks and drafts. Any payment for labor by check, draft, note, memorandum or other acknowledgment of indebtedness must be payable in cash on demand, without discount, at some established place of business within the state. The name and address of the place of business where it is payable must be on the instrument, and at the time of issuance and for thirty days thereafter, there must be sufficient funds to cover it.

Direct deposit. The above rules do not prohibit direct deposit of funds, but a payor of wages may not fire an employee for refusing to have his or her wages directly deposited. A violation of this rule can result in an employee's having his attorney's fees paid by the violator in an enforcement action.

Migrant and farm labor. Employers who hire migrant or farm labor should read Florida Statutes, Sections 450.181 through 450.38.

ADVERTISING AND PROMOTION LAWS 12

ADVERTISING LAWS AND RULES

FEDERAL LAWS The federal government regulates advertising through the Federal Trade Commission (FTC). The rules are contained in the Code of Federal Regulations (C.F.R.). You can find these rules in most law libraries and many public libraries. If you plan any advertising that you think may be questionable, you might want to check the rules. As you read the rules below, you will probably think of many violations you see every day.

Federal rules do not apply to every business; and small businesses that operate only within the state and do not use the postal service may be exempt. However, many of the federal rules have been adopted into law by the state of Florida. Therefore, a violation could be prosecuted by the state rather than the federal government.

Some of the important rules are summarized below. If you wish to learn more details about the rules you should obtain copies from your library.

Deceptive pricing (C.F.R., Title 16, Ch. I, Part 233.) When prices are being compared, it is required that actual and not inflated prices are used. For example, if an object would usually be sold for $7, you should not first offer it for $10 and then start offering it at 30% off. It is considered misleading to suggest that a discount from list price is a bargain if the item is seldom actually sold at list price. If most surrounding stores sell an item for $7 it is considered misleading to say it has a "retail value of $10" even if there are some stores elsewhere selling it at that price.

Bait advertising (C.F.R., Title 16, Ch. I, Part 238.) *Bait advertising* is placing an ad when you do not really want the respondents to buy the product offered, but want them to switch to another item. The factors used to determine if there was a violation are similar to those used by Florida, as explained on pages 109-110.

Use of "free," "half-off," and similar words (C.F.R., Title 16, Ch. I, Part 251.) Use of words such as "free," "1¢ sale" and the like must not be misleading. This means that the "regular price" must not include a mark-up to cover the "free" item. The seller must expect to sell the product without the free item at some time in the future.

Substantiation of claims (C.F.R., Title 16; Federal Regulations (F.R.), Title 48, Page 10471 (1983).) The FTC requires that advertisers be able to substantiate their claims. Some information on this policy is contained on the Internet at:

http://www.ftc.gov/bcp/guides/ad3subst.htm

Endorsements (C.F.R., Title 16, Ch. I, Part 255.) This rule forbids endorsements that are misleading. An example is a quote from a film review that is used in such a way as to change the substance of the review. It is not necessary to use the exact words of the person endorsing the product as long as the opinion is not distorted. If a product is changed, an endorsement that does not apply to the new version cannot be used. For some items, such as drugs, claims cannot be used without scientific proof. Endorsements by organizations cannot be used unless one is sure that the membership holds the same opinion.

Unfairness (U.S.C., Title 15, Section 45.) Any advertising practices that can be deemed to be "unfair" are forbidden by the FTC. An explanation of this policy is located on the Internet at:

http://www.ftc.gov/bcp/policy stmt/ad-unfair.htm

Negative option plans (C.F.R., Title 16, Ch. I, Part 425.) When a seller uses a sales system in which the buyer must notify the seller if he does not want the goods, the seller must provide the buyer with a form to decline the sale and at least ten days in which to decline. Bonus merchandise must be shipped promptly and the seller must promptly terminate any who so request after completion of the contract.

Laser eye surgery (U.S.C., Title 15, Secs. 45, 52-57.) Under the laws governing deceptive advertising, the FTC and the FDA are regulating the advertising of laser eye surgery. Anyone involved in this area should obtain a copy of these rules. They are located on the Internet at:

> http://www.ftc.gov/bcp/guides/eyecare2.htm

Food and dietary supplements (U.S.C., Title 21, Sec. 343.) Under the Nutritional Labeling Education Act of 1990, the FTC and the FDA regulate the packaging and advertising of food and dietary products. Anyone involved in this area should obtain a copy of these rules. They are located on the Internet at:

> http://www.ftc.gov/bcp/guides/ad4diet.htm
> http://www.ftc.gov/bcp/guides/ad-food.htm

Jewelry and precious metals (F.R., Title 61, Page 27212.) The FTC has numerous rules governing the sale and advertising of jewelry and precious metals. Anyone in this business should obtain a copy of these rules. They are located on the Internet at:

> http://www.ftc.gov/bcp/guides/jewel-gd.htm

FLORIDA LAWS
Most of Florida's advertising laws are included with the criminal statutes. Violation of the first three below is a misdemeanor and a second offense is punishable with a fine of up to $10,000.

Misleading advertising (Fla. Stat., Sec. 817.41.) It is illegal to use advertising that is "misleading," or to use words like "wholesale" or "below cost" unless the goods are actually at or below the retailer's net cost. If demanded by a consumer, a retailer must provide to the Better Business Bureau, the Chamber of Commerce, or the State Attorney's office proof of his cost, and must help that person figure out the net cost. Retailers may not advertise items at a special price unless they have reasonable quantities or state in the ad the quantity available (unless they give rain checks). A customer may sue a business under this law and receive his attorney's fees, court costs, actual and punitive damages.

Under the rules of the Department of Legal Affairs (Florida Administrative Code (Fla. Admin. Code), Sec. 2-9.02), it is forbidden to make any misrepresentations of goods or services to the public including any of the following:

- misrepresenting the owner, manufacturer, distributor, source or geographical origin of goods, but sellers may use their own brand names on goods;

- misrepresenting the age, model, grade, style or standard of goods.

- misrepresenting the sponsorship, endorsement, approval or certification of goods or services;

- misrepresenting the affiliation, connection, or association of any goods or services;

- misrepresenting the nature, characteristics, standard ingredients, uses, benefits, warranties, guarantees, quantities or qualities of goods or services;

- misrepresenting used, altered, deteriorated or repossessed goods as new; however, goods returned to a seller undamaged may be sold as new;

- disparaging goods, services or business of another by false or misleading representation; or

- advertising goods or services with intent not to sell them as advertised.

False information (Fla. Stat., Sec. 817.411.) No advertisement may state that an item or investment is insured when it is not.

Intentional false advertising (Fla. Stat., Sec. 817.44.) No advertisements may be used as part of a plan not to sell the items at the advertised price.

Free gifts (Fla. Stat., Sec. 817.415). Any item offered as free must be absolutely free of any obligation on the part of the customer except for postage. If there are any conditions on the free gift, the conditions must be in a type-size at least half of that of the word "free."

Under the rules of the Department of Legal Affairs (Fla. Admin. Code, Sec. 2-9.03), it is forbidden to:

- Advertise that a product or service is free, using the word "free" or any other wording, when the item is not actually free. However, actual delivery charges may be charged for free items if paid directly to the postal service or carrier.

- Advertise a price as reduced unless:

  1. It has been sold previously at the higher price, or

  2. Others are selling it in the area at the higher price.

- Advertise a price as below cost unless it actually is below cost.

- Advertise an item as free or discounted if it must be purchased with another product on which the price has been raised.

Bait and switch. (Fla. Admin. Code, Sec. 2-9.04.) It is forbidden to advertise a product or service when there is no intention to fulfill the offer in the ad. Some factors considered in determining whether an ad is real are:

- refusing to show or sell the item offered;

- criticizing the offered item or the terms available;

- not having a reasonable quantity of the sale item unless it is disclosed that the supply is limited;

- refusing to take orders for unstocked merchandise for a reasonable time;

- showing of an item that is defective, unusable, or impractical for the purpose represented;

- using a method of compensating salesmen that discourages them from selling advertised items; and

- delivering of an advertised item that is defective, unusable or impractical for the purpose represented or implied in the advertisement.

Language other than English (Fla. Admin. Code, Sec. 2-9.05.) It is forbidden to:

- Use any advertisement that includes limitations in a language different from the one used in the major part of the ad.

- Execute a document in a language other than the one it was negotiated in, unless a translation is provided. But this does not apply:

  1. if less than five percent of the transactions at a location are negotiated in the second language and there is no intention to deceive consumers;

  2. to licenses or registrations consumers must execute;

  3. to delivery or cash sales receipts;

  4. to transactions of under $150; or

  5. to revolving accounts existing prior to March 1, 1974.

Offer conditions (Fla. Admin. Code, Sec. 2-9.06.) All conditions of an advertised offer must be conspicuously stated within the offer.

Game promotion (Fla. Admin. Code, Sec. 2-9.07.) Any type of game, contest, sweepstakes, giveaway, or other game promotion must follow these rules:

- It must not be like a lottery, which consists of chance, payment, and a prize. (To avoid this, game participation must not require any payment or purchase.)

- The promotion must not be misleading as to chances of winning, number of winners, value of prizes, or availability of prizes.

- No publication, literature, or written or verbal promotion can be false or misleading.

It is also forbidden to tell a person he or she is a "winner" or "selected," or is entering a contest, when

- the enterprise is a scheme to make contacts with prospective - customers; or

- all or a substantial number of those "entering" receive the same "prize" or "opportunity."

Insurance advertising (Fla. Stat., Sec. 817.47.) None of the above rules apply to insurance advertising, which is covered by insurance laws.

Names and photographs (Fla. Stat., Sec. 540.08). It is unlawful to use for trade or advertising purposes the name or likeness of any person who has not been dead at least forty years without the permission of the person, his agent or heirs. This does not apply to a picture of people in public who are not identified.

INTERNET SALES LAWS

There are not yet specific laws governing Internet transactions that are different from laws governing other transactions. The FTC feels that its current rules regarding deceptive advertising, substantiation, disclaimers, refunds, and related matters must be followed by Internet businesses and that consumers are adequately protected by them. See the first three pages of this chapter and Chapter 9 for that information.

For some specific guidelines on Internet advertising, see the FTC's site at:

http://ftc.gov/bcp/conline/pubs/buspubs/ruleroad.htm

HOME SOLICITATION LAWS

FEDERAL LAW   The Federal Trade Commission has rules governing door-to-door sales. In any such sale it is a deceptive trade practice to fail to furnish a receipt explaining the sale (in the language of the presentation) and giving notice that there is a right to back out of the contract within three days, known as a right of *rescission*. The notice must be supplied in duplicate, must be in at least 10-point type, and must be captioned either "Notice of Right to Cancel" or "Notice of Cancellation." The notice must be worded as follows:

NOTICE OF CANCELLATION

_____
Date

YOU MAY CANCEL THIS TRANSACTION, WITHOUT ANY PENALTY OR OBLIGATION, WITHIN THREE BUSINESS DAYS FROM THE ABOVE DATE.

IF YOU CANCEL, ANY PROPERTY TRADED IN, ANY PAYMENTS MADE BY YOU UNDER THE CONTRACT OR SALE, AND ANY NEGOTIABLE INSTRUMENT EXECUTED BY YOU WILL BE RETURNED TO YOU WITHIN 10 BUSINESS DAYS FOLLOWING RECEIPT BY THE SELLER OF YOUR CANCELLATION NOTICE, AND ANY SECURITY INTEREST ARISING OUT OF THE TRANSACTION WILL BE CANCELLED.

IF YOU CANCEL, YOU MUST MAKE AVAILABLE TO THE SELLER AT YOUR RESIDENCE, IN SUBSTANTIALLY AS GOOD CONDITION AS WHEN RECEIVED, ANY GOODS DELIVERED TO YOU UNDER THIS CONTRACT OR SALE; OR YOU MAY IF YOU WISH, COMPLY WITH THE INSTRUCTIONS OF THE SELLER REGARDING THE RETURN SHIPMENT OF THE GOODS AT THE SELLER'S EXPENSE AND RISK.

IF YOU DO MAKE THE GOODS AVAILABLE TO THE SELLER AND THE SELLER DOES NOT PICK THEM UP WITHIN 20 DAYS OF THE DATE OF YOUR NOTICE OF CANCELLATION, YOU MAY RETAIN OR DISPOSE OF THE GOODS WITHOUT ANY FURTHER OBLIGATION. IF YOU FAIL TO MAKE THE GOODS AVAILABLE TO THE SELLER, OR IF YOU AGREE TO RETURN THE GOODS AND FAIL TO DO SO, THEN YOU REMAIN LIABLE FOR PERFORMANCE OF ALL OBLIGATIONS UNDER THE CONTRACT.

TO CANCEL THIS TRANSACTION, MAIL OR DELIVER A SIGNED AND DATED COPY OF THIS CANCELLATION NOTICE OR ANY OTHER WRITTEN NOTICE, OR SEND A TELEGRAM, TO [name of seller], AT [address of seller's place of business] NOT LATER THAN MIDNIGHT OF _____ (date).

I HEREBY CANCEL THIS TRANSACTION.

_____   _____

(Buyer's signature)   (Date)

The seller must complete the notice and orally inform the buyer of the right to cancel. He cannot misrepresent the right to cancel, assign the contract until the fifth business day, nor include a confession of judgment in the contract. For more specific details see the rules contained in the Code of Federal Regulations, Title 16, Chapter I, Part 429.

FLORIDA LAW

Florida Statutes, Sections 501.021 through 501.055 are titled Home Solicitation Sales, but the definition of such sales is much broader. These sections actually cover all transactions that are:

- consumer transactions (sale, rental, lease);

- over $25 (including all charges, interest, etc.);

- solicited other than at the seller's regular place of business;

- consummated other than at the seller's regular place of business; and

- unsolicited telephone sales.

Sales at trade shows are included under the law, but it does not include sales at fairs; sales from a purchaser's request for specific goods; sales by motor vehicle dealers at a place open to the public or to a designated group; sales of insurance; and sales of farm equipment or machinery.

Right to cancel. Any such sale described above may be cancelled by the buyer by written notice, in any form, postmarked any time before midnight of the "third business day" after the sales day. Business days do not include Sunday, New Year's Day, Washington's Birthday, Memorial Day, Independence Day, Labor Day, Columbus Day, Veterans Day, Thanksgiving Day, and Christmas Day.

Written agreement. Every such sale must be in writing, contain the buyer's signature and the date the buyer signed, and must contain the following notice:

> ### BUYER'S RIGHT TO CANCEL
>
> This is a home solicitation sale, and if you do not want the goods or services, you may cancel this agreement by providing written notice to the Seller in person, by telegram, or by mail. This notice must indicate that you do not want the goods or services and must be delivered or postmarked before midnight of the third business day after you sign this agreement. If you cancel this agreement, the Seller may not keep all or part of any cash down payment.

Refund. The refund must be made to the Buyer within ten days. If it is not, the seller may be subject to criminal and civil penalties.

Buyer's duty. Within a reasonable time after cancellation and demand by seller, a buyer must return any goods received under the contract unless the seller fails to refund the buyer's deposit as required. If the seller has not made demand within forty days, the buyer may keep the goods. If the seller does not refund the buyer's deposit, the buyer may retain possession of the goods and has a lien on them for the amount due him. The buyer must take reasonable care of the goods in his possession but does not have to deliver them to the seller at any place other than the buyer's residence.

Seller's duty. All businesses conducting solicitation sales must:

- ensure that all employees have the required permits;

- provide identification to salesmen for face to face sales, which includes the seller's name, description, and signature: the name, address, and phone number of the company; and the name, address, and signature of seller's supervisor; and

- direct sales agents to leave a business card, contract, or receipt with the buyer including the following information: name, address, and phone number of the company, and of the sales agent, and the buyer's Right to Cancel Notice described above.

In telephone solicitations, the name, address, and phone number of the company must be clearly disclosed on sales materials and contracts sent to the buyer.

Prohibitions. In conducting "home" solicitations, no person shall:

- misrepresent terms of the sale;

- misrepresent seller's affiliation with the company;

- misrepresent reasons for solicitation (such as contests, handicaps, etc. which are not true);

- imply the contract is non-cancelable; or

- misrepresent anything else.

TELEPHONE SOLICITATION LAWS

FEDERAL LAWS
Phone calls. Telephone solicitations are governed by the Telephone Consumer Protection Act (U.S.C., Title 47, Sec. 227) and the Federal Communications Commission rules implementing the act (C.F.R., Title 47, Sec. 64.1200). Violators of the act can be sued for $500 damages by consumers and can be fined $10,000 by the FCC. Some of the requirements under the law are:

- Calls can only be made between 8 a.m. and 9 p.m.

- Solicitors must keep a "do not call" list and honor requests not to call.

- There must be a written policy that the parties called are told the name of the caller, the callers business name and phone number or address, that the call is a sales call, and the nature of the goods or services.

- Personnel must be trained in the policies.

- Recorded messages cannot be used to call residences.

Faxes. It is illegal under the act to send advertising faxes to anyone who has not consented to receiving such faxes or is an existing customer.

FLORIDA LAW

Florida Statutes, Section 501.059, the telephone solicitation law, applies to any transaction involving real or personal property normally used primarily for personal, family, or household purposes. It includes cemetery lots and time shares. It does not apply to calls to businesses. Penalties for violations include a fine of up to $10,000, attorney's fees, and court costs. The law contains these main provisions:

Identification. Any person who makes a telephone solicitation call must identify himself or herself by true first and last name and the name of the business represented immediately upon making contact.

Prohibition. No solicitation calls may be made to any person who is listed in a quarterly directory published by the Division of Consumer Services of the Florida Department of Agriculture and Consumer Services. The fee for a listing in the directory is $10 for the first year and $5 for each additional year. Businesses may purchase a copy of this directory from the Division.

Enforceability. A contract agreed to after a telephone solicitation is not enforceable unless the seller obtains a signed contract from the buyer that accurately describes the goods; contains the name, address and phone number of the seller; contains in bold conspicuous type the following clause, "You are not obligated to pay any money unless you sign this contract and return it to the seller;" includes all oral representations made by the seller; and complies with "all applicable laws and rules." However, this rule does not apply to contractual sales that are regulated by other sections of Florida Statutes, to telephone companies, securities or financial services, or cable television companies.

Credit cards. A merchant (except a charity or newspaper) may not charge an amount to a person's credit card for a sale procured through a telephone solicitation until the merchant receives a signed contract from the customer unless:

- The customer has first visited a permanent place of business where the merchant has the goods on display, or

- The customer may receive a full refund by giving notice of cancellation within seven days and the refund will be processed within thirty days, or

- The consumer made the purchase pursuant to television, radio, or print advertising or a brochure, sample, or catalog that contains the name, address, and telephone number of the merchant, a description of the goods or services being sold, and any conditions of the offer.

This law does not apply to calls to persons who have made contact with the businesses, or to newspapers, or charities. Also exempt are real estate agents who make calls in response to yard signs or other ads by property owners.

Automatic dialing (Fla. Stat., Sec. 501.059(7).) Except in limited circumstances, it is forbidden to use any machine for automatic dialing or playing a recorded message. An automatic dialing system may be used with live messages if:

- the calls are made only to persons who have requested information;

- if the dialing is screened to exclude persons who are on the "no solicitation calls" list;

- the people called have unlisted numbers; or

- the calls concern goods or services previously ordered or purchased.

There are both civil and criminal penalties for violation of this law.

Fax advertising (Fla. Stat., Sec. 365.1657.) It is illegal to send unsolicited advertising materials by fax within the state of Florida.

PRICING, WEIGHTS, AND LABELING

FEDERAL LAW **Food products.** Beginning in 1994, all food products were required to have labels with information on the product's nutritional values such as calories, fat, and protein. For most products, the label must be in the required format so that consumers can easily compare products.

117

However, if such a format will not fit on the product label, the information may be in another format that is easily readable.

Metric measures. In 1994, federal rules requiring metric measurement of products took effect. Some federal agencies, such as the federal highway department, indefinitely postponed implementation of the rules, but the Federal Trade Commission (FTC) and the Food and Drug Administration intend to enforce the rules against businesses.

Under these rules, metric measures do not have to be the first measurement on the container, but they must be included. Food items that are packaged as they are sold (such as delicatessen items), do not have to contain metric labels.

FLORIDA LAW Under Florida Statutes, Chapter 531, it is a second degree misdemeanor (meaning a fine of up to $500 and up to sixty days in jail) to violate any of the following rules:

Misrepresenting quantity. No person shall misrepresent the quantity of goods offered for sale or goods purchased.

Misrepresenting price. No person shall misrepresent the price of any commodity, or represent the price in any manner calculated to confuse. When a price includes a fraction of a cent, all elements of the fraction must be prominently displayed.

Method of sale. Generally, commodities in liquid form must be sold by liquid measure or weight, and those not sold in liquid form, sold only by weight, area or volume, or by count, as long as the method of sale provides accurate quantity information.

Bulk sale. Bulk sales of over $20 must be accompanied by a delivery ticket containing the following information:

- the name and address of the seller and buyer;
- date delivered;

- net quantity delivered and net quantity for basis of price if this differs from quantity delivered;

- identity of the commodity in commercially practicable terms, including representations made in connection with the sale; and

- the count of individually wrapped packages, if there are more than one of such packages;

Information required on packages. Generally, all packages of commodities for sale must bear a conspicuous statement of:

- identity of commodity unless it can be identified through wrapper;

- net quantity of contents in terms of weight, measure or count; and

- for goods sold other than where they are packed, the name and place of business of the manufacturer, packer, or distributor.

Declarations of unit price on random packages. In addition to the bulk sales requirements above, when goods are offered in packages of different weights, with the price stated on them, the price per single unit of weight must also be stated.

Advertising packages for sale. When a packaged commodity is advertised for sale with a price stated, the quantity must also be conspicuously stated.

DECEPTIVE PRACTICES

FLORIDA LAW

If a business engages in practices that may be regarded as "deceptive or unfair" in a consumer transaction, it may be subject to the following penalties (Florida Statutes, Secs. 501.201 to 501.213):

- The State Attorney or the Department of Legal Affairs may bring court action for injunctions, for damages to consumers, and for fines of up to $10,000 for each violation. If the victim is a senior citizen or a handicapped person, the fine may be up to $15,000 plus restitution.

- A consumer may bring a suit for damages plus attorney's fees.

No damages can be recovered against a retailer who acted in good faith in repeating claims of a manufacturer or wholesaler and did not know they were in violation of this law.

REFUNDS

REFUND POLICY

If a retail establishment has a policy of no refunds or exchanges, a notice of such policy must be posted at the point of sale. If no notice is posted, a seller must grant a refund to purchasers requesting one within seven days of purchase and producing proof of purchase. However, the merchandise must be unused and in the original packaging (Fla. Stat., Sec. 501.142). This rule does not apply to food that cannot be resold by a merchant because of a law or regulation, perishables, goods that are custom-made or altered, or goods that cannot be resold.

STATEMENT OF SATISFACTION

If a seller uses any type of receipt on delivery of a packaged item in which the buyer is requested or required to agree in writing that the goods are satisfactory, the statement must also contain this notice (Fla. Stat., Sec. 501.141):

BUYER'S RIGHT TO CANCEL

If the goods you have received are not in satisfactory condition or operation, you may cancel this statement of satisfaction by mailing a notice to the Seller. This notice must indicate that you do not want the goods in the condition in which they were delivered and must be postmarked before midnight of the fifth business day after you sign.

PAYMENT AND COLLECTION 13

Depending on the business you are in, you may be paid by cash, checks, credit cards, or some sort of financing arrangement such as a promissory note and mortgage. Both state and federal laws affect the type of payments you collect, and failure to follow the laws can cost you considerably.

CASH

Cash is probably the easiest form of payment and it is subject to few restrictions. The most important one is that you keep an accurate accounting of your cash transactions and that you report all of your cash income on your tax return. Recent efforts to stop the drug trade have resulted in some serious penalties for failing to report cash transactions and for money laundering. The laws are so sweeping that even if you deal in cash in an ordinary business you may violate the law and face huge fines and imprisonment. A Florida Congressman stated that he thought a grocer selling food to drug dealers should be subject to forfeiture laws!

The most important law to be concerned with is the one requiring the filing of the REPORT OF CASH PAYMENTS OVER $10,000 (IRS form 8300). (see form 12, p.236.) A transaction does not have to happen in one day. If a person brings you smaller amounts of cash that add up to

$10,000 and the government can construe them as one transaction, then the form must be filed. Under this law, "cash" also includes travelers' checks, and money orders, but not cashier's checks or bank checks.

CHECKS

ACCEPTING
CHECKS

It is important to accept checks in your business. While there is a small percentage which will be bad, most checks will be good, and you will be able to accommodate more customers. To avoid having problems with checks, you should follow the following rules.

A business may not require a customer to provide a credit card number or expiration date in order to pay by or cash a check. (Fla. Stat., Sec. 832.75.) The business can request to see a card to establish that the customer is credit-worthy or for additional identification and can record the type of credit card and issuing company. The business cannot record the number of the card. The penalty for a violation is a fine of $250 for the first violation and $1000 for each subsequent violation.

BAD CHECKS

Florida has a fairly effective bad check collection process. If you follow the rules you will probably be able to collect on a bad check. Some counties even have special divisions of the sheriff's department that actively help you collect on bad checks.

The first rule is that you must be able to identify the person who gave you the check. To do this you should require identification and write down the sources of identification on the face of the check. Another rule is that you cannot accept post-dated checks. Also, you must send a demand to the person by certified mail that they pay the amount of the check plus a penalty of $10 or 5% of the face amount of the check, whichever is greater. The notice is contained in the Florida Statutes. (Fla. Stat., Sec. 832.07.)

REFUNDS AFTER
CASHING CHECK

A popular scam is for a person to purchase something by using a check and then come back the next day demanding a refund. After making the refund the business discovers the initial payment check bounced. Do not make refunds until checks clear!

CREDIT CARDS

In our buy-now, pay-later society, charge cards can add greatly to your sales potential, especially with large, discretionary purchases. For MasterCard, Visa, and Discover, the fees are about 2%, and this amount is easily paid for by the extra purchases that the cards allow. American Express charges 4% to 5% and you may decide this is not worth paying, since almost everyone who has an American Express card also has another card.

For businesses which have a retail outlet, there is usually no problem getting merchant status. Most commercial banks can handle it. Discover can also set you up to accept their card as well as MasterCard and Visa, and they will wire the money into your bank account daily.

For mail order businesses, especially those operating out of the home, it is much harder to get merchant status. This is because of the number of scams in which large amounts are charged, no products are shipped and the company folds. At one point, even a business offering to post a large cash bond and let the bank hold the charges for six months was refused.

Today things are a little better. Some companies are even soliciting merchants. But beware of those that charge exorbitant fees (such as $5 or $10 per order for "processing"). One good thing about American Express is that they will accept mail order companies operating out of the home. However, not as many people have their cards as others.

Some companies open a small storefront (or share one) to get merchant status, then process mostly mail orders. The processors usually do not want to accept you if you will do more than fifty percent mail order; but if you do not have many complaints, you may be allowed to process mostly mail orders. Whatever you do, keep your charge customers happy so that they do not complain!

You might be tempted to try to run your charges through another business. This may be okay if you actually sell your products through them, but if you run your business charges through their account the other business may lose its merchant status. People who bought a book by mail from you and then have a charge on their statement from a florist shop will probably call the credit card company saying that they never bought anything from the florist shop. Too many of these and the account will be closed.

A new money-making scheme by the credit card companies is to offer "business credit cards" that the merchants are charged a higher fee for accepting. To make these more profitable the credit card companies are telling customers they are not allowed to use their personal credit cards for business purposes! To keep your processing fees down, you can tell your customers you prefer personal, not business credit cards.

FINANCING LAWS

Some businesses can more easily make sales if they finance the purchases themselves. If the business has enough capital to do this, it can earn extra profits on the financing terms. Nonetheless, because of abuses, many consumer protection laws have been passed by both the federal and state governments.

FEDERAL LAW   ***Reg. Z.*** Two important federal laws regarding financing are called the *Truth in Lending Act* and the *Fair Credit Billing Act*. These are implemented by what is called *Regulation Z* (commonly known as *Reg. Z*), issued by the Board of Governors of the Federal Reserve System. It is contained in Volume 12 of the Code of Federal Regulations, page 226. (1 C.F.R., Vol. 12, p. 226.) This is a very complicated law and some have said that no business can be sure to be in compliance with it.

The regulation covers all transactions in which four conditions are met:

1. credit is offered;
2. the offering of credit is regularly done;
3. there is a finance charge for the credit or there is a written - agreement with more than four payments; and
4. the credit is for personal, family, or household purposes.

It also covers credit card transactions where only the first two conditions are met. It applies to leases if the consumer ends up paying the full value and keeping the item leased. It does not apply to the following transactions:

- transactions with businesses or agricultural purposes;

- transactions with organizations such as corporations or the government;

- transactions of over $25,000 that are not secured by the consumer's dwelling;

- credit involving public utilities;

- credit involving securities or commodities; and

- home fuel budget plans.

The way for a small business to avoid Reg. Z violations is to avoid transactions that meet the conditions or to make sure all transactions fall under the exceptions. For many businesses this is easy. Instead of extending credit to customers, accept credit cards and let the credit card company extend the credit. However, if your customers usually do not have credit cards or if you are in a business, such as used car sales, which often extends credit, you should consult a lawyer knowledgeable about Reg. Z or get a copy for yourself at:

http://www.cardreport.com/laws/tila/tila.html

FLORIDA LAW
Florida also has laws regarding financing arrangements. Anyone engaged in retail installment selling must be licensed by the Florida Department of Banking and Finance. The law specifies what size type must be used in printed contracts, what notices must be included in them and many other details. Anyone engaged in installment sales in Florida should carefully review the latest versions of the following statutes:

- Florida Consumer Finance Act. (Fla. Stat., Secs. 516.001-.36.)

- Motor Vehicle Sales Finance. (Fla. Stat., Ch. 520, Part I.)

- Retail Installment Sales. (Fla. Stat., Ch. 520, Part II.)

- Installment Sales Finance. (Fla. Stat., Ch. 520, Part II.)

- Home Improvement Sales and Finance. (Fla. Stat., Ch. 520, Part IV.)

- Department Regulation of Sales and Finance. (Fla. Stat., Ch. 520, Part V.)

- Rental-Purchase Agreement Act, (Fla. Stat., Secs. 559.9231-.9241.)

In addition to these acts, Florida forbids discrimination based upon sex, marital status, or race in the areas of loaning money, granting credit, or providing equal pay for equal services performed. (Fla. Stat., Sec. 725.07.) Discrimination is forbidden in the financing of residential real estate based upon race, color, national origin, sex, handicap, familial status, or religion. (Fla. Stat., Sec. 760.25.)

USURY

Usury is the charging of an illegally high rate of interest. In Florida, if you have a written agreement, the maximum rate of interest you may charge is 18%, except on loans of over $500,000 on which the maximum rate is 25%. If there is no written agreement as to the rate of interest, the rate is set by law. It previously was 12%, but beginning December 1, 1994, the Comptroller of Florida was required to set the rate of interest each year, to take effect the following January. Some businesses, such as banks are excluded from this law.

The penalty for charging in excess of the legal rate is that the borrower does not have to pay any interest and the lender has to repay double the amounts received.

Anyone charging or receiving interest at a rate of over 25% but less than 45% is guilty of a misdemeanor; and anyone charging or receiving interest of 45% or greater is guilty of a felony. The borrower may also sue for damages, costs, punitive damages, and attorney's fees.

COLLECTIONS

FEDERAL LAW

The Fair Debt Collection Practices Act of 1977 bans the use of deception, harassment, and other unreasonable acts in the collection of debts. It has strict requirements whenever someone is collecting a debt for someone else. If you are in the collection business, you must get a copy of this law.

The Federal Trade Commission has issued some rules that prohibit deceptive representations such as pretending to be in the motion picture industry, the government, or a credit bureau and/or using questionnaires that do not say that they are for the purpose of collecting a debt. (C.F.R., Title 16, Ch. I, Part 237.)

FLORIDA LAW

The Consumer Collection Practices Law applies to debts owed by persons (not corporations) for transactions that were for personal, family, or household purposes. (Fla. Stat., Sec. 559.55.) The law forbids:

- simulating a law enforcement officer or government agency;

- using or threatening force or violence;

- threatening to disclose the debt to others without explaining that the fact that there is a dispute over the debt will also be disclosed;

- contacting or threatening to contact a debtor's employer prior to obtaining a final judgment, unless the debtor has given permission in writing or unless the debtor has agreed in writing as to the debt, after the debt goes to collection;

- disclosing information affecting the debtor's reputation to persons outside the debtor's family who do not have a legitimate business need for the information;

- disclosing information affecting the debtor's reputation, knowing the information to be false;

- disclosing information about a disputed debt without disclosing the dispute;

- willfully harassing the debtor or his family;

- using profane, obscene, vulgar, or willfully abusive language with the debtor or his family;

- attempting to collect a debt that is not legitimate;

- claiming a legal right knowing that this right does not exist;

- using communication that looks like it is from a court, government or attorney if it is not;

- pretending to be an attorney by using attorney's stationery or forms;

- orally pretending to be an attorney or associated with an attorney;

- advertising or threatening to advertise sale of a claim unless under court order or as assignee;

- publishing or posting a "deadbeat" list;

- refusing to identify one's self or employer when requested by a debtor;

- mailing any communication to a debtor that contains embarrassing words on the outside of the envelope; and

- communicating with a debtor between 9 p.m. and 8 a.m. without prior consent of the debtor.

A debtor who is a victim of any of the above violations may sue the creditor for actual damages or $500 (whichever is greater), costs, and attorney fees, and in some cases *punitive* damages. (If a debtor wrongly brings a suit, he may have to pay the creditor's attorney fees and court costs.)

The Division of Consumer Services also investigates complaints by debtors of violations of this law. The agency may issue warnings, reprimands, revocation of licensing, and fines. The State Attorney may seek criminal penalties and injunctions for certain violations.

BUSINESS RELATIONS LAWS 14

THE UNIFORM COMMERCIAL CODE

The Uniform Commercial Code (UCC) is a set of laws regulating numerous aspects of doing business. A national group drafted this set of uniform laws to avoid having a patchwork of different laws around the fifty states. Although some states modified some sections of the laws, the code is basically the same in most of the states. In Florida, the UCC is contained in Chapters 670 to 680 of the Florida Statutes. Each chapter is concerned with a different aspect of commercial relations such as sales, warranties, bank deposits, commercial paper, and bulk transfers.

Businesses that wish to know their rights in all types of transactions should obtain a copy of the UCC and become familiar with it. It is especially useful in transactions between merchants. However, the meaning is not always clear from a reading of the statutes. In law school, students usually spend a full semester studying each chapter of this law.

COMMERCIAL DISCRIMINATION

FEDERAL LAW   The Robinson-Patman Act of 1936 prohibits businesses from injuring competition by offering the same goods at different prices to different buyers. This means that the large chain stores should not be getting a better price than your small shop. It also requires that promotional allowances must be made on proportionally the same terms to all buyers.

As a small business, you may be a victim of Robinson-Patman Act violations. A good place to look for information on the act is the following website:

http://www.lawmall.com/rpa/

FLORIDA LAW

It is unlawful for anyone who is engaged in the production, manufacture, sale, or distribution of any "article, product, thing of value, service or output of a service trade" to attempt to destroy the business of a competitor, by discriminating between different sections, communities or cities, by selling at a lower rate in one section. (Fla. Stat., Sec. 542.18.) The law also provides:

- It is not unlawful to discriminate in prices in a good faith effort to meet competition.

- Complaints may be made to a State Attorney or to the Department of State in Tallahassee.

- Violation is a first degree misdemeanor punishable by a fine of up to $1,000 or a year in prison.

RESTRAINING TRADE

FEDERAL LAW

One of the earliest federal laws affecting business is the Sherman Antitrust Act of 1890. The purpose of the law was to protect - competition in the marketplace by prohibiting monopolies. For example, one large company might buy out all of its competitors and then raise prices to astronomical levels. In recent years, this law was used to break up AT&T.

Examples of some things that are prohibited are:

- agreements between competitors to sell at the same prices;

- agreements between competitors on how much will be sold or produced;

- agreements between competitors to divide up a market;

- refusing to sell one product without a second product; or

- exchanging information among competitors which results in similarity of prices.

As a new business you probably will not be in a position to violate the act, but you should be aware of it in case a larger competitor tries to put you out of business. A good place to find information on the act is the following Internet site:

http://www.lawmall.com/sherman.act/index.html

FLORIDA LAW   It is unlawful to have any contract, combination or conspiracy to restrain trade or to monopolize, attempt to monopolize, or combine or conspire with any other person to monopolize, any part of trade or commerce. (Fla. Stat., Sec. 542.19.)

- The penalty for any violation is up to $100,000 for a natural person, and up to $1,000,000 for a company.

- Anyone "knowingly" violating or knowingly aiding or advising a violation can be guilty of a felony and sentenced to up to three years in prison in addition to the fines.

- A person whose business is hurt by a violation can seek an injunction to prohibit violations and may collect triple his damages in a suit against a violator, along with costs and attorney fees.

COMMERCIAL BRIBERY

FLORIDA LAW   In 1990, the Florida legislature created a new felony called *commercial bribery*. (Fla. Stat., Secs. 838.15 and 838.16.) *Commercial bribe receiving* is defined as soliciting, accepting or agreeing to accept a benefit with intent to violate a law. It applies to agents, employees, trustees, guardians, fiduciaries, lawyers, physicians, accountants, appraisers or other professional advisors, arbitrators, or officers, directors, managers, partners or others in control of an organization. Commercial bribery is committed by anyone on the other side of the above-described transaction.

In 1995, the Florida Supreme Court ruled that the law was unconstitutional because it was too vague. The court noted that the law could even be used to convict a head waiter who gave someone a better table for a tip. The legislature has not yet rewritten the law, but it is possible that this will be done in the future.

Intellectual Property Protection

As a business owner you should know enough about intellectual property law to protect your own creations and to keep from violating the rights of others. *Intellectual property* is that which is the product of human creativity, such as writings, designs, inventions, melodies and processes. They are things that can be stolen without being physically taken. For example, if you write a book, someone can steal the words from your book without stealing a physical copy of it.

As the Internet grows, intellectual property is becoming more valuable. Business owners should take the action necessary to protect their company's intellectual property. Additionally, business owners should know intellectual property law to be sure that they do not violate the rights of others. Even an unknowing violation of the law can result in stiff fines and penalties.

The following are the types of intellectual property and the ways to protect them.

PATENT | A *patent* is protection given to new and useful inventions, discoveries and designs. To be entitled to a patent, a work must be completely new and "unobvious." A patent is granted to the first inventor who files for the patent. Once an invention is patented, no one else can make use of that invention, even if they discover it independently after a lifetime of research. A patent protects an invention for 17 years; for designs it is 3-1/2, 7 or 14 years. Patents cannot be renewed. The patent application must clearly explain how to make the invention so that when the patent expires, others will be able to freely make and use the invention. Patents are registered with the United States Patent and Trademark Office (PTO). Examples of things that would be patentable would be mechanical devices or new drug formulas.

COPYRIGHT   A *copyright* is protection given to "original works of authorship," such as written works, musical works, visual works, performance works, or computer software programs. A copyright exists from the moment of creation, but one cannot register a copyright until it has been fixed in tangible form. Also, one cannot copyright titles, names, or slogans. A copyright currently gives the author and his heirs exclusive right to his work for the life of the author plus seventy years.

Copyrights first registered before 1978 last for 95 years. (This was previously 75 years but was extended 20 years to match the European system.) Copyrights are registered with the Register of Copyrights at the Library of Congress. Examples of works that would be copyrightable are books, paintings, songs, poems, plays, drawings, and films.

TRADEMARK   A *trademark* is protection given to a name or symbol which is used to distinguish one person's goods or services from those of others. It can consist of letters, numerals, packaging, labeling, musical notes, colors or a combination of these. If a trademark is used on services as opposed to goods, it is called a *service mark*.

A trademark lasts indefinitely if it is used continuously and renewed properly. Trademarks are registered with the United States Patent and Trademark Office and with individual states. (This is explained further in Chapter 3.) Examples of trademarks are the "Chrysler" name on automobiles, the red border on TIME magazine and the shape of the Coca-Cola bottle.

TRADE SECRETS   A *trade secret* is some information or process that provides a commercial advantage that is protected by keeping it a secret. Examples of trade secrets may be a list of successful distributors, the formula for Coca-Cola, or some unique source code in a computer program. Trade secrets are not registered anywhere, they are protected by the fact that they are not disclosed. They are protected only for as long as they are kept secret. If you independently discover the formula for Coca-Cola tomorrow, you can freely market it. (But you cannot use the trademark "Coca-Cola" on your product to market it.)

Florida law. Florida has passed the Uniform Trade Secrets Act, which protects trade secrets from appropriation by other businesses. (Fla. Stat., Ch. 688.) It provides for injunctions, damages, and attorney's fees for violation of the act.

There are numerous other Florida laws dealing with trade secrets. If you have some concerns about trade secrets in your business you should check the index to Florida statutes under "trade secrets."

NON-PROTECTABLE CREATIONS

Some things are just not protectable. Such things as ideas, systems and discoveries are not allowed any protection under any law. If you have a great idea, such as selling packets of hangover medicine in bars, you cannot stop others from doing the same thing. If you invent a new medicine, you can patent it; if you pick a distinctive name for it, you can register it as a trademark; if you create a unique picture or instructions for the package, you can copyright them. But you cannot stop others from using your basic business idea of marketing hangover medicine in bars.

Notice the subtle differences between the protective systems available. If you invent something two days after someone else does, you cannot even use it yourself if the other person has patented it. But if you write the same poem as someone else and neither of you copied the other, both of you can copyright the poem. If you patent something, you can have the exclusive rights to it for the term of the patent, but you must disclose how others can make it after the patent expires. However, if you keep it a trade secret, you have exclusive rights as long as no one learns the secret.

We are in a time of transition of the law of intellectual property. Every year new changes are made in the laws and new forms of creativity win protection. For more information, you should consult a new edition of a book on these types of property. Some are listed at the end of this book.

ENDLESS LAWS 15

The state of Florida and the federal government have numerous laws and rules that apply to every aspect of every type of business. There are laws governing even such things as fence posts, hosiery, rabbit raising, refund policies, frozen desserts, and advertising. Every business is affected by one or another of these laws.

Some activities are covered by both state and federal laws. In such cases, you must obey the stricter of the rules. In addition, more than one agency of the state or federal government may have rules governing your business. Each of these may have the power to investigate violations and impose fines or other penalties.

Penalties for violations of these laws can range from a warning to a criminal fine and even jail time. In some cases, employees can sue for damages. Recently, employees have been given awards of millions of dollars from employers who violated the law. Since "ignorance of the law is no excuse," it is your duty to learn which laws apply to your business, or to risk these penalties.

Very few people in business know the laws that apply to their businesses. If you take the time to learn them, you can become an expert in your field, and avoid problems with regulators. You can also fight back if one of your competitors uses some illegal method to compete with you.

The laws and rules that affect the most businesses are explained in this section. Following that is a list of more specialized laws. You should read through this list and see which ones may apply to your business. Then go to your public library or law library and read them. Some may not apply to your phase of the business, but if any of them do apply, you should make copies to keep on hand.

No one could possibly know all the rules that affect business, much less comply with them all. (The Interstate Commerce Commission alone has 40 trillion (that is 40 million million or 40,000,000,000,000) rates on its books telling the transportation industry what it should charge!) But if you keep up with the important rules you will stay out of trouble and have more chance of success.

FEDERAL LAWS

The federal laws that are most likely to affect small businesses are rules of the Federal Trade Commission (FTC). The FTC has some rules that affect many businesses such as the rules about labeling, warranties, and mail order sales. Other rules affect only certain industries.

If you sell goods by mail you should send for their booklet, *A Business Guide to the Federal Trade Commission's Mail Order Rule*. If you are going to be involved in a certain industry such as those listed below, or using warranties or your own labeling, you should ask for their latest information on the subject. The address is:

Federal Trade Commission
Washington, DC 20580

The rules of the FTC are contained in the Code of Federal Regulations (C.F.R.) in Chapter 16. Some of the industries covered are:

INDUSTRY	PART
Adhesive Compositions	235
Aerosol Products Used for Frosting Cocktail Glasses	417
Automobiles (New car fuel economy advertising)	259
Barber Equipment and Supplies	248
Binoculars	402
Business Opportunities and Franchises	436
Cigarettes	408

Tires	228
Used Automobile Parts	20
Used Lubricating Oil	406
Used Motor Vehicles	455
Waist Belts	405
Watches	245
Wigs and Hairpieces	252

Some other federal laws that affect businesses are as follows:

- Alcohol Administration Act (U.S.C., Title 29, beginning with Section 201.)

- Child Protection and Toy Safety Act (1969)

- Clean Water Act (U.S.C., Title 33)

- Comprehensive Smokeless Tobacco Health Education Act (1986). See also C.F.R., Title 16, Ch. I, Part 307 for rules.

- Consumer Credit Protection Act (1968)

- Consumer Product Safety Act (1972)

- Energy Policy and Conservation Act. See also C.F.R., Title 16, Ch. I, Part 305 for rules about energy cost labeling.

- Environmental Pesticide Control Act of 1972

- Fair Credit Reporting Act (1970)

- Fair Packaging and Labeling Act (1966). See also C.F.R., Title 16, Ch. I, Parts 500-503 for rules.

- Flammable Fabrics Act (1953). See also C.F.R., Title 16, Ch. II, Parts 1602-1632 for rules.

- Food, Drug, and Cosmetic Act (U.S.C., Title 21, beginning with Sec. 301.)

- Fur Products Labeling Act (1951). See also C.F.R., Title 16, Ch. I, Part 301 for rules.

- Hazardous Substances Act (1960)

- Hobby Protection Act. See also C.F.R., Title 16, Ch. I, Part 304 for rules.

- Insecticide, Fungicide, and Rodenticide Act (U.S.C., Title 7, beginning with Sec. 136.)

- Magnuson-Moss Warranty Act. See also C.F.R., Title 16, Ch. I, Part 239 for rules.

- Poison Prevention Packaging Act of 1970. See also C.F.R., Title 16, Ch. II, Parts 1700-1702 for rules.

- Solid Waste Disposal Act (U.S.C., Title 42, beginning with Sec. 6901.)

- Textile Fiber Products Identification Act. See also C.F.R., Title 16, Ch. I, Part 303 for rules.

- Toxic Substance Control Act (U.S.C., Title 15.)

- Wool Products Labeling Act (1939). See also C.F.R., Title 16, Ch. I, Part 300 for rules.

- Nutrition Labeling and Education Act of 1990. See also C.F.R., Title 21, Ch. 1, Subchapter B

- Food Safety Enforcement Enhancement Act of 1997.

FLORIDA LAWS

Florida has numerous laws regulating specific types of businesses or certain activities of businesses. The following is a list of those laws that are most likely to affect small businesses. If you are running a type of business that is not mentioned here, or using some sales technique that could come under government regulation, you should check the indexes to the Florida Statutes (Fla. Stat.) and the Florida Administrative Code (Fla. Admin. Code). Since these indexes are not well done, you should look up every possible synonym or related word to be sure not to miss anything.

Adoption agencies	Fla. Stat., Ch. 63
Adult congregate living facilities	Fla. Stat., Secs. 400.401-.454
Adult day care facilities	Fla. Stat., Secs. 400.55-.564
Adult foster home care	Fla. Stat., Secs. 400.616-.702
Air conditioning	Fla. Admin. Code, Chs. 2-14

Aircraft, Pilots & Airports	Fla. Stat., Ch. 330
Alcoholic beverages	Fla. Stat., Chs. 561-565
	Fla. Admin. Code, Ch. 61A
Ambulance service contracts	Fla. Stat., Ch. 638
Anatomical matter	Fla. Stat., Ch. 873
Animals	Fla. Stat., Secs. 585, 877.14; 877.16
	Fla. Admin. Code, Ch. 5C
Antifreeze	Fla. Stat., Secs. 501.91-.923
Aquaculture	Fla. Stat., Ch. 597
Art & craft material	Fla. Stat., Sec. 501.124
Auctions	Fla. Stat., Ch. 559, Part III
Automobile racing	Fla. Stat., Ch. 549
Bail bondsmen	Fla. Stat., Ch. 648
Banking	Fla. Admin. Code, Ch. 3
Boiler safety	Fla. Stat., Ch. 554
Bottles and boxes, markings	Fla. Stat., Ch. 506
Boxing & fighting	Fla. Stat., Ch. 548
	Fla. Admin. Code, Ch. 61K1
Brake fluid	Fla. Stat., Ch. 526
Budget planning	Fla. Stat., Ch. 559, Part II
Buildings, radon resistance stds.	Fla. Stat., Ch. 553
Burial contracts	Fla. Stat., Ch. 639
Business opportunities	Fla. Stat., Ch. 559, Part VII
	Fla. Admin. Code, Chs. 5J-10
Cemeteries	Fla. Stat., Secs. 497, 817.35
Charitable solicitation	Fla. Stat., Ch. 496
Citrus	Fla. Stat., Ch. 600-601
Collections	Fla. Stat., Ch. 559 Part V
Commissions merchants	Fla. Stat., Ch. 522
Condominiums	Fla. Stat., Ch. 718
	Fla. Admin. Code, Chs. 2-16; 61B
Construction	Fla. Admin. Code, Ch. 61G4
Consumer finance	Fla. Stat., Ch. 516
Cooperatives	Fla. Stat., Ch. 719
Cosmetics	Fla. Stat., Chs. 500, 544
Counseling & Psychotherapy	Fla. Stat., Ch. 491
Crash parts	Fla. Stat., Secs. 501.30-.34
Credit cards	Fla. Stat., Secs. 501.011-.0117

Credit service organizations	Fla. Stat., Ch. 817, Part III
Dairies	Fla. Stat., Ch. 502
	Fla. Admin. Code, Ch. 5D
Dance studios	Fla. Stat., Secs. 205.1969; 501.143
	Fla. Admin. Code, Ch. 5J-8
Desserts, frozen	Fla. Stat., Ch. 503
Dog racing & horseracing	Fla. Stat., Ch. 550
Drinking water	Fla. Stat., Secs. 403.850-.864
Driving schools	Fla. Stat., Ch. 488
Drugs	Fla. Stat., Chs. 499; 500; 544; 893
Eggs & poultry	Fla. Stat., Ch. 583
Electrical	Fla. Stat., Ch. 553
Electronic repair	Fla. Admin. Code, Chs. 2-28
Elevators, Escalators	Fla. Stat., Ch. 399,
	Fla. Admin. Code, Ch. 61C-5
Energy conservation standards	Fla. Stat., Ch. 553
Equity exchanges	Fla. Stat., Ch. 519
Explosives	Fla. Stat., Ch. 552
Factory built housing	Fla. Stat., Ch. 553
Fence posts	Fla. Stat., Sec. 501.90
Fences and livestock at large	Fla. Stat., Ch. 588
Fiduciary funds	Fla. Stat., Ch. 518
Fireworks	Fla. Stat., Ch. 791
Food	Fla. Stat., Chs. 500, 544
Franchises	Fla. Stat., Sec. 817.416
	Fla. Admin. Code, Chs. 2-17
Frontons	Fla. Stat., Ch. 551
Fruits & vegetables	Fla. Stat., Ch. 504
	Fla. Admin. Code, Ch. 5G; 5H
Fuels, liquid	Fla. Stat., Ch. 526
Future consumer services	Fla. Admin. Code, Chs. 2-18
Gambling & lotteries	Fla. Stat., Ch. 849
Gas, liquefied petroleum	Fla. Stat., Ch. 527
	Fla. Admin. Code, Chs. 2-20; 4B
Gasoline & oil	Fla. Stat., Ch. 525
Glass	Fla. Stat., Ch. 553
Hazardous substances	Fla. Stat., Secs. 501.061-.121
Hazardous waste amnesty	Fla. Stat., Sec. 403.7264

Health care	Fla. Stat., Chs. 381; 383-85; 390-92; 395; 400
	Fla. Admin. Code, Ch. 7G
Health studios	Fla. Stat., Sec. 501.012
	Fla. Admin. Code, Ch. 5J-4
Home health agencies	Fla. Stat., Secs. 401.461-.505
Home improvement sales & fin.	Fla. Stat., Secs. 520.60-.98
Home solicitation sales	Fla. Stat., Ch. 501
	Fla. Admin. Code, Ch. 5J-2
Honey	Fla. Stat., Ch. 586
Horse sales, shows, exhibitions	Fla. Stat., Ch. 535
Hospices	Fla. Stat., Secs. 400.601-.614
Hotels	Fla. Stat., Ch. 509
	Fla. Admin. Code, Ch. 61C
Household products	Fla. Stat., Ch. 499
Housing codes, state minimum	Fla. Stat., Ch. 553
Identification cards	Fla. Stat., Sec. 877.18
Insurance and service plans	Fla. Stat., Chs. 624-651; 865.02
	Fla. Admin. Code, Ch. 4
Invention development	Fla. Stat., Sec. 501.136
Land sales	Fla. Stat., Ch. 498
	Fla. Admin. Code, Ch. 61B
Lasers & non-ionizing radiation	Fla. Stat., Sec.. 501.122
Lead acid batteries	Fla. Stat., Sec. 403.718
Legal services	Fla. Stat., Secs. 877.01-.02
Linen suppliers	Fla. Stat., Secs. 865.10
Liquor	Fla. Stat., Chs. 561-568
Livestock	Fla. Stat., Secs. 534; 877.05-.06
Lodging	Fla. Admin. Code, Ch. 61C
Marketing establishments	Fla. Stat., Sec. 877.061
Meats	Fla. Stat., Ch. 544
Mental health	Fla. Stat., Ch. 394
Metal recyclers	Fla. Stat., Ch. 538
Milk & milk products	Fla. Stat., Ch. 502
	Fla. Admin. Code, Ch. 5D
Mining waste	Fla. Stat., Ch. 533
Mobile homes	Fla. Stat., Ch. 723
	Fla. Admin. Code, Chs. 2-12; 61B

Money orders	Fla. Stat., Ch. 560
Motion pictures	Fla. Stat., Sec. 501.138
Motor vehicle lemon law	Fla. Stat., Ch. 681
	Fla. Admin. Code, Chs. 2-30
Motor vehicles	Fla. Stat., Secs. 520.01-.13; Ch. 545; Ch. 559, Part VIII
	Fla. Admin. Code, Chs. 5J-11, 5J-12
Multi-level marketing	Fla. Admin. Code, Chs. 2-17
Naval stores	Fla. Stat., Ch. 523
Newsprint	Fla. Stat., Sec. 403.7195
Nursing homes	Fla. Stat., Secs. 400.011-.332
Obscene literature	Fla. Stat., Ch. 847
Occupational therapists	Fla. Stat., Ch. 468, Fla. Admin. Code, Ch. 61F6
Oil	Fla. Stat., Secs. 403.75-.769
Outdoor advertising	Fla. Stat., Ch. 479
Outdoor theatres	Fla. Stat., Ch. 555
Pari-mutual wagering	Fla. Admin. Code, Ch. 61D
Peanut marketing	Fla. Stat., Ch. 573, Part VI
Pest control	Fla. Stat., Ch. 487
Photos of admission parks	Fla. Stat., Sec. 540.09
Plants & nurseries	Fla. Stat., Ch. 573, Part II; 575-581; 865.05
	Fla. Admin. Code, Ch. 5B
Plumbing	Fla. Stat., Ch. 553
Private investigators	Fla. Stat., Ch. 493
Prostitution	Fla. Stat., Ch. 796
Pyramid schemes	Fla. Admin. Code, Chs. 2-17
Radiation	Fla. Stat., Ch. 404
Radio & television repairs	Fla. Stat., Sec. 817.53
Real estate sales	Fla. Stat., Secs. 501.1375; 877.10
	Fla. Admin. Code, Chs. 2-13
Rental housing	Fla. Stat., Ch. 83
	Fla. Admin. Code, Chs. 2-11
Restaurants	Fla. Stat., Ch. 509
	Fla. Admin. Code, Ch. 7C
Sanitarians	Fla. Stat., Sec. 381.0101

Secondhand dealers	Fla. Stat., Ch. 538
Securities transactions	Fla. Stat., Ch. 517
	Fla. Admin. Code, Ch. 3E
Soybean marketing	Fla. Stat., Ch. 573, Part IV
Swimming & bathing places	Fla. Stat., Ch. 514
Syrup	Fla. Stat., Sec. 865.07
Telegraph & cable companies	Fla. Stat., Ch. 363
Telemarketing	Fla. Stat., Ch. 501
	Fla. Admin. Code, Chs. 5J-6
Telephone companies	Fla. Stat., Ch. 364
Television picture tubes	Fla. Stat., Secs. 817.559-.56
Term papers, dissertations	Fla. Stat., Sec. 877.17
Thermal efficiency standards	Fla. Stat., Ch. 553
Timber and lumber	Fla. Stat., Ch. 536
Time shares	Fla. Stat., Ch. 721;
	Fla. Admin. Code, Chs. 2-23
Tires	Fla. Stat., Sec . 403.718
Tobacco	Fla. Stat., Ch. 573, Part V; 574; 865.08
	Fla. Admin. Code, Ch. 7A
Tourist attraction	Fla. Stat., Sec. 817.55
Tourist camps	Fla. Stat., Ch. 513
Travel services	Fla. Stat., Ch. 559, Part IX; 817.554
	Fla. Admin. Code, Ch. 5J-3, 5J-9
Sound & film, copying	Fla. Stat., Ch. 540
Viticulture	Fla. Stat., Ch. 599
Watches, used	Fla. Stat., Sec. 501.925
Watermelon marketing	Fla. Stat., Ch. 573, Part III
Weapons and firearms	Fla. Stat., Ch. 790
Yacht/ship brokers	Fla. Stat., Ch. 326, Fla. Admin. Code, Chs. 61B-60

BOOKKEEPING AND ACCOUNTING 16

It is beyond the scope of this book to explain all the intricacies of setting up a business's bookkeeping and accounting systems. But the important thing is to realize that if you do not set up an understandable bookkeeping system your business will undoubtedly fail.

Without accurate records of where your income is coming from and where it is going you will be unable to increase your profits, lower your expenses, obtain needed financing or make the right decisions in all areas of your business. The time to decide how you will handle your bookkeeping is when you open your business; not a year later when it is tax time.

INITIAL BOOKKEEPING

If you do not understand business taxation you should pick up a good book on the subject as well as the IRS tax guide for your type of business (proprietorship, partnership, corporation, or limited liability company).

The IRS tax book for small businesses is Publication 334, *Tax Guide for Small Businesses*. There are also instruction booklets for each type of business form: Schedule C for proprietorships, Form 1120 or 1120S for

C corporations and S corporations, and 1165 for partnerships and businesses which are taxed like partnerships (LLCs, LLPs).

Keep in mind that the IRS does not give you the best advice for saving on taxes and does not give you the other side of contested issues. For that you need a private tax guide or advisor.

The most important thing to do is to set up your bookkeeping so that you can easily fill out your monthly, quarterly, and annual tax returns.

The best way to do this is to get copies of the returns—not the totals that you will need to supply—and set up your bookkeeping system to group those totals.

For example, for a sole proprietorship you will use "Schedule C" to report business income and expenses to the IRS at the end of the year. Use the categories on that form to sort your expenses. To make your job especially easy, every time you pay a bill, put the category number on the check.

ACCOUNTANTS

Most likely your new business will not be able to afford hiring an accountant right off to handle your books. But that is good. Doing them yourself will force you to learn about business accounting and taxation. The worst way to run a business is to know nothing about the tax laws and turn everything over to an accountant at the end of the year to find out what is due.

You should know the basics of tax law before making basic decisions such as whether to buy or rent equipment or premises. You should understand accounting so you can time your financial affairs appropriately. If you were a boxer who only needed to win fights, you could turn everything over to an accountant. If your business needs to buy supplies, inventory, or equipment and provides goods or services throughout the year, you need to at least have a basic understanding of the system within which you are working.

Once you can afford an accountant you should weigh the cost against your time and the risk that you will make an error. Even if you think you know enough to do your own corporate tax return, you should still take it to an accountant one year to see if you have been missing any - deductions. You might decide that the money saved is worth the cost of the accountant's services.

COMPUTER PROGRAMS

Today every business should keep its books by computer. There are inexpensive programs such as Quicken which can instantly provide you with reports of your income and expenses and the right figures to plug into your tax returns.

Most programs even offer a tax program each year that will take all of your information and print it out on the current year's tax forms.

TAX TIPS

Here are a few tax tips for small businesses that will help you save money:

- Usually when you buy equipment for a business, you must amortize the cost over several years. That is, you don't deduct it all when you buy it, you take, say, twenty-five percent of the cost off your taxes each year for four years. (The time is determined by the theoretical usefulness of the item.) However, small businesses are allowed to write off the entire cost of a limited amount of items under Internal Revenue Code (I.R.C.) Sec. 179. If you have income to shelter, use it.

- Owners of S corporations do not have to pay social security or medicare taxes on the part of their profits that is not considered salary. As long as you pay yourself a reasonable salary, other money you take out is not subject to these taxes.

- You should not neglect to deposit withholding taxes for your own salary or profits. Besides being a large sum to come up with at once in April, there are penalties that must be paid for failure to do so.

- Do not fail to keep track of and remit your employees' withholding. You will be personally liable for them even if you are a corporation.

- If you keep track of the use of your car for business you can deduct 31.5¢ per mile (this may go up or down each year). If you use your car for business a considerable amount of time you may be able to depreciate it.

- If your business is a corporation and if you designate the stock as "section 1244 stock," then if the business fails you are able to get a much better deduction for the loss.

- By setting up a retirement plan you can exempt up to twenty percent of your salary from income tax. See Chapter 11. But do not use money you might need later. There are penalties for taking it out of the retirement plan.

- When you buy things that will be resold or made into products which will be resold, you do not have to pay sales taxes on those purchases. (See Chapter 18.)

PAYING FEDERAL TAXES 17

INCOME TAX

The manner in which each type of business pays taxes is as follows:

PROPRIETORSHIP   A proprietor reports profits and expenses on Schedule C attached to the usual Form 1040 and pays tax on all of the net income of the business. Each quarter Form ES-1040 must be filed along with payment of one-quarter of the amount of income tax and social security taxes estimated to be due for the year.

PARTNERSHIP   The partnership files a return showing the income and expenses but pays no tax. Each partner is given a form showing his share of the profits or losses and reports these on Schedule E of Form 1040. Each quarter, Form ES-1040 must be filed by each partner along with payment of one-quarter of the amount of income tax and social security taxes estimated to be due for the year.

C CORPORATION   A regular corporation is a separate taxpayer, and pays tax on its profits after deducting all expenses, including officers' salaries. If dividends are distributed, they are paid out of after-tax dollars, and the shareholders pay tax a second time when they receive the dividends. If a corporation needs to accumulate money for investment, it may be able to do so at lower tax rates than the shareholders. But if all profits will be distributed to shareholders, the double-taxation may be excessive unless all income is paid as salaries. (A C corporation files Form 1120.)

S Corporation

A small corporation has the option of being taxed like a partnership. If Form 2553 is filed by the corporation and accepted by the Internal Revenue Service, the S corporation will only file an informational return listing profits and expenses. Then each shareholder will be taxed on a proportional share of the profits (or be able to deduct a proportional share of the losses). Unless a corporation will make a large profit that will not be distributed, S-status is usually best in the beginning. An S corporation files Form 1120S and distributes Form K-1 to each shareholder. If any money is taken out by a shareholder that is not listed as wages subject to withholding, then the shareholder will usually have to file form ES-1040 each quarter along with payment of the estimated withholding on the withdrawals.

Limited Liability Companies and Partnerships

Limited liability companies and professional limited liability companies are allowed by the IRS to elect to be taxed either as a partnership or a corporation. To make this election you file Form 8832, Entity Classification Election with the IRS.

Tax Workshops and Booklets

The IRS conducts workshops to inform businesses about the tax laws. (Do not expect in-depth study of the loopholes.) For more information call or write to the IRS at the following addresses:

Jacksonville:
400 W. Bay St. Stop 6450
Jacksonville, FL 32202-0045
(904) 232-2514
(800) 829-1040

Ft. Lauderdale:
Building A, Room 270
Stop 6030
Ft. Lauderdale, FL 33324-2019
(954) 423-7636
(800) 829-1040

WITHHOLDING, SOCIAL SECURITY, AND MEDICARE TAXES

If you need basic information on business tax returns, the IRS publishes a rather large booklet that answers most questions and is available free of charge. Call or write them and ask for Publication No. 334. If you have any questions, look up their toll-free number in the phone book under United States Government/Internal Revenue Service. If you want more creative answers and tax saving information, you should find a good local accountant. But to get started you will need the following:

EMPLOYER IDENTIFICATION NUMBER

If you are a sole proprietor with no employees, you can use your social security number for your business. If you are a corporation, a partnership or a proprietorship with employees, you must obtain an Employer Identification Number. This is done by filing the **APPLICATION FOR EMPLOYER IDENTIFICATION NUMBER (IRS FORM SS-4)**. (see form 5, p.211.) It usually takes a week or two to receive. You will need this number to open bank accounts for the business, so you should file this form a soon as you decide to go into business. A sample filled-in form is in Appendix A, and the blank form with instructions is in Appendix B.

EMPLOYEE'S WITHHOLDING ALLOWANCE CERTIFICATE

You must have each employee fill out an **EMPLOYEE'S WITHHOLDING ALLOWANCE CERTIFICATE (IRS FORM W-4)** to calculate the amount of federal taxes to be deducted and to obtain their social security numbers. (see form 7, p.219.) (The number of allowances on this form is used with IRS Circular E, Publication 15, to figure out the exact deductions.) A sample filled-in form is in Appendix A.

FEDERAL TAX DEPOSIT COUPONS

After taking withholdings from employees' wages, you must deposit them at a bank that is authorized to accept such funds. If at the end of any month you have over $1000 in withheld taxes (including your contribution to FICA) you must make a deposit prior to the 15th of the following month. If on the 3rd, 7th, 11th, 15th, 19th, 22nd, or 25th of any month you have over $3,000 in withheld taxes, you must make a deposit within three banking days. The deposit is made using the coupons in the form 8109 booklet. A sample 8109-B coupon, which you will use to order your booklet, is shown in Appendix A on page 193.

ELECTRONIC FILING

Businesses that make $50,000 or more a year in federal tax deposits are required to begin electronic filing by June 30, 1999. However, this deadline has been extended in the past and may be again. (It was originally scheduled for July 1, 1997, but faced strong business opposition.)

ESTIMATED TAX PAYMENT VOUCHER

Sole proprietors and partners usually take draws from their businesses without the formality of withholding. However, they are still required to make deposits of income and FICA taxes each quarter. If more than $500 is due in April on a person's 1040 form, then not enough money was withheld each quarter and a penalty is assessed unless the person falls into an exception. The quarterly withholding is submitted on form 1040-ES on April 15th, June 15th, September 15th, and January 15th each year. If these days fall on a weekend then the due date is the following Monday. The worksheet with form 1040-ES can be used to determine the amount to pay. A sample filled-in form 1040-ES is in Appendix A on page 194.

NOTE: *One of the exceptions to the rule is that if you withhold the same amount as last year's tax bill, then you do not have to pay a penalty. This is usually a lot easier than filling out the 1040-ES worksheet.*

EMPLOYER'S QUARTERLY TAX RETURN

Each quarter you must file Form 941 reporting your federal withholding and FICA taxes. If you owe more than $1000 at the end of a quarter, you are required to make a deposit at the end of any month that you have $1000 in withholding. The deposits are made to the Federal Reserve Bank or an authorized financial institution on Form 501. Most banks are authorized to accept deposits. If you owe more than $3,000 for any month, you must make a deposit at any point in the month in which you owe $3,000. After you file form SS-4, the 941 forms will be sent to you automatically if you checked the box saying that you expect to have employees.

WAGE AND TAX
STATEMENT

At the end of each year, you are required to issue a W-2 Form to each employee. This form shows the amount of wages paid to the employee during the year as well as the amounts withheld for taxes, social security, medicare, and other purposes. A sample filled-in W-2 is in Appendix A on page 195.

MISCELLANEOUS

If you pay at least $600 to a person other than an employee (such as independent contractors) you are required to file a Form 1099 for that person. Along with the 1099s, you must file a form 1096, which is a summary sheet.

Many people are not aware of this law and fail to file these forms, but they are required for such things as services, royalties, rents, awards and prizes that you pay to individuals (but not corporations). The rules for this are quite complicated so you should either obtain "Package 1099" from the IRS or consult your accountant. Sample filled-in forms 1099 and 1096 are in Appendix A on pages 196 and 197.

EARNED
INCOME CREDIT

Persons who are not liable to pay income tax may have the right to a check from the government because of the "Earned Income Credit." You are required to notify your employees of this. You can satisfy this requirement with one of the following:

- a W-2 Form with the notice on the back;

- a substitute for the W-2 Form with the notice on it;

- a copy of Notice 797; or

- a written statement with the wording from Notice 797.

A Notice 797 can be obtained by calling 800-829-3676.

EXCISE TAXES

Excise taxes are taxes on certain activities or items. Most federal excise taxes have been eliminated since World War II, but a few remain.

Some of the things that are subject to federal excise taxes are tobacco and alcohol, gasoline, tires and inner tubes, some trucks and trailers, firearms, ammunition, bows, arrows, fishing equipment, the use of highway vehicles of over 55,000 pounds, aircraft, wagering, telephone and teletype services, coal, hazardous wastes, and vaccines. If you are involved with any of these, you should obtain from the IRS publication No. 510, *Information on Excise Taxes*.

UNEMPLOYMENT COMPENSATION TAX

You must pay federal unemployment taxes if you paid wages of $1,500 in any quarter, or if you had at least one employee for twenty calendar weeks. The federal tax amount is 0.8% of the first $7,000 of wages paid each employee. If more than $100 is due by the end of any quarter (if you paid $12,500 in wages for the quarter), then Form 508 must be filed with an authorized financial institution or the Federal Reserve Bank in your area. You will receive Form 508 when you obtain your employer identification number.

For more information on unemployment compensation in Florida, write to:

Division of Unemployment Compensation
107 E. Madison St.
Tallahassee, FL 32399-0233

At the end of each year, you must file Form 940 or Form 940EZ. This is your annual report of federal unemployment taxes. You will receive an original form from the IRS.

PAYING FLORIDA TAXES 18

SALES AND USE TAXES

If you will be selling or renting goods or services at retail, you must collect Florida Sales and Use Tax. Some services such as doctors and attorney's fees and newspaper advertising are not taxed, but most others are. If you have any doubt, check with the Florida Department of Revenue.

First, you must obtain a tax number by filling out the APPLICATION TO COLLECT AND/OR REPORT TAX IN FLORIDA (DR-1) and paying a $5 fee. (see form 8, p.221.) A sample filled-in copy of the form is in Appendix A. Some information for filling out the form and a blank form are in Appendix B. (see form 8, p.221.) For more details about the tax you should obtain the booklet, *Sales and Use Tax Registration Handbook for Business Operators*, from the Department of Revenue. You can find the local office in the blue pages of your phone book, or call their main number, 800-352-3671. If you cannot get through, their address is:

> Department of Revenue
> Carlton Building
> Tallahassee, FL 32301

The SALES AND USE TAX RETURNS (DR-15CS) are due for each month on the 20th of the following month. (see form 10, p.229.) You are allowed to deduct 2.5% of the tax as your reimbursement for collecting the tax.

Rest assured the amount will never be near enough to compensate for the work. In some cases, if your sales are very limited (under $100 a quarter), you may be allowed to file returns quarterly, or semi-annually.

Once you file your Application for Sales and Use Tax Registration, you will have to start filing monthly returns whether you have any sales or not. If you do not file the return, even if you had no sales, then you must pay a $5 penalty. If you do not expect to have any sales for the first few months while you are setting up your business, you probably should wait before sending in the registration. Otherwise you may forget to file the returns marked with zeros and end up paying the penalties.

One reason to get a tax number early is to exempt your purchases from tax. When you buy a product which you will resell, or use as part of a product which you will sell, you are exempt from paying tax on it. To get the exemption you need to submit a copy of your Annual Resale Certificate for Sales Tax (form DR-13). This form comes with your booklet of tax coupons each year. A sample is on page 198.

If you will only be selling items wholesale or out of state, you might think that you would not need a tax number or to submit returns, but you will need to be registered to obtain the tax number to exempt your purchases.

If you have any sales before you get your monthly tax return forms, you should calculate the tax anyway and submit the tax before the 20th of the following month. Otherwise, you will be charged a penalty even if it was not your fault that they did not send you the forms.

You should be aware that the Florida Department of Revenue has not been very well organized in the past. They have been known to give incorrect tax information, fail to send out refunds when due, take a year to send refunds, and fail to send out forms on time or to the correct address. This is improving but be sure to stay on top of your state tax situation.

After you obtain your tax number, you will be required to collect sales tax on all purchases. In some cases, new businesses are required to post a bond to insure taxes are paid.

If you sell to someone who claims to be exempt from sales and use taxes, (for example, if they plan to resell merchandise they have purchased from you) then you must have them complete the Certificate of Resale mentioned above. Following the application is an instruction sheet for filing a monthly return and a Blanket Certificate of Resale form.

SELLING TO TAX
EXEMPT
PURCHASERS

You are required to collect sales and use taxes for all sales you make unless you have documentation on file proving that a purchase was exempt from the tax. A purchaser who claims to be exempt should give you a signed copy of their form DR-13. Each year you need to obtain a copy of their new form DR-13.

UNEMPLOYMENT COMPENSATION TAX

You are not liable to pay unemployment compensation taxes until you have had an employee work a part of a day in any twenty calendar weeks or paid $1500 in wages in a quarter. But once you reach that point, you are liable for all back taxes. The rate starts at 2.7% but if your record is clear it may drop to 0.1%. The tax is paid on the first $7000 of wages of each employee.

When you have had an employee work for twenty weeks, you should send in an **EMPLOYER REGISTRATION REPORT**. A sample filled-in form is in Appendix A. You can use the blank form in Appendix B. (see form 9, p.227.) You will be sent quarterly returns to fill out.

Some businesses try to keep taxes low by having all work done by independent contractors instead of employees. One thing to be aware of is that if a business has no employees for several quarters, the Florida unemployment tax rate doubles. A payment of a small wage to someone each quarter will avoid this problem.

TANGIBLE AND INTANGIBLE PROPERTY TAXES

TANGIBLE
PROPERTY TAX

This is a tax on all personal property used in a business and on inventory. It includes such things as dishes, machinery, furniture, tools, signs, carpeting, appliances, laboratory equipment, and just about everything else.

Property is taxed on its value January 1st. A return must be filed by April 1st listing the property of the business, and a tax bill is sent out in November, the same time as the real property tax bill.

A "TRIM" (Truth in Millage) Notice is sent out in August by the county tax assessor letting taxpayers know the assessed value of their property and the tax rate that will apply. If you feel there is an error in the valuation of your property, you may discuss it with an appraiser or file a petition for review.

It is not unusual to see the assessed value of personal property remain the same or even go up over the years while the actual value depreciates greatly. Filing a petition protesting the assessment occasionally helps, but for the small amount of money involved, it is usually not worth it. For the property assessors, this is the easiest way to collect taxes that are not due.

INTANGIBLE
PROPERTY TAX

This is a tax on the value of such things as promissory notes, mortgages, accounts receivable, stocks, bonds, and mutual funds. The tax is one-tenth of one percent ($1 per $1000) of the value of the property on January 1st. The tax must be paid by individuals as well as businesses, but individuals have an exemption on the first $20,000 ($40,000 for married couples filing jointly.)

The tax applies to all intangibles owned on January 1st and must be paid by June 30th. There is a discount of 1% per month for paying early (up to a maximum of 4% for paying in February).

The tax does not apply to deposits in banks, but it does apply to money market mutual funds. (For large amounts, some people save taxes by transferring the funds from a mutual fund to a bank just before January

1st and then back again after the 1st. The tax does not apply to promissory notes secured by mortgages on real property or to IRA accounts.)

A corporation can pay the tax on its own tax held by stockholders in lieu of them paying it. The advantage is that the corporation can deduct the tax as a business expense. The shareholders can deduct the tax only if they itemize deduction. But they get a $20,000 exclusion, which may eliminate the tax completely.

INCOME TAX

Yes, Florida does have an income tax. It only applies to C corporations and entities that elect to be taxed as corporations under federal law. Prior to 1998, limited liability companies were subject to the corporate income tax but now they can elect partnership taxation. The tax is 5.5% of the Florida net income.

NOTE: *Professional service corporations that do not elect "S" status must pay the tax.*

Occasionally there is a proposal to extend this tax to S corporations. It has not yet passed, but it may if there is another budget crisis. Most proposals exempt *small* S corporations.

Forms and instructions can be obtained from your local Department of Revenue office or from:

Florida Department of Revenue
Carlton Building
Tallahassee, FL 32301

EXCISE TAXES

Florida imposes taxes on the following businesses:

- wholesale tobacco dealers and tobacco vending machine operators. (Contact the Division of Alcoholic Beverages and Tobacco of the Department of Business Regulation);

- alcohol manufacturers and distributors. (Contact the Division of Alcoholic Beverages and Tobacco of the Department of Business Regulation);

- mineral, oil, and gas producers. (Contact the Department of Revenue); and

- motor fuel dealers. (Contact the Department of Revenue).

OUT-OF-STATE TAXES 19

STATE SALES TAXES

In 1992, the United States Supreme Court struck a blow for the rights of small businesses by ruling that state tax authorities cannot force them to collect sales taxes on interstate mail orders (*Quill Corporation v. North Dakota*).

Unfortunately, the court left open the possibility that Congress could allow interstate taxation of mail order sales, and since then several bills have been introduced that would do so. One, introduced by Arkansas senator Dale Bumpers, was given the Orwellian "newspeak" title, *The Consumer and Main Street Protection Act*.

At present, companies are only required to collect sales taxes for states in which they *do business*. Exactly what business is enough to trigger taxation is a legal question and some states try to define it as broadly as possible.

If you have an office in a state, you are doing business there and any goods shipped to consumers in that state are subject to sales taxes. If you have a full time employee working in the state much of the year many states will consider you doing business there. In some states, attending a two-day trade show is enough business to trigger taxation for the entire year for every order shipped to the state. One loophole that often works is to be represented at shows by persons who are not your employees.

Because the laws are different in each state you will have to do some research on a state-by-state basis to find out how much business you can do in a state without being subject to their taxation. You can request a state's rules from its department of revenue, but keep in mind that what a department of revenue wants the law to be is not always what the courts will rule that it is.

Business Taxes

Even worse than being subject to a state's sales taxes is to be subject to their income or other business taxes. For example, California charges every company doing business in the state a minimum $800 a year fee and charges income tax on a portion of the company's worldwide income. Doing a small amount of business in the state is clearly not worth getting mired in California taxation.

For this reason some trade shows have been moved from the state and this has resulted in a review of the tax policies and some "safe-harbor" guidelines to advise companies on what they can do without becoming subject to taxation.

Write to the Department of Revenue of any state with which you have business contacts to see what might trigger your taxation.

Internet Taxes

State revenue departments are drooling at the prospect of taxing commerce on the Internet. Theories have already been proposed that websites available to state residents mean a company is doing business in a state.

Fortunately, Congress has passed a moratorium on taxation of the Internet. This will be extended, hopefully, and will give us a new tax-free world, but do not count on it. It would take a tremendous outcry to keep the Internet tax-free. (Keep an eye out for any news stories on proposals to tax the Internet and petition your representatives against them.)

CANADIAN TAXES

The Canadian government expects American companies, which sell goods by mail order to Canadians, to collect taxes for them and file returns with Revenue Canada, their tax department.

Those that receive an occasional unsolicited order are not expected to register and Canadian customers, who order things from the U.S., pay the tax plus a $5 fee upon receipt of the goods. But companies that solicit Canadian orders are expected to be registered if their worldwide income is $30,000 or more per year. In some cases, a company may be required to post a bond and to pay for the cost of Canadian auditors visiting its premises and auditing its books! For these reasons you may notice that some companies decline to accept orders from Canada.

THE END...AND THE BEGINNING 20

If you have read through this whole book, you know more about the rules and laws for operating a Florida business than most people in business today. However, after learning about all the governmental regulations, you may become discouraged. You are probably wondering how you can keep track of all the laws and how you will have any time left to make money after complying with the laws. It is not that bad. People are starting businesses every day and they are making money, lots of money. American business owners are lucky, some countries have marginal tax rates as high as 105%!

The regulations that exist right now are enough to strangle some businesses. Consider the Armour meat-packing plant. The Federal Meat Inspection Service required that an opening be made in a conveyor to allow inspection or they would shut down the plant. OSHA told them that if they made that opening they would be shut down for safety reasons. Government regulations made it impossible for that plant to be in business!

But what you have to realize is that the same bureaucrats who are creating laws to slow down businesses are the ones who are responsible for enforcing the laws. And just as most government programs cost more than expected and fail to achieve their goals, most government regulations cannot be enforced against millions of people.

In a pure democracy, fifty-one percent of the voters can decide that all left-handed people must wear green shirts and that everyone must go to church three days a week. It is the Bill of Rights in our constitution that protects us from the whims of the majority.

In America today, there are no laws regarding left-handed people or going to church but there are laws controlling minute aspects of our personal and business lives. Does a majority have the right to decide what hours you can work, what you can sell, or where you can sell it? You must decide for yourself and act accordingly.

One way to avoid problems with the government is to keep a low profile and avoid open confrontation. For a lawyer, it can be fun going to appeals court over an unfair parking ticket or making a federal case out of a $25 fine. But for most people the expenses of a fight with the government are unbearable. If you start a mass protest against the IRS or OSHA they will have to make an example of you.

The important thing is that you know the laws and the penalties for violations before making your decision. Knowing the laws will also allow you to use the loopholes in the laws to avoid violations.

Congratulations on deciding to start a business in Florida! If you have any unusual experiences along the way, drop us a line at the following address. The information may be useful for a future book.

Sphinx Publishing
P.O. Box 4410
Naperville, IL 60567-4410

GLOSSARY

A

acceptance. Agreeing to the terms of an offer and creating a contract.

affirmative action. Hiring an employee to achieve a balance in the workplace, and avoid existing or continuing discrimination based on minority status.

alien. A person who is not a citizen of the country.

articles of incorporation. The document that sets forth the organization of a corporation.

B

bait advertising. Offering a product for sale with the intention of selling another product.

bulk sales. Selling substantially all of a company's inventory.

C

C corporation. A corporation that pays taxes on its profits.

collections. The collection of money owed to a business.

common law.   Laws that are determined in court cases rather than statutes.

consideration.   The exchange of value or promises in a contract.

contract.   An agreement between two or more parties.

copyright.   Legal protection given to "original works of authorship."

corporation.   An artificial person which is set up to conduct a business owned by shareholders and run by officers and directors.

D

deceptive pricing.   Pricing goods or services in a manner intended to deceive the customers.

discrimination.   The choosing among various options based on their characteristics.

domain name.   The address of a website.

E

employee.   Person who works for another under that person's control and direction.

endorsements.   Positive statements about goods or services.

excise tax.   A tax paid on the sale or consumption of goods or services.

express warranty.   A specific guarantee of a product or service.

F

fictitious name.   A name used by a business that is not its personal or legal name.

G

general partnership. A business that is owned by two or more persons.

goods. Items of personal property.

guarantee/guaranty. A promise of quality of a good or service.

I

implied warranty. A guarantee of a product or service that is not specifically made, but can be implied from the circumstances of the sale.

independent contractor. Person who works for another as a separate business, not as an employee.

intangible property. Personal property that does not have physical presence, such as the ownership interest in a corporation.

intellectual property. Legal rights to the products of the mind, such as writings, musical compositions, formulas and designs.

L

liability. The legal responsibility to pay for an injury.

limited liability company. An entity recognized as a legal "person" that is set up to conduct a business owned and run by members.

limited liability partnership. An entity recognized as a legal "person" that is set up to conduct a business owned and run by members that is set up for professionals such as attorneys or doctors.

limited partnership. A business that is owned by two or more persons of which one or more is liable for the debts of the business and one or more has no liability for the debts.

limited warranty. A guarantee covering certain aspects of a good or service.

M

merchant. A person who is in business.

merchant's firm offer. An offer by a business made under specific terms.

N

nonprofit corporation. An entity recognized as a legal "person" that is set up to run an operation in which none of the profits are distributed to controlling members.

O

occupational license. A government-issued permit to transact business.

offer. A proposal to enter into a contract.

overtime. Hours worked in excess of forty hours in one week, or eight hours in one day.

P

partnership. A business formed by two or more persons.

patent. Protection given to inventions, discoveries and designs.

personal property. Any type of property other than land and the structures attached to it.

pierce the corporate veil. When a court ignores the structure of a corporation and holds its owners responsible for its debts or liabilities.

professional association. An entity recognized as a legal "person" that is set up to conduct a business of professionals such as attorneys or doctors.

proprietorship. A business that is owned by one person.

R

real property. Land and the structures attached to it.

resident alien. A person who is not a citizen of the country but who may legally reside and work there.

S

S corporation. A corporation in which the profits are taxed to the shareholders.

sale on approval. Selling an item with the agreement that it may be brought back and the sale cancelled.

sale or return. An agreement whereby goods are to be purchased or returned to the vendor.

securities. Interests in a business such as stocks or bonds.

sexual harassment. Activity that causes an employee to feel or be sexually threatened.

shares. Units of stock in a corporation.

statute of frauds. Law that requires certain contracts to be in writing.

stock. Ownership interests in a corporation.

sublease. An agreement to rent premises from an existing tenant.

T

tangible property. Physical personal property such as desks and tables.

trade secret. Commercially valuable information or process that is protected by being kept a secret.

trademark. A name or symbol used to identify the source of goods or services.

U

unemployment compensation. Payments to a former employee who was terminated from a job for a reason not based on his or her fault.

usury. Charging an interest rate higher than that allowed by law.

W

withholding. Money taken out of an employee's salary and remitted to the government.

workers compensation. Insurance program to cover injuries or deaths of employees.

For Further Reference

The following books will provide valuable information to those who are starting new businesses. Some are out of print, but they are classics that are worth tracking down.

For inspiration to give you the drive to succeed:

Hill, Napoleon, *Think and Grow Rich*. New York: Fawcett Books, 1990, 233 pages.

Karbo, Joe, *The Lazy Man's Way to Riches*. Sunset Beach: F P Publishing, 1974, 156 pages.

Schwartz, David J., *The Magic of Thinking Big*. Fireside, 1987, 234 pages.

For hints on what it takes to be successful:

Carnegie, Dale, *How to Win Friends and Influence People*. New York: Pocket Books, 1994, 276 pages.

Ringer, Robert J., *Looking Out for #1*. New York: Fawcett Books, 1993.

Ringer, Robert J., *Million Dollar Habits*. New York: Fawcett Books, 1991.

Ringer, Robert J., *Winning Through Intimidation*. New York: Fawcett Books, 1993.

For advice on bookkeeping and organization:

Kamoroff, Bernard, *Small Time Operator (25th Edition)*. Bell Springs Publishing, 2000, 200 pages.

For a very practical guide to investing:

Tobias, Andrew, *The Only Investment Guide You'll Ever Need*. Harvest Books, 1999, 239 pages.

For advice on how to avoid problems with government agencies:

Browne, Harry, *How I Found Freedom in an Unfree World*. Great Falls: Liam Works, 1998, 387 pages.

The following are other books published by **Sphinx Publishing** that may be helpful to your business:

Eckert, W. Kelsea, Sartorius, Arthur, III, & Warda, Mark, *How to Form Your Own Corporation*. 2001.

Haman, Edward A., *How to Form Your Own Partnership*. 1999.

Ray, James C., *The Most Valuable Business Legal Forms You'll Ever Need*. 1998.

Ray, James C., *The Most Valuable Corporate Forms You'll Ever Need*. 1998.

Warda, Mark, *How to Form a Delaware Corporation from Any State*. 1999.

Warda, Mark, *Incorporate in Nevada from Any State*. 2001.

Warda, Mark, *How to Form a Limited Liability Company*. 1999.

Warda, Mark, *How to Register Your Own Copyright*. 2000.

Warda, Mark, *How to Register Your Own Trademark.*. 1999.

The following are books published by **Sourcebooks, Inc.** that may be helpful to your business:

Fleury, Robert E., *The Small Business Survival Guide.*. 1995.

Gutman, Jean E., *Accounting Made Easy*. 1998.

Milling, Bryan E., *How to Get a Small Business Loan (2nd Edition)*. 1998.

The following websites provide information that may be useful to you in starting your business:

Internal Revenue Service: http://www.irs.gov

Small Business Administration: http://www.sba.gov

Social Security Administration: http://www.ssa.gov

U. S. Business Advisor: http://www.business.gov

APPENDIX A
SAMPLE FILLED-IN FORMS

The following forms are selected filled-in forms for demonstration purposes. Most have a corresponding blank form in Appendix B. The form numbers in this appendix correspond to the form numbers in Appendix B. If there is no blank for a particular form, it is because you must obtain it from a government agency. If you need instructions for these forms as you follow how they are filled out, they can be found in Appendix B, or in those pages in the chapters that discuss those forms.

APPLICATION FOR REGISTRATION OF FICTITIOUS NAME

Note: Acknowledgements/certificates will be sent to the address in Section 1 only.

Section 1

1. Krebbs Company

Fictitious Name to be Registered

2. 100 Maynard Drive

Mailing Address of Business

Jacksonville   FL   32100

City   State   Zip Code

3. Florida County of principal place of business: _____

Bradford

4. FEI Number: 69-09090909

This space for office use only

Section 2

A. Owner(s) of Fictitious Name If Individual(s): (Use an attachment if necessary):

1. Krebbs   Darron   T   2. _____

    Last   First   M.I.   Last   First   M.I.

761 Ivy Grey Lane

Address   Address

Jacksonville, FL   32100

City   State   Zip Code   City   State   Zip Code

SS# 410 - 00 - 300 (optional)   SS# _____ - _____ - _____ (optional)

B. Owner(s) of Fictitious Name If other than individuals(s): (Use attachment if necessary):

1. _____   2. _____

   Entity Name   Entity Name

   Address   Address

   City   State   Zip Code   City   State   Zip Code

Florida Registration Number _____   Florida Registration Number _____

FEI Number: _____   FEI Number: _____

☐ Applied for   ☐ Not Applicable   ☐ Applied for   ☐ Not Applicable

Section 3

I (we) the undersigned, being the sole (all the) party(ies) owning interest in the above fictitious name, certify that the information indicated on this form is true and accurate. In accordance with Section 865.09, F.S., I (we) further certify that the fictitious name shown in Section 1 of this form has been advertised at least once in a newspaper as defined in chapter 50, Florida Statutes, in the county where the applicant's principal place of business is located. I (we) understand that the signature(s) below shall have the same legal effect as if made under oath. (At Least One Signature Required)

Darron Krebbs   *Jan. 2, 2004*

Signature of Owner   Date   Signature of Owner   Date

Phone Number: 904-594-1111   Phone Number: _____

Section 4

FOR CANCELLATION COMPLETE SECTION 4 ONLY:

FOR FICTITIOUS NAME OR OWNERSHIP CHANGE COMPLETE SECTIONS 1 THROUGH 4:

I (we) the undersigned, hereby cancel the fictitious name _____

_____, which was registered on _____ and was assigned registration number _____

Signature of Owner   Date   Signature of Owner   Date

Mark the applicable boxes   ☐ Certificate of Status - $10   ☐ Certified Copy - $30

Filing Fee: $50

CR4E-001

APPLICATION FOR THE REGISTRATION OF A TRADEMARK OR SERVICE MARK
PURSUANT TO CHAPTER 495, FLORIDA STATUTES

TO: **Division of Corporations**
Post Office Box 6327
Tallahassee, FL 32314

Name & address to whom acknowledgment should be sent:

Krebbs Company/Darron Krebbs

100 Maynard Drive

Jacksonville, FL 32100

(904) 594-0000
Daytime Telephone number

PART I

1. (a) Applicant's name: _Darron Krebbs/Krebbs Company_

   (b) Applicant's business address: 100 Maynard Drive

   Jacksonville, FL 32100
   City/State/Zip

   (c) Applicant's telephone number: (904)594-0000
   ☒ Individual   ❑ Corporation   ❑Joint Venture   ❑ Other:_____
   ❑ General Partnership   ❑ Limited Partnership   ❑Union

If other than an individual,

(1) Florida registration number: _____ (2) Domicile State: _____

(3) Federal Employer Identification Number: _____

2. (a) If the mark to be registered is a service mark, the services in connection with which the mark is used:
(i.e., furniture moving services, diaper services, house painting services, etc.)

_____

_____

   (b) If the mark to be registered is a trademark, the goods in connection with which the mark is used:
(i.e., ladies sportswear, cat food, barbecue grills, shoe laces, etc.)

Wines and Spirits in Class 33

_____

   (c) The mode or manner in which the mark is used:(i.e., labels, decals, newspaper advertisements, brochures, etc.)

   Labels are glued onto front of goods

_____

_____

(Continued)

177

d) The class(es) in which goods or services fall:

Class 33

PART II

1. Date first used by the applicant, predecessor, or a related company (must include month, day and year):

(a) Date first used anywhere: _June 19, 2001_ (b) Date first used in Florida: _June 19, 2001_

PART III

1. The mark to be registered is: (If logo/design is included, please give brief written description which must be 25 words or less.)

Logo is small, crab-like figure holding a bunch of

grapes in one claw and grains in the other. Claws

are crossing his chest.

English Translation_____

2. DISCLAIMER (if applicable)

NO CLAIM IS MADE TO THE EXCLUSIVE RIGHT TO USE THE TERM " _____
_____ " APART FROM THE MARK AS SHOWN.

I,_____ Darron Krebbs _____, *being sworn, depose and say that I am the owner and the applicant herein, or that I am authorized to sign on behalf of the owner and applicant herein, and no other person except a related company has the right to use such mark in Florida either in the identical form or in such near resemblance as to be likely to deceive or confuse or to be mistaken therefor. I make this affidavit and verification on my/the applicant's behalf. I further acknowledge that I have read the application and know the contents thereof and that the facts stated herein are true and correct*

_____ Darron Krebbs _____
Typed or printed name of applicant

Darron Krebbs
Applicant's signature or authorized person's signature
(List name and title)

STATE OF _Florida_

COUNTY OF _Florida_

On this _23rd_ day of _____ May _____ , 2002, _____ Darron Krebbs _____ personally appeared before me,

☐ who is personally known to me   ☒ whose identity I proved on the basis of _____
FL Dr. Lic. # K123-45-67-890   .

(Seal)

_____ Joan Nichte _____
Notary Public Signature

Joan Nichte
Notary's Printed Name

My Commission Expires: _Jan. 02, 2004_

FEE: $87.50 per class

U.S. Department of Justice
Immigration and Naturalization Service

OMB No. 1115-0136
Employment Eligibility Verification

Please read instructions carefully before completing this form. The instructions must be available during completion of this form. **ANTI-DISCRIMINATION NOTICE.** It is illegal to discriminate against work eligible individuals. Employers CANNOT specify which document(s) they will accept from an employee. The refusal to hire an individual because of a future expiration date may also constitute illegal discrimination.

Section 1. Employee Information and Verification. To be completed and signed by employee at the time employment begins

Print Name: Last	First	Middle Initial	Maiden Name
REDDENBACHER	MARY	J.	HASSENFUSS

Address (Street Name and Number)	Apt. #	Date of Birth (month/day/year)
1234 LIBERTY LANE		1/26/69

City	State	Zip Code	Social Security #
TAMPA	FL	33613	123-45-6789

I am aware that federal law provides for imprisonment and/or fines for false statements or *use of false documents* in connection with the completion of this form.

I attest, under penalty of perjury, that I am (check one of the following):
- ☒ A citizen or national of the United States
- ☐ A Lawful Permanent Resident (Alien # A_____)
- ☐ An alien authorized to work until___/___/___
  (Alien # or Admission #_____)

Employee's Signature	Date (month/day/year)
Mary Reddenbacher	1/29/00

Preparer and/or Translator Certification. *(To be completed and signed if Section 1 is prepared by a person other than the employee.) I attest, under penalty of perjury, that I have assisted in the completion of this form and that to the best of my knowledge the information is true and correct.*

Preparer's/Translator's Signature	Print Name

Address (Street Name and Number, City, State, Zip Code)	Date (month/day/year)

Section 2. Employer Review and Verification. To be completed and signed by employer. **Examine one document from List A OR** examine one document from List B **and** one from List C as listed on the reverse of this form and record the title, number and expiration date, if any, of the document(s)

List A	OR	List B	AND	List C
Document title: PASSPORT		_____		_____
Issuing authority: PASSPORT AGENCY TPA		_____		_____
Document #: 123456789		_____		_____
Expiration Date (if any): 10 / 5 /06		___/___/___		___/___/___
Document #: _____				
Expiration Date (if any): ___/___/___				

CERTIFICATION - I attest, under penalty of perjury, that I have examined the document(s) presented by the above-named employee, that the above-listed document(s) appear to be genuine and to relate to the employee named, that the employee began employment on (month/day/year) 02 / 02 / 02 **and that to the best of my knowledge the employee is eligible to work in the United States.** (State employment agencies may omit the date the employee began employment).

Signature of Employer or Authorized Representative	Print Name	Title
Darron Krebbs	Darron Krebbs	owner

Business or Organization Name	Address (Street Name and Number, City, State, Zip Code)	Date (month/day/year)
Krebbs Company	100 Maynard Dr., Jacksonville FL 32100	2/2/02

Section 3. Updating and Reverification. To be completed and signed by employer

A. New Name (if applicable)	B. Date of rehire (month/day/year) (if applicable)

C. If employee's previous grant of work authorization has expired, provide the information below for the document that establishes current employment eligibility.

Document Title:_____ Document #:_____ Expiration Date (if any):___/___/___

I attest, under penalty of perjury, that to the best of my knowledge, this employee is eligible to work in the United States, and if the employee presented document(s), the document(s) I have examined appear to be genuine and to relate to the individual.

Signature of Employer or Authorized Representative	Date (month/day/year)

Form I-9 (Rev. 11-21-91) N

Form **SS-4**

(Rev. April 2000)

Department of the Treasury
Internal Revenue Service

Application for Employer Identification Number

(For use by employers, corporations, partnerships, trusts, estates, churches, government agencies, certain individuals, and others. See instructions.)

▶ Keep a copy for your records.

EIN

OMB No. 1545-0003

Please type or print clearly.

1 Name of applicant (legal name) (see instructions)

John Doe and James Doe

2 Trade name of business (if different from name on line 1)

Doe Company

3 Executor, trustee, "care of" name

4a Mailing address (street address) (room, apt., or suite no.)

123 Main Street

5a Business address (if different from address on lines 4a and 4b)

4b City, state, and ZIP code

Libertyville, FL 33461

5b City, state, and ZIP code

6 County and state where principal business is located

Libertyville, FL

7 Name of principal officer, general partner, grantor, owner, or trustor—SSN or ITIN may be required (see instructions) ▶ 123-45-6789

John Doe

8a Type of entity (Check only one box.) (see instructions)

Caution: *If applicant is a limited liability company, see the instructions for line 8a.*

- ☐ Sole proprietor (SSN) _____
- ☒ Partnership
- ☐ REMIC
- ☐ State/local government
- ☐ Church or church-controlled organization
- ☐ Other nonprofit organization (specify) ▶ _____
- ☐ Other (specify) ▶
- ☐ Personal service corp.
- ☐ National Guard
- ☐ Farmers' cooperative
- ☐ Estate (SSN of decedent) _____
- ☐ Plan administrator (SSN) _____
- ☐ Other corporation (specify) ▶ _____
- ☐ Trust
- ☐ Federal government/military
  (enter GEN if applicable) _____

8b If a corporation, name the state or foreign country (if applicable) where incorporated

State

Foreign country

9 Reason for applying (Check only one box.) (see instructions)

- ☒ Started new business (specify type) ▶ _____
  clothing manufacturer
- ☐ Hired employees (Check the box and see line 12.)
- ☐ Created a pension plan (specify type) ▶
- ☐ Banking purpose (specify purpose) ▶ _____
- ☐ Changed type of organization (specify new type) ▶ _____
- ☐ Purchased going business
- ☐ Created a trust (specify type) ▶ _____
- ☐ Other (specify) ▶

10 Date business started or acquired (month, day, year) (see instructions)

10-15-2001

11 Closing month of accounting year (see instructions)

December

12 First date wages or annuities were paid or will be paid (month, day, year). **Note:** *If applicant is a withholding agent, enter date income will first be paid to nonresident alien. (month, day, year)* . . . . ▶ 10-22-2001

13 Highest number of employees expected in the next 12 months. **Note:** *If the applicant does not expect to have any employees during the period, enter -0-. (see instructions)* . . . . ▶

Nonagricultural	Agricultural	Household

14 Principal activity (see instructions) ▶ clothing manufacturing

15 Is the principal business activity manufacturing? . . . . ☒ Yes ☐ No

If "Yes," principal product and raw material used ▶ fabric

16 To whom are most of the products or services sold? Please check one box.   ☒ Business (wholesale)

☐ Public (retail)   ☐ Other (specify) ▶   ☐ N/A

17a Has the applicant ever applied for an employer identification number for this or any other business? . . . . ☐ Yes ☒ No

Note: *If "Yes," please complete lines 17b and 17c.*

17b If you checked "Yes" on line 17a, give applicant's legal name and trade name shown on prior application, if different from line 1 or 2 above.

Legal name ▶   Trade name ▶

17c Approximate date when and city and state where the application was filed. Enter previous employer identification number if known.

Approximate date when filed (mo., day, year)	City and state where filed	Previous EIN

Under penalties of perjury, I declare that I have examined this application, and to the best of my knowledge and belief, it is true, correct, and complete.

Business telephone number (include area code)

(518) 555-0000

Fax telephone number (include area code)

( )

Name and title (Please type or print clearly.) ▶ John Doe, Partner

Signature ▶ *John Doe*   Date ▶ *10/15/01*

Note: *Do not write below this line. For official use only.*

Please leave blank ▶	Geo.	Ind.	Class	Size	Reason for applying

For Privacy Act and Paperwork Reduction Act Notice, see page 4.

Cat. No. 16055N

Form **SS-4** (Rev. 4-2000)

| Form **SS-8**
(Rev. June 1997)
Department of the Treasury
Internal Revenue Service | **Determination of Employee Work Status
for Purposes of Federal Employment Taxes
and Income Tax Withholding** | OMB No. 1545-0004 |

Paperwork Reduction Act Notice

We ask for the information on this form to carry out the Internal Revenue laws of the United States. You are required to give us the information. We need it to ensure that you are complying with these laws and to allow us to figure and collect the right amount of tax.

You are not required to provide the information requested on a form that is subject to the Paperwork Reduction Act unless the form displays a valid OMB control number. Books or records relating to a form or its instructions must be retained as long as their contents may become material in the administration of any Internal Revenue law. Generally, tax returns and return information are confidential, as required by Code section 6103.

The time needed to complete and file this form will vary depending on individual circumstances. The estimated average time is: **Recordkeeping, 34 hr., 55 min.; Learning about the law or the form, 12 min.;** and **Preparing and sending the form to the IRS, 46 min.** If you have comments concerning the accuracy of these time estimates or suggestions for making this form simpler, we would be happy to hear from you. You can write to the Tax Forms Committee, Western Area Distribution Center, Rancho Cordova, CA 95743-0001. **DO NOT** send the tax form to this address. Instead, see **General Information** for where to file.

Purpose

Employers and workers file Form SS-8 to get a determination as to whether a worker is an employee for purposes of Federal employment taxes and income tax withholding.

General Information

Complete this form carefully. If the firm is completing the form, complete it for **ONE** individual who is representative of the class of workers whose status is in question. If you want a written determination for more than one class of workers, complete a separate Form SS-8 for one worker

from each class whose status is typical of that class. A written determination for any worker will apply to other workers of the same class if the facts are not materially different from those of the worker whose status was ruled upon.

Caution: Form SS-8 is not a claim for refund of social security and Medicare taxes or Federal income tax withholding. Also, a determination that an individual is an employee does not necessarily reduce any current or prior tax liability. A worker must file his or her income tax return even if a determination has not been made by the due date of the return.

Where to file.—In the list below, find the state where your legal residence, principal place of business, office, or agency is located. Send Form SS-8 to the address listed for your location.

Location:	Send to:
Alaska, Arizona, Arkansas, California, Colorado, Hawaii, Idaho, Illinois, Iowa, Kansas, Minnesota, Missouri, Montana, Nebraska, Nevada, New Mexico, North Dakota, Oklahoma, Oregon, South Dakota, Texas, Utah, Washington, Wisconsin, Wyoming	Internal Revenue Service SS-8 Determinations P.O. Box 1231, Stop 4106 AUSC Austin, TX 78767
Alabama, Connecticut, Delaware, District of Columbia, Florida, Georgia, Indiana, Kentucky, Louisiana, Maine, Maryland, Massachusetts, Michigan, Mississippi, New Hampshire, New Jersey, New York, North Carolina, Ohio, Pennsylvania, Rhode Island, South Carolina, Tennessee, Vermont, Virginia, West Virginia, All other locations not listed	Internal Revenue Service SS-8 Determinations Two Lakemont Road Newport, VT 05855-1555
American Samoa, Guam, Puerto Rico, U.S. Virgin Islands	Internal Revenue Service Mercantile Plaza 2 Avenue Ponce de Leon San Juan, Puerto Rico 00918

Name of firm (or person) for whom the worker performed services Doe Company	Name of worker Mary Reddenbacher
Address of firm (include street address, apt. or suite no., city, state, and ZIP code) 123 Main St. Libertyville, FL 33461	Address of worker (include street address, apt. or suite no., city, state, and ZIP code) 1234 Liberty Ln. Tampa, FL 33613

Trade name	Telephone number (include area code) (813) 555-2000	Worker's social security number 123 : 45 : 6789

Telephone number (include area code) (813) 555-0000	Firm's employer identification number 59 : 123 , 45678	

Check type of firm for which the work relationship is in question:

☐ **Individual**   ☐ **Partnership**   ☐ **Corporation**   ☐ **Other** (specify) ▶ ....

Important Information Needed To Process Your Request

This form is being completed by: ☒ Firm   ☐ Worker

If this form is being completed by the worker, the IRS **must** have your permission to disclose your name to the firm.

Do you object to disclosing your name and the information on this form to the firm? . . . .   ☐ Yes   ☐ No

If you answer "Yes," the IRS cannot act on your request. **Do not complete the rest of this form unless the IRS asks for it.**

Under section 6110 of the Internal Revenue Code, the information on this form and related file documents will be open to the public if any ruling or determination is made. However, names, addresses, and taxpayer identification numbers will be removed before the information is made public.

Is there any other information you want removed? . . . .   ☐ Yes   ☒ No

If you check "Yes," we cannot process your request unless you submit a copy of this form and copies of all supporting documents showing, in brackets, the information you want removed. Attach a separate statement showing which specific exemption of section 6110(c) applies to each bracketed part.

This form is designed to cover many work activities, so some of the questions may not apply to you. You must answer ALL items or mark them "Unknown" or "Does not apply." If you need more space, attach another sheet.

Total number of workers in this class. (Attach names and addresses. If more than 10 workers, list only 10.) ▶ _____

This information is about services performed by the worker from __5/2/01__   to   __Present__
                                                                (month, day, year)   (month, day, year)

Is the worker still performing services for the firm? . . . . ☐ **Yes** ☐ **No**

● If "No," what was the date of termination? ▶ _____
                                              (month, day, year)

1a Describe the firm's business ..Clothing.manufacturing...

  b Describe the work done by the worker .personalized.embroidering...

    ....

2a If the work is done under a written agreement between the firm and the worker, attach a copy.

  b If the agreement is not in writing, describe the terms and conditions of the work arrangement ....

    ....

    ....

  c If the actual working arrangement differs in any way from the agreement, explain the differences and why they occur ....

    ....

3a Is the worker given training by the firm? . . . . ☐ **Yes** ☒ **No**

  ● If "Yes," what kind? ....

  ● How often? ....

  b Is the worker given instructions in the way the work is to be done (exclusive of actual training in 3a)? . ☐ **Yes** ☒ **No**

  ● If "Yes," give specific examples ....

  c Attach samples of any written instructions or procedures.

  d Does the firm have the right to change the methods used by the worker or direct that person on how to
      do the work? . . . . ☐ **Yes** ☒ **No**

  ● Explain your answer ....

    ....

  e Does the operation of the firm's business require that the worker be supervised or controlled in the
      performance of the service? . . . . ☐ **Yes** ☒ **No**

  ● Explain your answer ....

4a The firm engages the worker:

  ☐ To perform and complete a particular job only

  ☐ To work at a job for an indefinite period of time

  ☐ Other (explain) ....

  b Is the worker required to follow a routine or a schedule established by the firm? . . . . ☐ **Yes** ☐ **No**

  ● If "Yes," what is the routine or schedule? ....

    ....

  c Does the worker report to the firm or its representative? . . . . ☐ **Yes** ☐ **No**

  ● If "Yes," how often? ....

  ● For what purpose? ....

  ● In what manner (in person, in writing, by telephone, etc.)? ....

  ● Attach copies of any report forms used in reporting to the firm.

  d Does the worker furnish a time record to the firm? . . . . ☐ **Yes** ☒ **No**

  ● If "Yes," attach copies of time records.

5a State the kind and value of tools, equipment, supplies, and materials furnished by:

  ● The firm .None...

    ....

  ● The worker Embroidery.machine..

    ....

  b What expenses are incurred by the worker in the performance of services for the firm? Worker sometimes hires
      ...help...

  c Does the firm reimburse the worker for any expenses? . . . . ☐ **Yes** ☒ **No**

  ● If "Yes," specify the reimbursed expenses ....

6a Will the worker perform the services personally? . . . . ☒ **Yes** ☐ **No**

  b Does the worker have helpers? . . . . ☒ **Yes** ☐ **No**
  - If "Yes," who hires the helpers? ☐ Firm ☐ Worker
  - If the helpers are hired by the worker, is the firm's approval necessary? . . . . ☐ **Yes** ☒ **No**
  - Who pays the helpers?   ☐ Firm ☐ Worker
  - If the worker pays the helpers, does the firm repay the worker? . . . . ☐ **Yes** ☒ **No**
  - Are social security and Medicare taxes and Federal income tax withheld from the helpers' pay? . . ☒ **Yes** ☐ **No**
  - If "Yes," who reports and pays these taxes?   ☐ Firm   ☒ Worker
  - Who reports the helpers' earnings to the Internal Revenue Service? ☐ Firm ☐ Worker
  - What services do the helpers perform? ...Embroidering...

7 At what location are the services performed? ☐ Firm's ☒ Worker's ☐ Other (specify) ....

8a Type of pay worker receives:
  ☐ Salary   ☐ Commission ☐ Hourly wage   ☒ Piecework ☐ Lump sum   ☐ Other (specify) ....

  b Does the firm guarantee a minimum amount of pay to the worker? . . . . ☐ **Yes** ☒ **No**

  c Does the firm allow the worker a drawing account or advances against pay? . . . . ☐ **Yes** ☒ **No**
  - If "Yes," is the worker paid such advances on a regular basis? . . . . ☐ **Yes** ☐ **No**

  d How does the worker repay such advances? ....

9a Is the worker eligible for a pension, bonus, paid vacations, sick pay, etc.? . . . . ☐ **Yes** ☒ **No**
  - If "Yes," specify ....

  b Does the firm carry worker's compensation insurance on the worker? . . . . ☐ **Yes** ☒ **No**

  c Does the firm withhold social security and Medicare taxes from amounts paid the worker? . . . . . ☐ **Yes** ☒ **No**

  d Does the firm withhold Federal income tax from amounts paid the worker? . . . . ☐ **Yes** ☒ **No**

  e How does the firm report the worker's earnings to the Internal Revenue Service?
  ☐ Form W-2 ☐ Form 1099-MISC   ☐ Does not report ☐ Other (specify) ....
  - Attach a copy.

  f Does the firm bond the worker? . . . . ☐ **Yes** ☒ **No**

10a Approximately how many hours a day does the worker perform services for the firm? ...3................

  b Does the firm set hours of work for the worker? . . . . ☐ **Yes** ☒ **No**
  - If "Yes," what are the worker's set hours? _____ a.m./p.m. to _____ a.m./p.m. (Circle whether a.m. or p.m.)

  c Does the worker perform similar services for others? . . . . ☒ **Yes** ☐ **No** ☐ **Unknown**
  - If "Yes," are these services performed on a daily basis for other firms? . . . . . ☒ **Yes** ☐ **No** ☐ **Unknown**
  - Percentage of time spent in performing these services for:
    This firm .... % Other firms .... %   ☐ **Unknown**
  - Does the firm have priority on the worker's time? . . . . ☐ **Yes** ☒ **No**
  - If "No," explain ....

  d Is the worker prohibited from competing with the firm either while performing services or during any later period? . . . . ☐ **Yes** ☒ **No**

11a Can the firm discharge the worker at any time without incurring a liability? . . . . ☒ **Yes** ☐ **No**
  - If "No," explain ....

  b Can the worker terminate the services at any time without incurring a liability? . . . . ☒ **Yes** ☐ **No**
  - If "No," explain ....

12a Does the worker perform services for the firm under:
  ☐ The firm's business name   ☐ The worker's own business name   ☐ Other (specify) ....

  b Does the worker advertise or maintain a business listing in the telephone directory, a trade journal, etc.? . . . . ☐ **Yes** ☐ **No** ☒ **Unknown**
  - If "Yes," specify ....

  c Does the worker represent himself or herself to the public as being in business to perform the same or similar services? . . . . ☐ **Yes** ☐ **No** ☒ **Unknown**
  - If "Yes," how? ....

  d Does the worker have his or her own shop or office? . . . . ☐ **Yes** ☒ **No** ☐ **Unknown**
  - If "Yes," where? ....

  e Does the firm represent the worker as an employee of the firm to its customers? . . . . ☐ **Yes** ☒ **No**
  - If "No," how is the worker represented? ....

  f How did the firm learn of the worker's services? .....Relative........

13 Is a license necessary for the work? . . . . ☐ **Yes** ☒ **No** ☐ **Unknown**
  - If "Yes," what kind of license is required? ....
  - Who issues the license? ....
  - Who pays the license fee?

14 Does the worker have a financial investment in a business related to the services performed? . . . . ☐ Yes ☐ No ☒ Unknown
  ● If "Yes," specify and give amount of the investment ....

15 Can the worker incur a loss in the performance of the service for the firm? . . . . . . ☐ Yes ☒ No
  ● If "Yes," how? ....

16a Has any other government agency ruled on the status of the firm's workers? . . . . ☐ Yes ☒ No
  ● If "Yes," attach a copy of the ruling.

  b Is the same issue being considered by any IRS office in connection with the audit of the worker's tax return or the firm's tax return, or has it been considered recently? . . . . ☐ Yes ☒ No
  ● If "Yes," for which year(s)? ....

17 Does the worker assemble or process a product at home or away from the firm's place of business? ☒ Yes ☐ No
  ● If "Yes," who furnishes materials or goods used by the worker? ☒ Firm ☐ Worker ☐ Other
  ● Is the worker furnished a pattern or given instructions to follow in making the product? . . . . . ☐ Yes ☒ No
  ● Is the worker required to return the finished product to the firm or to someone designated by the firm? ☒ Yes ☐ No

18 Attach a detailed explanation of any other reason why you believe the worker is an employee or an independent contractor.

Answer items 19a through o only if the worker is a salesperson or provides a service directly to customers.

19a Are leads to prospective customers furnished by the firm? . . . . ☐ Yes ☐ No ☐ Does not apply
  b Is the worker required to pursue or report on leads? . . . . ☐ Yes ☐ No ☐ Does not apply
  c Is the worker required to adhere to prices, terms, and conditions of sale established by the firm? . . ☐ Yes ☐ No
  d Are orders submitted to and subject to approval by the firm? . . . . ☐ Yes ☐ No
  e Is the worker expected to attend sales meetings? . . . . ☐ Yes ☐ No
  ● If "Yes," is the worker subject to any kind of penalty for failing to attend? . . . . ☐ Yes ☐ No
  f Does the firm assign a specific territory to the worker? . . . . ☐ Yes ☐ No
  g Whom does the customer pay? ☐ Firm ☐ Worker
  ● If worker, does the worker remit the total amount to the firm? . . . . ☐ Yes ☐ No
  h Does the worker sell a consumer product in a home or establishment other than a permanent retail establishment? . . . . ☐ Yes ☐ No
  i List the products and/or services distributed by the worker, such as meat, vegetables, fruit, bakery products, beverages (other than milk), or laundry or dry cleaning services. If more than one type of product and/or service is distributed, specify the principal one ....
  j Did the firm or another person assign the route or territory and a list of customers to the worker? . . ☐ Yes ☐ No
  ● If "Yes," enter the name and job title of the person who made the assignment ....
  k Did the worker pay the firm or person for the privilege of serving customers on the route or in the territory? ☐ Yes ☐ No
  ● If "Yes," how much did the worker pay (not including any amount paid for a truck or racks, etc.)? $ ....
  ● What factors were considered in determining the value of the route or territory? ....
  l How are new customers obtained by the worker? Explain fully, showing whether the new customers called the firm for service, were solicited by the worker, or both ....
  m Does the worker sell life insurance? . . . . ☐ Yes ☐ No
  ● If "Yes," is the selling of life insurance or annuity contracts for the firm the worker's entire business activity? . . . . ☐ Yes ☐ No
  ● If "No," list the other business activities and the amount of time spent on them ....
  n Does the worker sell other types of insurance for the firm? . . . . ☐ Yes ☐ No
  ● If "Yes," state the percentage of the worker's total working time spent in selling other types of insurance .... %
  ● At the time the contract was entered into between the firm and the worker, was it their intention that the worker sell life insurance for the firm: ☐ on a full-time basis ☐ on a part-time basis
  ● State the manner in which the intention was expressed ....
  o Is the worker a traveling or city salesperson? . . . . ☐ Yes ☐ No
  ● If "Yes," from whom does the worker principally solicit orders for the firm? ....
  ● If the worker solicits orders from wholesalers, retailers, contractors, or operators of hotels, restaurants, or other similar establishments, specify the percentage of the worker's time spent in the solicitation .... %
  ● Is the merchandise purchased by the customers for resale or for use in their business operations? If used by the customers in their business operations, describe the merchandise and state whether it is equipment installed on their premises or a consumable supply

Under penalties of perjury, I declare that I have examined this request, including accompanying documents, and to the best of my knowledge and belief, the facts presented are true, correct, and complete.

Signature ▶ *John Doe* Title ▶ Partner Date ▶ 10/10/01

If the firm is completing this form, an officer or member of the firm must sign it. If the worker is completing this form, the worker must sign it. If the worker wants a written determination about services performed for two or more firms, a separate form must be completed and signed for each firm. Additional copies of this form may be obtained by calling 1-800-TAX-FORM (1-800-829-3676).

Form W-4 (2001)

Purpose. Complete Form W-4 so your employer can withhold the correct Federal income tax from your pay. Because your tax situation may change, you may want to refigure your withholding each year.

Exemption from withholding. If you are exempt, complete only lines 1, 2, 3, 4, and 7, and sign the form to validate it. Your exemption for 2001 expires February 18, 2002.

Note: *You cannot claim exemption from withholding if (1) your income exceeds $750 and includes more than $250 of unearned income (e.g., interest and dividends) and (2) another person can claim you as a dependent on their tax return.*

Basic instructions. If you are not exempt, complete the **Personal Allowances Worksheet** below. The worksheets on page 2 adjust your withholding allowances based on itemized deductions, certain credits, adjustments to

income, or two-earner/two-job situations. Complete all worksheets that apply. They will help you figure the number of withholding allowances you are entitled to claim. However, **you may claim fewer (or zero) allowances.**

Head of household. Generally, you may claim head of household filing status on your tax return only if you are unmarried and pay more than 50% of the costs of keeping up a home for yourself and your dependent(s) or other qualifying individuals. See line E below.

Tax credits. You can take projected tax credits into account in figuring your allowable number of withholding allowances. Credits for child or dependent care expenses and the child tax credit may be claimed using the **Personal Allowances Worksheet** below. See **Pub. 919,** How Do I Adjust My Tax Withholding? for information on converting your other credits into withholding allowances.

Nonwage income. If you have a large amount of nonwage income, such as interest or dividends,

consider making estimated tax payments using **Form 1040-ES,** Estimated Tax for Individuals. Otherwise, you may owe additional tax.

Two earners/two jobs. If you have a working spouse or more than one job, figure the total number of allowances you are entitled to claim on all jobs using worksheets from only one Form W-4. Your withholding usually will be most accurate when all allowances are claimed on the Form W-4 for the highest paying job and zero allowances are claimed on the others.

Check your withholding. After your Form W-4 takes effect, use Pub. 919 to see how the dollar amount you are having withheld compares to your projected total tax for 2001. Get Pub. 919 especially if you used the **Two-Earner/Two-Job Worksheet** on page 2 and your earnings exceed $150,000 (Single) or $200,000 (Married).

Recent name change? If your name on line 1 differs from that shown on your social security card, call 1-800-772-1213 for a new social security card.

Personal Allowances Worksheet (Keep for your records.)

A Enter "1" for **yourself** if no one else can claim you as a dependent . . . . **A** _____

B Enter "1" if:
- You are single and have only one job; or
- You are married, have only one job, and your spouse does not work; or
- Your wages from a second job or your spouse's wages (or the total of both) are $1,000 or less.

B __1__

C Enter "1" for your **spouse.** But, you may choose to enter -0- if you are married and have either a working spouse or more than one job. (Entering -0- may help you avoid having too little tax withheld.) . . . . **C** _____

D Enter number of **dependents** (other than your spouse or yourself) you will claim on your tax return . . . . . . **D** _____

E Enter "1" if you will file as **head of household** on your tax return (see conditions under **Head of household** above) . **E** _____

F Enter "1" if you have at least $1,500 of **child or dependent care expenses** for which you plan to claim a credit . . **F** _____
(**Note:** *Do **not** include child support payments. See **Pub. 503,** Child and Dependent Care Expenses, for details.*)

G **Child Tax Credit** (including additional child tax credit).
- If your total income will be between $18,000 and $50,000 ($23,000 and $63,000 if married), enter "1" for each eligible child.
- If your total income will be between $50,000 and $80,000 ($63,000 and $115,000 if married), enter "1" if you have two eligible children, enter "2" if you have three or four eligible children, or enter "3" if you have five or more eligible children. **G** __1__

H Add lines A through G and enter total here. (**Note:** *This may be different from the number of exemptions you claim on your tax return.*) ▶ **H** _____

For accuracy, complete all worksheets that apply.
- If you plan to **itemize or claim adjustments to income** and want to reduce your withholding, see the **Deductions and Adjustments Worksheet** on page 2.
- If you are **single,** have **more than one job** and your combined earnings from all jobs exceed $35,000, **or** if you are **married** and have a **working spouse or more than one job** and the combined earnings from all jobs exceed $60,000, see the **Two-Earner/Two-Job Worksheet** on page 2 to avoid having too little tax withheld.
- If **neither** of the above situations applies, **stop here** and enter the number from line H on line 5 of Form W-4 below.

- - - - - - - - - - - - - - - - - - **Cut here and give Form W-4 to your employer. Keep the top part for your records.** - - - - - - - - - - - - - - -

Form **W-4**
Department of the Treasury
Internal Revenue Service

Employee's Withholding Allowance Certificate

▶ **For Privacy Act and Paperwork Reduction Act Notice, see page 2.**

OMB No. 1545-0010

2001

1 Type or print your first name and middle initial	Last name		2 Your social security number
John A.	Smith		123 45 6789

Home address (number and street or rural route)
567 Wharf Blvd.

City or town, state, and ZIP code
Jacksonville, FL 33490

3 ☒ Single ☐ Married ☐ Married, but withhold at higher Single rate.
Note: *If married, but legally separated, or spouse is a nonresident alien, check the Single box.*

4 If your last name differs from that on your social security card, check here. You must call 1-800-772-1213 for a new card. ▶ ☐

5 Total number of allowances you are claiming (from line H above **or** from the applicable worksheet on page 2) | **5** | 1

6 Additional amount, if any, you want withheld from each paycheck . . . . | **6** $ | 0

7 I claim exemption from withholding for 2001, and I certify that I meet **both** of the following conditions for exemption:
- Last year I had a right to a refund of **all** Federal income tax withheld because I had **no** tax liability **and**
- This year I expect a refund of **all** Federal income tax withheld because I expect to have **no** tax liability.

If you meet both conditions, write "Exempt" here . . . . ▶ | **7** |

Under penalties of perjury, I certify that I am entitled to the number of withholding allowances claimed on this certificate, or I am entitled to claim exempt status.
Employee's signature
(Form is not valid
unless you sign it.) ▶ *John A. Smith* | Date ▶ *June 6* *2000*

8 Employer's name and address (Employer: Complete lines 8 and 10 only if sending to the IRS.)	9 Office code (optional)	10 Employer identification number

Cat. No. 10220Q

185

Deductions and Adjustments Worksheet

Note: *Use this worksheet only if you plan to itemize deductions, claim certain credits, or claim adjustments to income on your 2001 tax return.*

1	Enter an estimate of your 2001 itemized deductions. These include qualifying home mortgage interest, charitable contributions, state and local taxes, medical expenses in excess of 7.5% of your income, and miscellaneous deductions. (For 2001, you may have to reduce your itemized deductions if your income is over $132,950 ($66,475 if married filing separately). See **Worksheet 3** in Pub. 919 for details.) . . .	**1**	$
2	Enter: $\left\{\begin{array}{l}\text{\$7,600 if married filing jointly or qualifying widow(er)}\\\text{\$6,650 if head of household}\\\text{\$4,550 if single}\\\text{\$3,800 if married filing separately}\end{array}\right\}$ . .	**2**	$
3	**Subtract** line 2 from line 1. If line 2 is greater than line 1, enter -0-	**3**	$
4	Enter an estimate of your 2001 adjustments to income, including alimony, deductible IRA contributions, and student loan interest	**4**	$
5	**Add** lines 3 and 4 and enter the total (Include any amount for credits from **Worksheet 7** in Pub. 919.) .	**5**	$
6	Enter an estimate of your 2001 nonwage income (such as dividends or interest)	**6**	$
7	**Subtract** line 6 from line 5. Enter the result, but not less than -0-	**7**	$
8	**Divide** the amount on line 7 by $3,000 and enter the result here. Drop any fraction	**8**	
9	Enter the number from the **Personal Allowances Worksheet**, line H, page 1	**9**	
10	**Add** lines 8 and 9 and enter the total here. If you plan to use the **Two-Earner/Two-Job Worksheet**, also enter this total on line 1 below. Otherwise, **stop here** and enter this total on Form W-4, line 5, page 1 .	**10**	

Two-Earner/Two-Job Worksheet

Note: *Use this worksheet only if the instructions under line H on page 1 direct you here.*

1	Enter the number from line H, page 1 (or from line 10 above if you used the **Deductions and Adjustments Worksheet**)	**1**	
2	Find the number in **Table 1** below that applies to the **lowest** paying job and enter it here	**2**	
3	If line 1 is **more than or equal to** line 2, subtract line 2 from line 1. Enter the result here (if zero, enter -0-) and on Form W-4, line 5, page 1. **Do not** use the rest of this worksheet	**3**	

Note: *If line 1 is **less than** line 2, enter -0- on Form W-4, line 5, page 1. Complete lines 4–9 below to calculate the additional withholding amount necessary to avoid a year end tax bill.*

4	Enter the number from line 2 of this worksheet	**4**	
5	Enter the number from line 1 of this worksheet	**5**	
6	**Subtract** line 5 from line 4	**6**	
7	Find the amount in **Table 2** below that applies to the **highest** paying job and enter it here	**7**	$
8	**Multiply** line 7 by line 6 and enter the result here. This is the additional annual withholding needed . .	**8**	$
9	Divide line 8 by the number of pay periods remaining in 2001. For example, divide by 26 if you are paid every two weeks and you complete this form in December 2000. Enter the result here and on Form W-4, line 6, page 1. This is the additional amount to be withheld from each paycheck	**9**	$

Table 1: Two-Earner/Two-Job Worksheet

Married Filing Jointly				All Others			
If wages from LOWEST paying job are—	Enter on line 2 above	If wages from LOWEST paying job are—	Enter on line 2 above	If wages from LOWEST paying job are—	Enter on line 2 above	If wages from LOWEST paying job are—	Enter on line 2 above
$0 - $4,000	0	42,001 - 47,000	8	$0 - $6,000	0	65,001 - 80,000	8
4,001 - 8,000	1	47,001 - 55,000	9	6,001 - 12,000	1	80,001 - 105,000	9
8,001 - 14,000	2	55,001 - 65,000	10	12,001 - 17,000	2	105,001 and over	10
14,001 - 19,000	3	65,001 - 70,000	11	17,001 - 22,000	3		
19,001 - 25,000	4	70,001 - 90,000	12	22,001 - 28,000	4		
25,001 - 32,000	5	90,001 - 105,000	13	28,001 - 40,000	5		
32,001 - 38,000	6	105,001 - 115,000	14	40,001 - 50,000	6		
38,001 - 42,000	7	115,001 and over	15	50,001 - 65,000	7		

Table 2: Two-Earner/Two-Job Worksheet

Married Filing Jointly		All Others	
If wages from HIGHEST paying job are—	Enter on line 7 above	If wages from HIGHEST paying job are—	Enter on line 7 above
$0 - $50,000	$440	$0 - $30,000	$440
50,001 - 100,000	800	30,001 - 60,000	800
100,001 - 130,000	900	60,001 - 120,000	900
130,001 - 250,000	1,000	120,001 - 270,000	1,000
250,001 and over	1,100	270,001 and over	1,100

APPLICATION TO COLLECT AND/OR REPORT TAX IN FLORIDA

iNET

DR-1
R. 08/00
Page 1

Please use BLACK or BLUE ink ONLY and type or print clearly.

Indicate tax registration you are seeking.
This application is for (check all that apply):

* The $5 registration fee does not apply if this application is for a business location outside the state of Florida.

✓	Tax Type	Fee Due	Complete Sections
X	Sales and Use Tax	$5.00*	A, B, F
	Use Tax Only	No fee	A, B, F
	Solid Waste Fees	No fee	A, B, C, F
	Gross Receipts Tax on Utilities	No fee	A, D, F
	Gross Receipts Tax on Dry Cleaning	$30.00	A, D, F
	Documentary Stamp Tax	No fee	A, E, F

SECTION A — BUSINESS INFORMATION

1. Check the box that applies:

[X] New business   [ ] New business location   [ ] Change of county location (from one Florida county to another)   [ ] Change of legal entity (proprietorship to partnership; partnership to corporation, etc.)

This change is effective (enter date): [ ] [ ] / [ ] [ ] / [ ] [ ] [ ] [ ]
month / day / year

List below your old account or registration number(s) to be canceled.
_____

a. If this is a seasonal business (not open year-round), list the first and last months of your season.   First month _____   Last month _____

2. Beginning date of business activity for this location: **1 1 / 1 0 / 2 0 0 1**
month / day / year

If incorporated, please provide incorporation date: [ ] [ ] / [ ] [ ] / [ ] [ ] [ ] [ ]
month / day / year

Provide the date this business location became or will become liable for Florida tax(es). Do not use your incorporation date unless that is the date your business became liable for the tax. If you have been in business longer than 30 days prior to registering, contact the taxpayer service center nearest you.

3. Business Name: business, trade, or fictitious (d/b/a) name
Frankenfurter's Red Hots

Business Telephone Number:
305-867-5309

4. Owner Name: legal name of individual, principal partner, or corporation
Rocky Frankenfurter

Owner Telephone Number:
305-705-5007

5. Business Location: Complete physical address of business or real property. Home-based businesses and flea market/craft show vendors must use their home address. Listing a post office box, private mailbox or rural route number is not permitted.

1234 Bayshore Boulevard

Is business located within city limits? [X] Yes [ ] No

City/State/ZIP:
Miami, Florida 33940

County:
Dade County

6. Mail to the Attention of:
Rocky Frankenfurter

Mailing Address:
6950 S. Miami Avenue

City/State/ZIP:
Miami, Florida 33940

County:
Dade County

Would you like to receive correspondence via e-mail? [X] Yes [ ] No

E-mail address:
redhot3@mindspring.com

** PLEASE TYPE OR PRINT CLEARLY **

7. If you have a **Consolidated Sales Tax Number** and want to include this business location, please complete the following:

_____
Consolidated registration name on record with the Florida Department of Revenue.
If you want to obtain a new consolidated number contact the Department and request Form DR-1CON.

8 0 [ ] [ ] [ ] [ ] [ ] [ ] [ ] [ ] [ ] [ ]

8. Business Entity Identification Number (If an FEIN is not required for your business entity, the Social Security Number of the owner will be accepted.)

a. Federal Employer Identification Number (FEIN): **3 3 — 6 7 8 9 0 2 1**

b. Social Security Number (SSN) of Owner: [ ] [ ] [ ] — [ ] [ ] — [ ] [ ] [ ] [ ]

187

9. Identify proprietors or owners, partners, officers, members, or trustees. Include the person whose Social Security Number is listed under Question 8. **Without this information, processing of your application may be delayed.**

Name Title	Social Security Number Driver License Number and State	Home Address City, State, ZIP Code	Telephone Number
Rocky Frankenfurter, owner	200 44 1000	6950 S. Miami Ave., Miami, FL 33940	305 705 5007

10. **Type of Ownership** - Check one box to describe the structure of your business entity.

☒ Sole Proprietorship - an individual or individual and spouse

☐ Partnership - two or more persons or entities that have entered into a voluntary contract

☐ Corporation - legal entity created under the authority of the corporation laws of a state (includes professional service corporation)

☐ Limited Liability Company - legal entity created under the authority of the limited liability company
laws of a state (includes professional limited liability company)

☐ Trust - legal entity created by a grantor for the benefit of designated beneficiaries under the laws of a state and valid trust agreement

☐ Other (please specify) _____

11. If a partnership, corporation or limited liability company, provide your fiscal year ending date: ☐☐ / ☐☐
month   day

12. If incorporated or registered in Florida, provide your corporate document/registration number: _____

If not incorporated or registered in Florida, attach a copy of your Articles of Incorporation as filed with your state's corporate registration authority. For Florida corporation information, call the Florida Department of State, Division of Corporations at 850-488-9000.

13. Business Bank Information – provide the following information about the bank where tax money from this business will be deposited:

_____Metwire Bank_____   ☐ Personal Account   ☒ Business Account
Bank Name
2345 Jones Street   Miami   Florida   33941
Bank Street Address   City   State   ZIP

14. Is your business location rented? Yes ☐ No ☒ If yes, and you <u>do not operate from your home</u>, provide the following information.

Owner or Landlord's Name _____

Address _____

City/State/ZIP _____

Telephone No. _____

15. Describe your primary (more than 50%) business activity that generates revenue.
_____Food and beverage sales_____

16. Does your business activity include (check all that apply):

☒ Sales of property or goods at retail (to consumers)?
☐ Sales of property or goods at wholesale (to registered dealers)?
☐ Sales of secondhand goods?
☐ Rental of commercial real property to individuals or businesses?
☐ Rental of transient living or sleeping accommodations (for six months or less)?
☐ Rental of equipment or other property or goods to individuals or businesses?
☐ Renting/leasing motor vehicles to others?
☐ Repair or alteration of tangible personal property?
☐ Charging admission or membership fees?

☐ Placing and operating coin-operated amusement machines at business locations belonging to others?
☐ Placing and operating vending machines at business locations belonging to others?

☐ Providing any of the following services? (Check all that apply.)
   ☐ Pest control for nonresidential buildings
   ☐ Cleaning services for nonresidential buildings
   ☐ Detective services
   ☐ Protection services
   ☐ Security alarm system monitoring

17. What products do you purchase for resale to your customers, or include in a finished product you manufacture for sale?

hot dogs, potatoes, buns, carbonated beverages

SECTION B — SALES TAX ACTIVITY

COIN-OPERATED AMUSEMENT MACHINES

18. Are coin-operated amusement machines being operated at your business location? If yes, answer question 19. .... ☐ Yes ☒ No

19. Do you have a written agreement that requires someone other than yourself to obtain Amusement Machine Certificates for any of the machines at your location? If yes, provide their information below. .... ☐ Yes ☒ No

Name   Address   Telephone No.

NOTE: You must complete an *Application for Amusement Machine Certificate* (Form DR-18) if you answered YES to question 18 **and** NO to question 19.

CONTRACTORS

20. Are you a contractor who improves real property? If yes, answer questions 21-24. .... ☐ Yes ☐ No
21. a. Do you operate under formal written contracts? .... ☐ Yes ☐ No
   b. If yes, under what type of contracts do you operate?
   ☐ Lump Sum ☐ Cost Plus ☐ Fixed Fee ☐ Other (please explain) _____
22. Do you purchase materials or supplies from vendors located outside of Florida? .... ☐ Yes ☐ No
23. Does your company have a current occupational license in any Florida county? .... ☐ Yes ☐ No
   If yes, please list all counties in which you are licensed and the corresponding license numbers.

24. Do you fabricate/manufacture any building component at a location other than contract sites? .... ☐ Yes ☐ No

MOTOR FUEL

25. Do you sell any type of fuel, or use off-road diesel fuel? If yes, answer questions 26 and 27. .... ☐ Yes ☐ No
26. a. Do you make retail sales of gasoline, diesel fuel, or aviation fuel at posted retail prices? .... ☐ Yes ☐ No
   b. If yes to #26a, does this business exist as a marina? .... ☐ Yes ☐ No
   c. If yes to #26a, provide your Florida Department of Environmental Protection Facility Registration Number for this location. ☐☐☐☐☐☐
27. Do you use non-taxed, dyed diesel fuel for non-highway purposes? .... ☐ Yes ☐ No

SECTION C — SOLID WASTE FEES

28. Do you sell tires or batteries, or rent/lease motor vehicles to others? If yes, answer questions 29-31. .... ☐ Yes ☐ No
29. Do you make retail sales of new tires for motorized vehicles (either separately or as a part of a vehicle)? .... ☐ Yes ☐ No
30. Do you make retail sales of new or remanufactured lead-acid batteries sold separately or as a component part of another product such as automobiles, golf carts, boats, etc.? .... ☐ Yes ☐ No
31. Are you in the business of renting or leasing vehicles that transport fewer than nine passengers to individuals or businesses? .... ☐ Yes ☐ No

32. Do you sell telecommunication services, electrical power, or gas? If yes, answer questions a-l and 33, below. .... ☐ Yes ☐ No
Do you sell:
   a. Electrical power? .... ☐ Yes ☐ No
   b. Natural or manufactured gas? .... ☐ Yes ☐ No
   c. Pay phone service? .... ☐ Yes ☐ No
   d. 2-way cable television service? .... ☐ Yes ☐ No
   e. Telex, telegram, teletype service? .... ☐ Yes ☐ No
   f. Cellular service? .... ☐ Yes ☐ No
   g. Pagers and beepers? .... ☐ Yes ☐ No
   h. Long distance (inter-exchange service)? .... ☐ Yes ☐ No
   i. Shared tenant utility service? .... ☐ Yes ☐ No
   j. Alternative access vendor service? .... ☐ Yes ☐ No
   k. Telephone service (local exchange)? .... ☐ Yes ☐ No
   l. Other telecommunication service (by-pass provider, etc.)? .... ☐ Yes ☐ No
   Describe _____

33. Do you provide billing services to telecommunication service providers? .... ☐ Yes ☐ No
34. Do you own or operate a dry-cleaning dry drop-off facility or plant in Florida? .... ☐ Yes ☐ No
   If yes, enclose the $30 dry-cleaning registration fee.
35. Do you produce or import perchloroethylene? .... ☐ Yes ☐ No
   If yes, you must complete an *Application for Florida License to Produce or Import Taxable Pollutants* (Form DR-166).

SECTION E — DOCUMENTARY STAMP TAX

36. Do you make sales, finalized by written agreements, that do not require recording by the
   Clerk of the Court, <u>but do require documentary stamp tax to be paid</u>? If yes, answer questions 37-39. .... ☐ Yes ☒ No
37. Do you anticipate five or more transactions subject to documentary stamp tax per month? .... ☐ Yes ☐ No
38. Do you anticipate your average monthly documentary stamp tax remittance to be less than $80 per month? .... ☐ Yes ☐ No
39. Is this application being completed to register your <u>first</u> location to collect documentary stamp tax? .... ☐ Yes ☐ No
   If no, and this application is for additional locations, please list name and address of each additional location.
   (Attach additional sheets if needed.)
   Location Name _____ Address _____
   City, State, ZIP _____ Telephone Number _____

SECTION F — APPLICANT DECLARATION AND SIGNATURE

This application will not be accepted if not signed by the applicant.

Please note that any person (including employees, corporate directors, corporate officers, etc.) who is required to collect, truthfully account for, and pay any taxes and willfully fails to do so shall be liable for penalties under the provisions of §213.29, Florida Statutes (F.S.). All information provided by the applicant is confidential as provided in §213.053, F.S., and is not subject to Florida Public Records Law (§119.07, F.S.).

Under penalties of perjury, I declare that I have read the foregoing application and that the facts stated in it are true.

SIGN HERE ▶ *Rocky Frankenfurter* Title ____owner____

Print Name ____Rocky Frankenfurter____ Date ____01/10/01____

Amount Enclosed: $_____ (See table on top of page 1 for <u>Fee Due</u> with this application.)

NOTE: If the applicant is a sole proprietorship, the proprietor or owner must sign; if a partnership, a partner must sign; if a corporation, an officer of the corporation authorized to sign on behalf of the corporation must sign; if a limited liability company, a member must sign; if a trust, the grantor or a trustee must sign. **The signature of any other person will not be accepted.**

USE THIS CHECKLIST TO ENSURE FAST PROCESSING OF YOUR APPLICATION.

✓ Complete application in its entirety.
✓ Sign and date the application.
✓ Attach check or money order for appropriate registration fee amount.

✓ Mail to: **FLORIDA DEPARTMENT OF REVENUE**
5050 W TENNESSEE ST
TALLAHASSEE FL 32399-0100

You may also mail or deliver to any service center listed on front page.

Employer Registration Report

iNET   UCS-1
R. 02/01

FLORIDA
DEPARTMENT
OF REVENUE

☐☐☐☐☐☐—☐
UC Employer Account Number

Please complete front and back in black ink. (Print or type)

1. **Federal Employer Identification Number (FEIN)** 5 9 — 1 2 3 4 5 6 7

2. **Legal name of employer** Rocky Frankenfurter
(Sole proprietor, partners, or corporate name, etc.)

3. **Trade name (d/b/a)** Rocky Frankenfurter   **Telephone No.** (305) 867-5309

4. **Mailing address** 6950 S. Miami Avenue   Miami, FL   33940
(Street address, City, State, ZIP)

5. **Business location** 1234 Bayshore Boulevard   Miami, FL   33940
(Florida street address, City, State, ZIP)

6. **Legal entity types** (check only one)

☒ Sole proprietor   ☐ Partnership   ☐ S corporation
☐ Limited partnership   ☐ Joint venture   ☐ Limited liability corp
☐ Corporation   ☐ Government instrumentality   ☐ Other
(state incorporated) _____   (city, county, special district, etc.)   (specify) _____

7. **Employer type** (check all that apply)

☒ Regular   ☐ Domestic (household)
☐ Agricultural   ☐ Agricultural citrus   ☐ Agricultural crew chief
☐ Non-profit organization   ☐ Political instrumentality   ☐ Purchased existing business
(501(c)(3) attached)   (city, county, or municipality)   (complete Form UCS-1S)

8. **Did your business pay federal unemployment tax in another state in the previous or current calendar year?**
☐ Yes   ☒ No   State(s) _____   Year(s) _____

9. **Date of first employment in Florida** January 10, 2001
(This includes full and part-time employees and officers of a corporation. If resuming employment, enter date resumed.)

10. **Do you use, or intend to use, the services of individuals you consider to be self-employed?**
☐ Yes   ☒ No   If yes, please explain type(s) of services performed. _____
_____

11. **Do you wish to elect to extend the coverage of the law to your workers who are not covered because they work in exempt employment or because you are not liable for the payment of unemployment tax?**
☐ Yes   ☒ No   If yes, proper forms will be furnished by this agency. The election would require liability for a period of at least one complete calendar year.

12. **General information**
A. Information regarding owner, partners, or officers. (Attach a separate sheet if necessary.)

Full name Rocky Frankenfurter   Title owner
Home address 6950 S. Miami Ave   City, State, ZIP Miami, FL 33940
Home phone number 305-705-5007   SSN 200-44-1000

Full name _____   Title _____
Home address _____   City, State, ZIP _____
Home phone number _____   SSN _____

Full name _____   Title _____
Home address _____   City, State, ZIP _____
Home phone number _____   SSN _____

Internet address: www.myflorida.com/dor

B. **Payroll maintained by** (accountant, bookkeeper, etc.)

Name Janet Frankenfurter

Address 6950 S. Miami Avenue

City, State, ZIP Miami, FL 33940

Phone # (305) 705-5007

13. Standard Industrial Classification (SIC) List the location and nature of business conducted in Florida. If you need more space, please attach separate page.

Enter city and county for each work site	Principal products or services (be specific)	Average # of employees
Miami, Dade County	Fast Food Restaurant	4

Does the above work site(s) provide support for any other units of the company? ☐ Yes ☒ No

If yes, please indicate whether these services are: ☐ Administrative ☐ Research ☐ Other (specify) _____

14. Did you acquire a business?

☒ Yes ☐ No If you answered yes, you must complete a *Report to Determine Succession* (Form UCS-1S). Please call 1-800-352-3671 to request one.

Note: The *Report to Determine Succession* must be **postmarked within 90 days of the acquisition date to be considered timely.**

15. Enter the number of weeks you had workers in the current year 4

Enter the number of weeks you had workers in the preceding year 3

16. Your Florida gross payroll by calendar quarters (may estimate if not available)

		Quarter ending March 31	Quarter ending June 30	Quarter ending September 30	Quarter ending December 31
Current year	2002	$ 11,349	$ 15,785	$ 17,435	$ 20,900
Prior year	2001	$ 9,632	$ 13,093	$ 16,765	$ 18,333

BE SURE THAT ALL QUESTIONS ARE ANSWERED BEFORE SIGNING

Pursuant to section 443.171(7), Florida Statutes, the information given above is true and correct and is given for the purpose of determining liability under said law and the undersigned is authorized to execute this report on behalf of the employing unit named.

Legal name of employing unit Frankenfurter's Red Hots

By (print name) Rocky Frankenfurter

Signature *Rocky Frankenfurter*

Date December 10, 2002 Title owner

This registration report is due by the end of the month that follows the calendar quarter in which your business commenced operation.
Return address: Department of Revenue   **For assistance call:**   P.O. Box 6510   1-800-482-8293   Tallahassee, FL 32314-6510

FEDERAL TAX DEPOSIT COUPON (IRS form 8109-B)

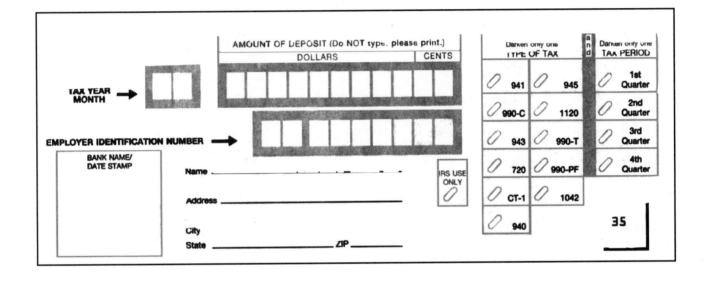

ESTIMATED TAX PAYMENT VOUCHER (IRS form 1040-ES)

Cat. No. 61900V

OMB No. 1545-0087

Form 1040-ES (OCR)

2000 Estimated Tax

Payment Voucher **4**

Calendar year—
Due Jan. 15, **2001**

Department of the Treasury
Internal Revenue Service

Cross out any errors and print the correct information. Get **Form 8822** to report a new address (see instructions). For Paperwork Reduction Act Notice, see instructions.

0746497

07 234-56-7890 DC

9712

234-56-7890   DC WARD 30 0 9712 430 07

JOHN DOE
123 ANYWHERE STREET
LARGO, FL 34006

LARGO FL 34006-0001

I.II.II....II..I..II..I..I.I.I.I..II...II...II...II..I.I

Enter the amount of your payment. File this voucher only if you are making a payment of **estimated** tax.	$	▶ Make your check or money order payable to **"Internal Revenue Service."** ▶ Write your social security number and "1997 Form 1040-ES" on your payment. ▶ Send your payment and payment voucher to the address above. ▶ Do not send cash. Do not staple your payment to the voucher.

WAGE AND TAX STATEMENT (IRS form W-2)

a Control number	22222	Void ☐	For Official Use Only ▶ OMB No. 1545-0008	
b Employer's identification number 59-123456			1 Wages, tips, other compensation 25,650.00	2 Federal income tax withheld 5,050.00
c Employer's name, address, and ZIP code Doe Company 123 Main Street Largo, FL 34600			3 Social security wages 25,650.00	4 Social security tax withheld 1,590.30
			5 Medicare wages and tips 25,650.00	6 Medicare tax withheld 371.93
			7 Social security tips 0	8 Allocated tips 0
d Employee's social security number 123-45-6789			9 Advance EIC payment 0	10 Dependent care benefits 0
e Employee's name (first, middle initial, last) John A. Smith 567 Wharf Boulevard Largo, FL 34006			11 Nonqualified plans 0	12 Benefits included in box 1 0
			13 See Instrs. for box 13	14 Other
f Employee's address and ZIP code			15 Statutory employee ☐ Deceased ☐ Pension plan ☐ Legal rep. ☐ Hshld. emp. ☐ Subtotal ☐ Deferred compensation ☐	

16 State Employer's state I.D. No.	17 State wages, tips, etc.	18 State income tax	19 Locality name	20 Local wages, tips, etc.	21 Local income tax

Cat. No. 10134D

Department of the Treasury—Internal Revenue Service

Form **W-2** **Wage and Tax Statement** **2000**

Copy A For Social Security Administration

For Paperwork Reduction Act Notice, see separate instructions.

MISCELLANEOUS INCOME (IRS form 1099)

9595	☐ VOID	☐ CORRECTED			
PAYER'S name, street address, city, state, and ZIP code Doe Company 123 Main Street Largo, FL 34006		**1** Rents $ 12,000.00	OMB No. 1545-0115 20**00** Form **1099-MISC**	**Miscellaneous Income**
		2 Royalties $		
		3 Other income $		

PAYER'S Federal identification number 59-123456	RECIPIENT'S identification number 9876532	**4** Federal income tax withheld $	**5** Fishing boat proceeds $	**Copy A** **For** **Internal Revenue Service Center**
RECIPIENT'S name John A. Smith		**6** Medical and health care payments $	**7** Nonemployee compensation $ 21,000	**File with Form 1096.**
		8 Substitute payments in lieu of dividends or interest $	**9** Payer made direct sales of $5,000 or more of consumer products to a buyer (recipient) for resale ▶ ☐	For Paperwork Reduction Act Notice and instructions for
Street address (including apt. no.) 567 Wharf Boulevard				completing this form,
City, state, and ZIP code Largo, FL 34006		**10** Crop insurance proceeds $	**11** State income tax withheld $ 00.00	see **Instructions for Forms 1099, 1098, 5498, and W-2G.**
Account number (optional)	2nd TIN Not. ☐	**12** State/Payer's state number 8884444		

Form **1099-MISC**   Cat. No. 14425J   Department of the Treasury - Internal Revenue Service

Do NOT Cut or Separate Forms on This Page

ANNUAL SUMMARY AND TRANSMITTAL OF U.S. INFORMATION RETURNS
(IRS form 1096)

DO NOT STAPLE 6969

Form **1096**	**Annual Summary and Transmittal of U.S. Information Returns**	OMB No. 1545-0108

Department of the Treasury
Internal Revenue Service

2000

FILER'S name

ATTACH IRS LABEL HERE

Doe Company

Street address (including room or suite number)

123 Main Street

City, state, and ZIP code

Largo, FL 94006

If you are not using a preprinted label, enter in box 1 or 2 below the identification number you used as the filer on the information returns being transmitted. Do not fill in both boxes 1 and 2.

Name of person to contact if the IRS needs more information

John Doe

Telephone number

(518) 5550000

For Official Use Only

1 Employer identification number	2 Social security number	3 Total number of forms	4 Federal income tax withheld	5 Total amount reported with this Form 1096
59-123456		3	$ 0	$ $63,000

If this is your FINAL return, enter an "X" here . . ▶ ☒

Enter an "X" in only one box below to indicate the type of form being filed.

W-2G 32	1098 81	1099-A 80	1099-B 79	1099-C 85	1099-DIV 91	1099-G 86	1099-INT 92	1099-MISC 95	1099-OID 96	1099-PATR 97	1099-R 98	1099-S 75	5498 28
☐	☐	☐	☐	☐	☐	☐	☐	☒	☐	☐	☐	☐	☐

form 19

FLORIDA
DEPARTMENT
OF REVENUE

2001 Florida Annual Resale Certificate for Sales Tax

THIS CERTIFICATE EXPIRES ON DECEMBER 31, 2001

DR-13
R. 10/00

Business Name and Location Address	Registration Effective Date	Certificate Number

DOE CO.

JOHN DOE

1234 MAIN ST.

JACKSON, FL 32100

JUNE 27, 1990

12-34-567890-12-3

This is to certify that all tangible personal property purchased or rented, real property rented, or services purchased after the above Registration Effective Date by the above business are being purchased or rented for one of the following purposes:

I Resale as tangible personal property.

I Re-rental as tangible personal property.

I Resale of services.

I Re-rental as real property

I Incorporation into and sale as part of the repair of tangible personal property by a repair dealer.

I Incorporation as a material, ingredient, or component part of tangible personal property that is being produced for sale by manufacturing, compounding, or processing.

This certificate cannot be reassigned or transferred. This certificate can only be used by the active dealer or its authorized employees. Misuse of this Annual Resale Certificate will subject the user to penalties as provided by law.

Presented to: _____   Presented by: _____

(insert name of seller on photocopy)   (date)   Authorized Signature (Purchaser)   (date)

198

APPENDIX B
BLANK FORMS

The following forms may be photocopied or removed from this book and used immediately. Some of the tax forms explained in this book are not included here because you should use original returns provided by the IRS (940, 941) or the Florida Department of Revenue (quarterly unemployment compensation form).

These forms are included on the following pages:

TAX TIMETABLE

form 1

<table>
<tr><th></th><th colspan="6">Florida</th><th colspan="3">Federal</th></tr>
<tr><th></th><th>Sales</th><th>Unem-ployment</th><th>Tangible</th><th>Intang-ible</th><th>Corp. Income</th><th>Est. Payment</th><th>Annual Return</th><th>Form 941*</th><th>Misc.</th></tr>
<tr><td>JAN.</td><td>20th</td><td>31st</td><td></td><td></td><td></td><td>15th</td><td></td><td>31st</td><td>940 508   31st W-2 1099</td></tr>
<tr><td>FEB.</td><td>20th</td><td></td><td></td><td>28th 4% disc.</td><td></td><td></td><td></td><td></td><td>28th W-3</td></tr>
<tr><td>MAR.</td><td>20th</td><td></td><td>31st</td><td>31st 3% disc.</td><td></td><td></td><td>15th Corp. & Partnership</td><td></td><td></td></tr>
<tr><td>APR.</td><td>20th</td><td>30th</td><td>1st</td><td>30th 2% disc.</td><td>1st</td><td>15th</td><td>15th Personal</td><td>30th</td><td>30th 508</td></tr>
<tr><td>MAY</td><td>20th</td><td></td><td></td><td>31st 1% disc.</td><td></td><td></td><td></td><td></td><td></td></tr>
<tr><td>JUN.</td><td>20th</td><td></td><td></td><td>30th tax due</td><td></td><td>15th</td><td></td><td></td><td></td></tr>
<tr><td>JUL.</td><td>20th</td><td>31st</td><td></td><td></td><td></td><td></td><td></td><td>31st</td><td>31st 508</td></tr>
<tr><td>AUG.</td><td>20th</td><td></td><td></td><td></td><td></td><td></td><td></td><td></td><td></td></tr>
<tr><td>SEP.</td><td>20th</td><td></td><td></td><td></td><td></td><td>15th</td><td></td><td></td><td></td></tr>
<tr><td>OCT.</td><td>20th</td><td>31st</td><td></td><td></td><td></td><td></td><td></td><td>31st</td><td>31st 508</td></tr>
<tr><td>NOV.</td><td>20th</td><td></td><td></td><td></td><td></td><td></td><td></td><td></td><td></td></tr>
<tr><td>DEC.</td><td>20th</td><td></td><td></td><td></td><td></td><td></td><td></td><td></td><td></td></tr>
</table>

* In addition to form 941, deposits must be made regularly if withholding exceeds $500 in any month

Instructions for Completing Application for Registration of Fictitious Name

Section 1:

Line 1: Enter the name as you wish it to be registered. A fictitious name may <u>not</u> contain the words "Corporation" or "Incorporated," or the abbreviations "Corp." or "Inc.," unless the person or business for which the name is registered is incorporated or has obtained a certificate of authority to transact business in this state pursuant to chapter 607 or chapter 617 Florida Statutes.

Line 2: Enter the mailing address of the business. This address does not have to be the principal place of business and can be directed to anyone's attention. DO NOT USE AN ADDRESS THAT IS NOT YET OCCUPIED. ALL FUTURE MAILINGS AND ANY CERTIFICATION REQUESTED ON THIS REGISTRATION FORM WILL BE SENT TO THE ADDRESS IN SECTION 1. An address may be changed at any future date with no charge by simply writing the Division.

Line 3: Enter the name of the county in Florida where the principal place of business of the fictitious name is located. If there is more than one county, list all applicable counties or state "multiple".

Line 4: Enter the Federal Employer Identification (FEI) number if known or if applicable.

Section 2:

Part A: Complete if the owner(s) of the fictitious name are individuals. The individual's name and address must be provided. The social security number is not mandatory. Information provided on this application is a public record and, as such, will be made accessible to the public.

Part B: Complete if the owner(s) are not individuals. Examples are a corporation, limited partnership, joint venture, general partnership, trusts, fictitious name, etc. Provide the name of the owner, their address, their registration number as registered with the Division of Corporations, and the Federal Employer Identification (FEI) number. An FEI number must be provided or the appropriate box must be checked.

Owners listed in Part B must be registered with the Division of Corporations or provide documentation as to why they are not required to register. Examples would be Federally Chartered Corporations, or Legislatively created entities.

Additional owners may be listed on an attached page as long as all of the information requested in Part A or Part B is provided.

Section 3:

Only one signature is required. It is preferred that a daytime phone number be provided in order to contact the applicant if there are any questions about the application.

Section 4:

TO CANCEL A REGISTRATION ON FILE: Provide fictitious name, date filed, and registration number of the fictitious name to be cancelled.

TO CHANGE OWNERSHIP OF A REGISTRATION: Complete section 4 to cancel the original registration. Complete sections 1 through 3 to re-register the fictitious name listing the new owner(s). An owner's signature is required in both sections 3 and 4.

TO CHANGE THE NAME OF A REGISTRATION: Complete section 4 to cancel the original registration. Complete sections 1 through 3 to re-register the new fictitious name. An owner's signature is required in both sections 3 and 4.

An acknowledgement letter will be mailed once the fictitious name registration has been filed.

If you wish to receive a certificate of status and/or certified copy at the time of filing of this registration, check the appropriate box at the bottom of the form. PLEASE NOTE: Acknowledgements/certificates will be sent to the address in Section 1. If a certificate of status is requested, an additional $10 is due. If a certified copy is requested, an additional $30 is due.

The registration and re-registration will be in effect until December 31 of the fifth year.

Send completed application with appropriate fees to:
Fictitious Name Registration
PO Box 1300
Tallahassee, FL 32302-1300

Internet Address:
http://www.sunbiz.org

The fee for registering a fictitious name is $50. Please make a separate check for each filing payable to the Department of State. Application must be typed or printed in ink and legible.

APPLICATION FOR REGISTRATION OF FICTITIOUS NAME

Note: Acknowledgements/certificates will be sent to the address in Section 1 only.

Section 1

1. _____

Fictitious Name to be Registered

_____

2. _____

Mailing Address of Business

_____

City   State   Zip Code

3. Florida County of principal place of business: _____

_____

4. FEI Number: _____

This space for office use only

Section 2

A. Owner(s) of Fictitious Name If Individual(s): (Use an attachment if necessary):

1. _____

Last   First   M.I.

_____

Address

_____

City   State   Zip Code

SS# _____ - _____ - _____ (optional)

2. _____

Last   First   M.I.

_____

Address

_____

City   State   Zip Code

SS#_____ - _____ - _____ (optional)

B. Owner(s) of Fictitious Name If other than Individuals(s): (Use attachment if necessary):

1. _____

Entity Name

_____

Address

_____

City   State   Zip Code

Florida Registration Number _____
FEI Number: _____
☐ Applied for   ☐ Not Applicable

2. _____

Entity Name

_____

Address

_____

City   State   Zip Code

Florida Registration Number _____
FEI Number: _____
☐ Applied for   ☐ Not Applicable

Section 3

I (we) the undersigned, being the sole (all the) party(ies) owning interest in the above fictitious name, certify that the information indicated on this form is true and accurate. In accordance with Section 865.09, F.S., I (we) further certify that the fictitious name shown in Section 1 of this form has been advertised at least once in a newspaper as defined in chapter 50, Florida Statutes, in the county where the applicant's principal place of business is located. I (we) understand that the signature(s) below shall have the same legal effect as if made under oath. (At Least One Signature Required)

_____   _____
Signature of Owner   Date
Phone Number: _____

_____   _____
Signature of Owner   Date
Phone Number: _____

Section 4

FOR CANCELLATION COMPLETE SECTION 4 ONLY:
FOR FICTITIOUS NAME OR OWNERSHIP CHANGE COMPLETE SECTIONS 1 THROUGH 4:

I (we) the undersigned, hereby cancel the fictitious name _____

_____, which was registered on _____ and was assigned registration number _____

_____   _____
Signature of Owner   Date   Signature of Owner   Date

Mark the applicable boxes   ☐ Certificate of Status - $10   ☐ Certified Copy - $30
Filing Fee: $50

CR4E-001

TRADEMARK/SERVICE MARK REGISTRATION GUIDELINES

I. GENERAL INFORMATION

Trade and Service Marks may be registered with the Florida Department of State pursuant to Chapter 495, Florida Statutes. Registration must be denied if a mark does not meet and comply with all of the requirements and provisions stipulated in Chapter 495, Florida Statutes. Marks are checked against other marks registered or reserved with this division and not against corporations, fictitious names or other entities. Rights to a name or mark are perfected by actual use in the ordinary pursuit of the specific endeavor; rights are not perfected by registration only, and the general rule of "FIRST IN USE, FIRST IN RIGHT" is applicable.

Our agency registers trade and service marks on a state level. If you need information concerning the federal registration of trademarks, service marks or patents, please contact the Commissioner of Patents and Trademarks in Washington, D. C. by calling 703-308-9000. If you need information concerning copyrights, contact the Copyright Office in Washington, D. C. by calling 202-707-3000. Although trade names are defined in Chapter 495, Florida Statutes, there is no provision for their registration.

If you wish to register a mark pursuant to Chapter 495, Florida Statutes, please submit one original and one photocopy of the Trade or Service Mark Registration application completed in its entirety, three specimens and a check made payable to the Florida Department of State for the appropriate amount. The application must be typed or neatly handwritten, signed and notarized.

The mark must be in use before it can be registered. If registering a trademark, the good(s) or product(s) must be on sale in the market place. If registering a service mark, you must be rendering the service(s) you are advertising. The mere advertising of future goods or services does not constitute use of a trade or service mark.

II. FEES AND CLASSES

The fee to register a mark is $87.50 per class. Please refer to section 495.111, Florida Statutes (attached), for a list of classes.

Should you need additional information concerning these classes or your classification, please contact the Registration Section by calling (850)487-6051.

III. SPECIMENS

If your mark is a trademark, we will need specimens that are affixed to the good(s) or product(s). Some acceptable trademark specimens are: labels, decals, tags, wrappers, boxes, and containers. If your mark is a service mark, we will need specimens which reflect the type of service(s) being provided. Some acceptable service mark specimens are: business cards, brochures, flyers, and newspaper advertisements. If your mark is both a trade and service mark, you must submit three appropriate trademark specimens and three appropriate service mark specimens.

CR2E014(1/00)

Do not submit photocopies, camera ready copies, letterhead stationery, envelopes, invoices or matchbooks as specimens. Photographs of bulky specimens are acceptable if the mark to be registered and the good(s) or product(s) are clearly legible. We will not accept any specimens that have been altered or defaced in any way.

IV. APPLICATION

Part I.

#1 - You must list the complete name and business address of the applicant. Please indicate if the applicant is an individual, a corporation, a limited partnership, a general partnership, etc. Enter the domicile state, Florida registration number and Federal Employer Identification number if the applicant is other than an individual.

#2(a) - If a service mark, list the services the mark is used in connection with (i.e., restaurant services, real estate agency, insurance agency, etc.).

#2(b) - If a trademark, list the goods/products the mark is used in connection with (i.e., window cleaner, furniture polish, ladies sportswear, etc.).

#2(c) - List how the mark is being used. If a trademark, tell how the mark is applied to the goods (i.e., label, decal, engraving, imprinting on the goods or products themselves, etc.).

If a service mark, tell how the mark is used in advertising (i.e., brochures, business cards, newspaper advertisements, etc.).

#2(d) - List the applicable class(es). Please refer to section 495.111, F.S., (attached) for a list of these classes.

Part II

#1(a) - Enter the date the mark was first used anywhere.

#1(b) - Enter the date the mark was first used in Florida.

Part III

#1 - Enter the mark to be registered. If the mark includes a design, include a brief written description. If your mark is in another language, please provide this office with an English translation of your mark in this section.

#2 - Disclaimer - Your mark may include a word or design that must be disclaimed. All geographical terms and representations of cities, states or countries must be disclaimed (i.e., Miami, Orlando, Florida, the design of the state of Florida, the design of the United States of America, etc.). Commonly used words, including corporate suffixes, must also be disclaimed.

Signature Portion

Complete the signature paragraph accordingly. Please note the applicant's signature must be notarized.

V. TRADEMARK/SERVICE MARK SEARCH

Due to the amount of time it takes to conduct a thorough search of the records, this office does not provide trademark/service mark searches over the telephone. However, you may submit a written request. The request must specify the exact mark to be used and the good(s) or service(s) the mark is to be used in connection with. Please direct all requests to the Trademark Registration Section, Division of Corporations, P. O. Box 6327, Tallahassee, FL 32314.

VI. PROCESSING TIME

The application should be processed within two to five business days from the date of receipt. The processing time may be longer during our peak periods. All applications meeting the requirements of Chapter 495, F. S., on the initial examination will be filed as of the date of receipt. Applications received by courier are not handled on an expedited basis.

VII. COURIER ADDRESS AND MAILING ADDRESS

Street Address	**Mailing Address**
Registration Section	Registration Section
Division of Corporations	Division of Corporations
409 E. Gaines St.	P. O. Box 6327
Tallahassee, FL 32399	Tallahassee, FL 32314

Applications received via a courier service are not handled on an expedited basis.

VIII. QUESTIONS

If you have any questions concerning the registration of a mark, please contact the Trademark Registration Section by calling (850)487-6051 between the hours of 8 a.m. and 5:00 p.m. or writing to an address listed above.

495.111 Classification. -

(1) The following general classes of goods and services are established for convenience of administration of this chapter:

(a) Goods:

Class 1 Chemicals

Class 2 Paints

Class 3 Cosmetics and cleaning preparations

Class 4 Lubricants and fuels

Class 5 Pharmaceuticals

Class 6 Metal goods

Class 7 Machinery

Class 8 Hand tools

Class 9 Electrical and scientific apparatus

Class 10 Medical Apparatus

Class 11 Environmental control apparatus

Class 12 Vehicles

Class 13 Firearms

Class 14 Jewelry

Class 15 Musical instruments

Class 16 Paper goods and printed matter

Class 17 Rubber goods

Class 18 Leather goods

Class 19 Nonmetallic building materials

Class 20 Furniture and articles not otherwise classified

Class 21 Housewares and glass

Class 22 Cordage and fibers

Class 23 Yarns and threads

Class 24 Fabrics

Class 25 Clothing

Class 26 Fancy goods

Class 27 Floor coverings

Class 28 Toys and sporting goods

Class 29 Meats and processed foods

Class 30 Staple foods

Class 31 Natural agricultural products

Class 32 Light beverages

Class 33 Wines and spirits

Class 34 Smoker's articles

(b) Services:

Class 35 Advertising and business

Class 36 Insurance and financial

Class 37 Construction and repair

Class 38 Communication

Class 39 Transportation and storage

Class 40 Material treatment

Class 41 Education and entertainment

Class 42 Miscellaneous

APPLICATION FOR THE REGISTRATION OF A TRADEMARK OR SERVICE MARK
PURSUANT TO CHAPTER 495, FLORIDA STATUTES

TO: **Division of Corporations**
Post Office Box 6327
Tallahassee, FL 32314

Name & address to whom acknowledgment should be sent:

_____

_____

_____

(_____)_____
Daytime Telephone number

PART I

1. (a) Applicant's name: _____

   (b) Applicant's business address: _____

   _____
   City/State/Zip

   (c) Applicant's telephone number: (_____)_____
   ☐ Individual   ☐ Corporation   ☐ Joint Venture   ☐ Other:_____
   ☐ General Partnership ☐ Limited Partnership   ☐ Union

   If other than an individual,

   (1) Florida registration number: _____ (2) Domicile State: _____

   (3) Federal Employer Identification Number: _____

2. (a) If the mark to be registered is a service mark, the services in connection with which the mark is used:
   (i.e., furniture moving services, diaper services, house painting services, etc.)

   _____

   _____

   (b) If the mark to be registered is a trademark, the goods in connection with which the mark is used:
   (i.e., ladies sportswear, cat food, barbecue grills, shoe laces, etc.)

   _____

   _____

   (c) The mode or manner in which the mark is used:(i.e., labels, decals, newspaper advertisements, brochures, etc.)

   _____

   _____

   _____
   (Continued)

207

d) The class(es) in which goods or services fall:

_____

_____

PART II
1. Date first used by the applicant, predecessor, or a related company (must include month, day and year):

(a) Date first used anywhere: _____   (b) Date first used in Florida: _____

PART III
1. The mark to be registered is: (If logo/design is included, please give brief written description which must be 25 words or less.)

_____

_____

_____

English Translation_____

2. DISCLAIMER (if applicable)
NO CLAIM IS MADE TO THE EXCLUSIVE RIGHT TO USE THE TERM " _____
_____ " APART FROM THE MARK AS SHOWN.

I,_____, *being sworn, depose and say that I am the owner and the applicant herein, or that I am authorized to sign on behalf of the owner and applicant herein, and no other person except a related company has the right to use such mark in Florida either in the identical form or in such near resemblance as to be likely to deceive or confuse or to be mistaken therefor. I make this affidavit and verification on my/the applicant's behalf. I further acknowledge that I have read the application and know the contents thereof and that the facts stated herein are true and correct*

_____
Typed or printed name of applicant

_____
Applicant's signature or authorized person's signature
(List name and title)

STATE OF _____

COUNTY OF _____

On this _____ day of _____ , _____ , _____personally
appeared before me,
  ☐ who is personally known to me   ☐ whose identity I proved on the basis of _____
_____ .

_____
Notary Public Signature

(Seal)

_____
Notary's Printed Name

My Commission Expires:_____

FEE: $87.50 per class

U.S. Department of Justice
Immigration and Naturalization Service

OMB No. 1115-0136
Employment Eligibility Verification

Please read instructions carefully before completing this form. The instructions must be available during completion of this form. ANTI-DISCRIMINATION NOTICE. It is illegal to discriminate against work eligible individuals. Employers CANNOT specify which document(s) they will accept from an employee. The refusal to hire an individual because of a future expiration date may also constitute illegal discrimination.

Section 1. Employee Information and Verification. To be completed and signed by employee at the time employment begins

Print Name: Last	First	Middle Initial	Maiden Name

Address *(Street Name and Number)*	Apt. #	Date of Birth *(month/day/year)*

City	State	Zip Code	Social Security #

I am aware that federal law provides for imprisonment and/or fines for false statements or use of false documents in connection with the completion of this form.

I attest, under penalty of perjury, that I am (check one of the following):
- ☐ A citizen or national of the United States
- ☐ A Lawful Permanent Resident (Alien # A_____
- ☐ An alien authorized to work until_____/_____/_____
   (Alien # or Admission # _____

Employee's Signature

Date *(month/day/year)*

Preparer and/or Translator Certification. *(To be completed and signed if Section 1 is prepared by a person other than the employee.) I attest, under penalty of perjury, that I have assisted in the completion of this form and that to the best of my knowledge the information is true and correct.*

Preparer's/Translator's Signature	Print Name

Address *(Street Name and Number, City, State, Zip Code)*	Date *(month/day/year)*

Section 2. Employer Review and Verification. To be completed and signed by employer. **Examine one document from List A OR examine one document from List B and one from List C** as listed on the reverse of this form and record the title, number and expiration date, if any, of the document(s)

List A	OR	List B	AND	List C

Document title: _____   _____   _____

Issuing authority: _____   _____   _____

Document #: _____   _____   _____

   Expiration Date *(if any):* ___/___/___   ___/___/___   ___/___/___

Document #: _____

   Expiration Date *(if any):* ___/___/___

CERTIFICATION - I attest, under penalty of perjury, that I have examined the document(s) presented by the above-named employee, that the above-listed document(s) appear to be genuine and to relate to the employee named, that the employee began employment on *(month/day/year)* _____/_____/_____ **and that to the best of my knowledge the employee is eligible to work in the United States. (State employment agencies may omit the date the employee began employment).**

Signature of Employer or Authorized Representative	Print Name	Title

Business or Organization Name	Address *(Street Name and Number, City, State, Zip Code)*	Date *(month/day/year)*

Section 3. Updating and Reverification. To be completed and signed by employer

A. New Name *(if applicable)*	B. Date of rehire *(month/day/year)* *(if applicable)*

C. If employee's previous grant of work authorization has expired, provide the information below for the document that establishes current employment eligibility.

   Document Title:_____   Document #:_____   Expiration Date (if any):___/___/___

I attest, under penalty of perjury, that to the best of my knowledge, this employee is eligible to work in the United States, and if the employee presented document(s), the document(s) I have examined appear to be genuine and to relate to the individual.

Signature of Employer or Authorized Representative	Date *(month/day/year)*

Form I-9 (Rev. 11-21-91) N

INSTRUCTIONS
PLEASE READ ALL INSTRUCTIONS CAREFULLY BEFORE COMPLETING THIS FORM.

Anti-Discrimination Notice. It is illegal to discriminate against any individual (other than an alien not authorized to work in the U.S.) in hiring, discharging, or recruiting or referring for a fee because of that individual's national origin or citizenship status. It is illegal to discriminate against work eligible individuals. Employers **CANNOT** specify which document(s) they will accept from an employee. The refusal to hire an individual because of a future expiration date may also constitute illegal discrimination.

Section 1 - Employee. All employees, citizens and noncitizens, hired after November 6, 1986, must complete Section 1 of this form at the time of hire, which is the actual beginning of employment. **The employer is responsible for ensuring that Section 1 is timely and properly completed.**

Preparer/Translator Certification. The Preparer/Translator Certification must be completed if Section 1 is prepared by a person other than the employee. A preparer/translator may be used only when the employee is unable to complete Section 1 on his/her own. However, the employee must still sign Section 1 personally.

Section 2 - Employer. For the purpose of completing this form, the term "employer" includes those recruiters and referrers for a fee who are agricultural associations, agricultural employers, or farm labor contractors.

Employers must complete Section 2 by examining evidence of identity and employment eligibility within three (3) business days of the date employment begins. If employees are authorized to work, but are unable to present the required document(s) within three business days, they must present a receipt for the application of the document(s) within three business days and the actual document(s) within ninety (90) days. However, if employers hire individuals for a duration of less than three business days, Section 2 must be completed at the time employment begins. **Employers must record: 1)** document title; **2)** issuing authority; **3)** document number, **4)** expiration date, if any; and **5)** the date employment begins. Employers must sign and date the certification. Employees must present original documents. Employers may, but are not required to, photocopy the document(s) presented. These photocopies may only be used for the verification process and must be retained with the I-9. **However, employers are still responsible for completing the I-9.**

Section 3 - Updating and Reverification. Employers must complete Section 3 when updating and/or reverifying the I-9. Employers must reverify employment eligibility of their employees on or before the expiration date recorded in Section 1. Employers **CANNOT** specify which document(s) they will accept from an employee.

- If an employee's name has changed at the time this form is being updated/ reverified, complete Block A.

- If an employee is rehired within three (3) years of the date this form was originally completed and the employee is still eligible to be employed on the same basis as previously indicated on this form (updating), complete Block B and the signature block.

- If an employee is rehired within three (3) years of the date this form was originally completed and the employee's work authorization has expired or if a current employee's work authorization is about to expire (reverification), complete Block B and:
  - examine any document that reflects that the employee is authorized to work in the U.S. (see List A or C),
  - record the document title, document number and expiration date (if any) in Block C, and
  - complete the signature block.

Photocopying and Retaining Form I-9. A blank I-9 may be reproduced provided both sides are copied. The Instructions must be available to all employees completing this form. Employers must retain completed I-9s for three (3) years after the date of hire **or** one (1) year after the date employment ends, whichever is later.

For more detailed information, you may refer to the INS Handbook for Employers, (Form M-274). You may obtain the handbook at your local INS office.

Privacy Act Notice. The authority for collecting this information is the Immigration Reform and Control Act of 1986, Pub. L. 99-603 (8 U.S.C. 1324a).

This information is for employers to verify the eligibility of individuals for employment to preclude the unlawful hiring, or recruiting or referring for a fee, of aliens who are not authorized to work in the United States.

This information will be used by employers as a record of their basis for determining eligibility of an employee to work in the United States. The form will be kept by the employer and made available for inspection by officials of the U.S. Immigration and Naturalization Service, the Department of Labor, and the Office of Special Counsel for Immigration Related Unfair Employment Practices.

Submission of the information required in this form is voluntary. However, an individual may not begin employment unless this form is completed since employers are subject to civil or criminal penalties if they do not comply with the Immigration Reform and Control Act of 1986.

Reporting Burden. We try to create forms and instructions that are accurate, can be easily understood, and which impose the least possible burden on you to provide us with information. Often this is difficult because some immigration laws are very complex. Accordingly, the reporting burden for this collection of information is computed as follows: 1) learning about this form, 5 minutes; 2) completing the form, 5 minutes; and 3) assembling and filing (recordkeeping) the form, 5 minutes, for an average of 15 minutes per response. If you have comments regarding the accuracy of this burden estimate, or suggestions for making this form simpler, you can write to both the Immigration and Naturalization Service, 425 I Street, N.W., Room 5304, Washington, D. C. 20536; and the Office of Management and Budget, Paperwork Reduction Project, OMB No. 1115-0136, Washington, D.C. 20503.

EMPLOYERS MUST RETAIN COMPLETED I-9
PLEASE DO NOT MAIL COMPLETED I-9 TO INS

Form SS-4
(Rev. April 2000)
Department of the Treasury
Internal Revenue Service

Application for Employer Identification Number

(For use by employers, corporations, partnerships, trusts, estates, churches, government agencies, certain individuals, and others. See instructions.)

▶ Keep a copy for your records.

EIN

OMB No. 1545-0003

Please type or print clearly.

1 Name of applicant (legal name) (see instructions)

2 Trade name of business (if different from name on line 1)

3 Executor, trustee, "care of" name

4a Mailing address (street address) (room, apt., or suite no.)

5a Business address (if different from address on lines 4a and 4b)

4b City, state, and ZIP code

5b City, state, and ZIP code

6 County and state where principal business is located

7 Name of principal officer, general partner, grantor, owner, or trustor—SSN or ITIN may be required (see instructions) ▶

8a Type of entity (Check only one box.) (see instructions)

Caution: *If applicant is a limited liability company, see the instructions for line 8a.*

☐ Sole proprietor (SSN) _____

☐ Partnership   ☐ Personal service corp.

☐ REMIC   ☐ National Guard

☐ State/local government   ☐ Farmers' cooperative

☐ Church or church-controlled organization

☐ Other nonprofit organization (specify) ▶ _____

☐ Other (specify) ▶

☐ Estate (SSN of decedent) _____

☐ Plan administrator (SSN) _____

☐ Other corporation (specify) ▶ _____

☐ Trust

☐ Federal government/military

(enter GEN if applicable) _____

8b If a corporation, name the state or foreign country (if applicable) where incorporated

State

Foreign country

9 Reason for applying (Check only one box.) (see instructions)

☐ Started new business (specify type) ▶ _____

☐ Hired employees (Check the box and see line 12.)

☐ Created a pension plan (specify type) ▶

☐ Banking purpose (specify purpose) ▶ _____

☐ Changed type of organization (specify new type) ▶ _____

☐ Purchased going business

☐ Created a trust (specify type) ▶ _____

☐ Other (specify) ▶

10 Date business started or acquired (month, day, year) (see instructions)

11 Closing month of accounting year (see instructions)

12 First date wages or annuities were paid or will be paid (month, day, year). **Note:** *If applicant is a withholding agent, enter date income will first be paid to nonresident alien. (month, day, year)* . . . . ▶

13 Highest number of employees expected in the next 12 months. **Note:** *If the applicant does not expect to have any employees during the period, enter -0-. (see instructions)* . . . . . ▶

Nonagricultural	Agricultural	Household

14 Principal activity (see instructions) ▶

15 Is the principal business activity manufacturing? . . . . ☐ Yes ☐ No
If "Yes," principal product and raw material used ▶

16 To whom are most of the products or services sold? Please check one box.   ☐ Business (wholesale)
☐ Public (retail)   ☐ Other (specify) ▶   ☐ N/A

17a Has the applicant ever applied for an employer identification number for this or any other business? . . . . . ☐ Yes ☐ No
Note: *If "Yes," please complete lines 17b and 17c.*

17b If you checked "Yes" on line 17a, give applicant's legal name and trade name shown on prior application, if different from line 1 or 2 above.
Legal name ▶   Trade name ▶

17c Approximate date when and city and state where the application was filed. Enter previous employer identification number if known.

Approximate date when filed (mo., day, year)	City and state where filed	Previous EIN

Under penalties of perjury, I declare that I have examined this application, and to the best of my knowledge and belief, it is true, correct, and complete.

Business telephone number (include area code)
( )

Fax telephone number (include area code)
( )

Name and title (Please type or print clearly.) ▶

Signature ▶   Date ▶

Note: *Do not write below this line. For official use only.*

Please leave blank ▶	Geo.	Ind.	Class	Size	Reason for applying

For Privacy Act and Paperwork Reduction Act Notice, see page 4.

Cat. No. 16055N

Form **SS-4** (Rev. 4-2000)

General Instructions

Section references are to the Internal Revenue Code unless otherwise noted.

Purpose of Form

Use Form SS-4 to apply for an employer identification number (EIN). An EIN is a nine-digit number (for example, 12-3456789) assigned to sole proprietors, corporations, partnerships, estates, trusts, and other entities for tax filing and reporting purposes. The information you provide on this form will establish your business tax account.

Caution: *An EIN is for use in connection with your business activities only. Do **not** use your EIN in place of your social security number (SSN).*

Who Must File

You must file this form if you have not been assigned an EIN before and:

• You pay wages to one or more employees including household employees.

• You are required to have an EIN to use on any return, statement, or other document, even if you are not an employer.

• You are a withholding agent required to withhold taxes on income, other than wages, paid to a nonresident alien (individual, corporation, partnership, etc.). A withholding agent may be an agent, broker, fiduciary, manager, tenant, or spouse, and is required to file **Form 1042,** Annual Withholding Tax Return for U.S. Source Income of Foreign Persons.

• You file **Schedule C,** Profit or Loss From Business, **Schedule C-EZ,** Net Profit From Business, or **Schedule F,** Profit or Loss From Farming, of **Form 1040,** U.S. Individual Income Tax Return, **and** have a Keogh plan or are required to file excise, employment, or alcohol, tobacco, or firearms returns.

The following must use EINs even if they do not have any employees:

• State and local agencies who serve as tax reporting agents for public assistance recipients, under Rev. Proc. 80-4, 1980-1 C.B. 581, should obtain a separate EIN for this reporting. See **Household employer** on page 3.

• Trusts, except the following:

   1. Certain grantor-owned trusts. (See the **Instructions for Form 1041,** U.S. Income Tax Return for Estates and Trusts.)

   2. Individual retirement arrangement (IRA) trusts, unless the trust has to file **Form 990-T,** Exempt Organization Business Income Tax Return. (See the **Instructions for Form 990-T.**)

• Estates

• Partnerships

• REMICs (real estate mortgage investment conduits) (See the **Instructions for Form 1066,** U.S. Real Estate Mortgage Investment Conduit (REMIC) Income Tax Return.)

• Corporations

• Nonprofit organizations (churches, clubs, etc.)

• Farmers' cooperatives

• Plan administrators (A plan administrator is the person or group of persons specified as the administrator by the instrument under which the plan is operated.)

When To Apply for a New EIN

New Business. If you become the new owner of an existing business, **do not** use the EIN of the former owner. **If you already have an EIN, use that number.** If you do not have an EIN, apply for one on this form. If you become the "owner" of a corporation by acquiring its stock, use the corporation's EIN.

Changes in Organization or Ownership. If you already have an EIN, you may need to get a new one if either the organization or ownership of your business changes. If you incorporate a sole proprietorship or form a partnership, you must get a new EIN. However, **do not** apply for a new EIN if:

• You change only the name of your business,

• You elected on **Form 8832,** Entity Classification Election, to change the way the entity is taxed, or

• A partnership terminates because at least 50% of the total interests in partnership capital and profits were sold or exchanged within a 12-month period. (See Regulations section 301.6109-1(d)(2)(iii).) The EIN for the terminated partnership should continue to be used.

Note: *If you are electing to be an "S corporation," be sure you file **Form 2553,** Election by a Small Business Corporation.*

File Only One Form SS-4. File only one Form SS-4, regardless of the number of businesses operated or trade names under which a business operates. However, each corporation in an affiliated group must file a separate application.

EIN Applied for, But Not Received. If you do not have an EIN by the time a return is due, write "Applied for" and the date you applied in the space shown for the number. **Do not** show your social security number (SSN) as an EIN on returns.

If you do not have an EIN by the time a tax deposit is due, send your payment to the Internal Revenue Service Center for your filing area. (See **Where To Apply** below.) Make your check or money order payable to "United States Treasury" and show your name (as shown on Form SS-4), address, type of tax, period covered, and date you applied for an EIN. Send an explanation with the deposit.

For more information about EINs, see **Pub. 583,** Starting a Business and Keeping Records, and **Pub. 1635,** Understanding Your EIN.

How To Apply

You can apply for an EIN either by mail or by telephone. You can get an EIN immediately by calling the Tele-TIN number for the service center for your state, or you can send the completed Form SS-4 directly to the service center to receive your EIN by mail.

Application by Tele-TIN. Under the Tele-TIN program, you can receive your EIN by telephone and use it immediately to file a return or make a payment. To receive an EIN by telephone, complete Form SS-4, then call the Tele-TIN number listed for your state under **Where To Apply.** The person making the call must be authorized to sign the form. (See **Signature** on page 4.)

An IRS representative will use the information from the Form SS-4 to establish your account and assign you an EIN. Write the number you are given on the upper right corner of the form and sign and date it.

Mail or fax (facsimile) the signed Form SS-4 **within 24 hours** to the Tele-TIN Unit at the service center address for your state. The IRS representative will give you the fax number. The fax numbers are also listed in Pub. 1635.

Taxpayer representatives can receive their client's EIN by telephone if they first send a fax of a completed **Form 2848,** Power of Attorney and Declaration of Representative, or **Form 8821,** Tax Information Authorization, to the Tele-TIN unit. The Form 2848 or Form 8821 will be used solely to release the EIN to the representative authorized on the form.

Application by Mail. Complete Form SS-4 at least 4 to 5 weeks before you will need an EIN. Sign and date the application and mail it to the service center address for your state. You will receive your EIN in the mail in approximately 4 weeks.

Where To Apply

The Tele-TIN numbers listed below will involve a long-distance charge to callers outside of the local calling area and can be used only to apply for an EIN. **The numbers may change without notice.** Call 1-800-829-1040 to verify a number or to ask about the status of an application by mail.

If your principal business, office or agency, or legal residence in the case of an individual, is located in:	Call the Tele-TIN number shown or file with the Internal Revenue Service Center at:
Florida, Georgia, South Carolina	Attn: Entity Control Atlanta, GA 39901 770-455-2360
New Jersey, New York (New York City and counties of Nassau, Rockland, Suffolk, and Westchester)	Attn: Entity Control Holtsville, NY 00501 516-447-4955
New York (all other counties), Connecticut, Maine, Massachusetts, New Hampshire, Rhode Island, Vermont	Attn: Entity Control Andover, MA 05501 978-474-9717
Illinois, Iowa, Minnesota, Missouri, Wisconsin	Attn: Entity Control Stop 6800 2306 E. Bannister Rd. Kansas City, MO 64999 816-926-5999
Delaware, District of Columbia, Maryland, Pennsylvania, Virginia	Attn: Entity Control Philadelphia, PA 19255 215-516-6999
Indiana, Kentucky, Michigan, Ohio, West Virginia	Attn: Entity Control Cincinnati, OH 45999 859-292-5467

Kansas, New Mexico, Oklahoma, Texas	Attn: Entity Control Austin, TX 73301 512-460-7843
Alaska, Arizona, California (counties of Alpine, Amador, Butte, Calaveras, Colusa, Contra Costa, Del Norte, El Dorado, Glenn, Humboldt, Lake, Lassen, Marin, Mendocino, Modoc, Napa, Nevada, Placer, Plumas, Sacramento, San Joaquin, Shasta, Sierra, Siskiyou, Solano, Sonoma, Sutter, Tehama, Trinity, Yolo, and Yuba), Colorado, Idaho, Montana, Nebraska, Nevada, North Dakota, Oregon, South Dakota, Utah, Washington, Wyoming	Attn: Entity Control Mail Stop 6271 P.O. Box 9941 Ogden, UT 84201 801-620-7645
California (all other counties), Hawaii	Attn: Entity Control Fresno, CA 93888 559-452-4010
Alabama, Arkansas, Louisiana, Mississippi, North Carolina, Tennessee	Attn: Entity Control Memphis, TN 37501 901-546-3920
If you have no legal residence, principal place of business, or principal office or agency in any state	Attn: Entity Control Philadelphia, PA 19255 215-516-6999

Specific Instructions

The instructions that follow are for those items that are not self-explanatory. Enter N/A (nonapplicable) on the lines that do not apply.

Line 1. Enter the legal name of the entity applying for the EIN exactly as it appears on the social security card, charter, or other applicable legal document.

Individuals. Enter your first name, middle initial, and last name. If you are a sole proprietor, enter your individual name, not your business name. Enter your business name on line 2. Do not use abbreviations or nicknames on line 1.

Trusts. Enter the name of the trust.

Estate of a decedent. Enter the name of the estate.

Partnerships. Enter the legal name of the partnership as it appears in the partnership agreement. **Do not** list the names of the partners on line 1. See the specific instructions for line 7.

Corporations. Enter the corporate name as it appears in the corporation charter or other legal document creating it.

Plan administrators. Enter the name of the plan administrator. A plan administrator who already has an EIN should use that number.

Line 2. Enter the trade name of the business if different from the legal name. The trade name is the "doing business as" name.

Note: *Use the full legal name on line 1 on all tax returns filed for the entity. However, if you enter a trade name on line 2 and choose to use the trade name instead of the legal name, enter the trade name on all returns you file. To prevent processing delays and errors, always use either the legal name only or the trade name only on all tax returns.*

Line 3. Trusts enter the name of the trustee. Estates enter the name of the executor, administrator, or other fiduciary. If the entity applying has a designated person to receive tax information, enter that person's name as the "care of" person. Print or type the first name, middle initial, and last name.

Line 7. Enter the first name, middle initial, last name, and SSN of a principal officer if the business is a corporation; of a general partner if a partnership; of the owner of a single member entity that is disregarded as an entity separate from its owner; or of a grantor, owner, or trustor if a trust. If the person in question is an alien individual with a previously assigned individual taxpayer identification number (ITIN), enter the ITIN in the space provided, instead of an SSN. You are not required to enter an SSN or ITIN if the reason you are applying for an EIN is to make an entity classification election (see Regulations section 301.7701-1 through 301.7701-3), and you are a nonresident alien with no effectively connected income from sources within the United States.

Line 8a. Check the box that best describes the type of entity applying for the EIN. If you are an alien individual with an ITIN previously assigned to you, enter the ITIN in place of a requested SSN.

Caution: *This is not an election for a tax classification of an entity. See "Limited liability company (LLC)" below.*

If not specifically mentioned, check the "Other" box, enter the type of entity and the type of return that will be filed (for example, common trust fund, Form 1065). Do not enter N/A. If you are an alien individual applying for an EIN, see the **Line 7** instructions above.

Sole proprietor. Check this box if you file Schedule C, C-EZ, or F (Form 1040) and have a qualified plan, or are required to file excise, employment, or alcohol, tobacco, or firearms returns, or are a payer of gambling winnings. Enter your SSN (or ITIN) in the space provided. If you are a nonresident alien with are a nonresident alien with no effectively

connected income from sources within the United States, you do not need to enter an SSN or ITIN.

REMIC. Check this box if the entity has elected to be treated as a real estate mortgage investment conduit (REMIC). See the Instructions for Form 1066 for more information.

Other nonprofit organization. Check this box if the nonprofit organization is other than a church or church-controlled organization and specify the type of nonprofit organization (for example, an educational organization).

If the organization also seeks tax-exempt status, you must file either **Package 1023,** Application for Recognition of Exemption, or **Package 1024,** Application for Recognition of Exemption Under Section 501(a). Get **Pub. 557,** Tax Exempt Status for Your Organization, for more information.

Group exemption number (GEN). If the organization is covered by a group exemption letter, enter the four-digit GEN. (Do not confuse the GEN with the nine-digit EIN.) If you do not know the GEN, contact the parent organization. Get Pub. 557 for more information about group exemption numbers.

Withholding agent. If you are a withholding agent required to file Form 1042, check the "Other" box and enter "Withholding agent."

Personal service corporation. Check this box if the entity is a personal service corporation. An entity is a personal service corporation for a tax year only if:

● The principal activity of the entity during the testing period (prior tax year) for the tax year is the performance of personal services substantially by employee-owners, and

● The employee-owners own at least 10% of the fair market value of the outstanding stock in the entity on the last day of the testing period.

Personal services include performance of services in such fields as health, law, accounting, or consulting. For more information about personal service corporations, see the **Instructions for Forms 1120 and 1120-A,** and **Pub. 542,** Corporations.

Limited liability company (LLC). See the definition of limited liability company in the **Instructions for Form 1065,** U.S. Partnership Return of Income. An LLC with two or more members can be a partnership or an association taxable as a corporation. An LLC with a single owner can be an association taxable as a corporation or an entity disregarded as an entity separate from its owner. See Form 8832 for more details.

Note: *A domestic LLC with at least two members that does not file Form 8832 is classified as a partnership for Federal income tax purposes.*

● If the entity is classified as a partnership for Federal income tax purposes, check the "partnership" box.

● If the entity is classified as a corporation for Federal income tax purposes, check the "Other corporation" box and write "limited liability co." in the space provided.

● If the entity is disregarded as an entity separate from its owner, check the "Other" box and write in "disregarded entity" in the space provided.

Plan administrator. If the plan administrator is an individual, enter the plan administrator's SSN in the space provided.

Other corporation. This box is for any corporation other than a personal service corporation. If you check this box, enter the type of corporation (such as insurance company) in the space provided.

Household employer. If you are an individual, check the "Other" box and enter "Household employer" and your SSN. If you are a state or local agency serving as a tax reporting agent for public assistance recipients who become household employers, check the "Other" box and enter "Household employer agent." If you are a trust that qualifies as a household employer, you do not need a separate EIN for reporting tax information relating to household employees; use the EIN of the trust.

QSub. For a qualified subchapter S subsidiary (QSub) check the "Other" box and specify "QSub."

Line 9. Check only **one** box. Do not enter N/A.

Started new business. Check this box if you are starting a new business that requires an EIN. If you check this box, enter the type of business being started. **Do not** apply if you already have an EIN and are only adding another place of business.

Hired employees. Check this box if the existing business is requesting an EIN because it has hired or is hiring employees and is therefore required to file employment tax returns. **Do not** apply if you already have an EIN and are only hiring employees. For information on the applicable employment taxes for family members, see **Circular E,** Employer's Tax Guide (Publication 15).

Created a pension plan. Check this box if you have created a pension plan and need an EIN for reporting purposes. Also, enter the type of plan.

Note: *Check this box if you are applying for a trust EIN when a new pension plan is established.*

Banking purpose. Check this box if you are requesting an EIN for banking purposes only, and enter the banking purpose (for example, a bowling league for depositing dues or an investment club for dividend and interest reporting).

Changed type of organization. Check this box if the business is changing its type of organization, for example, if the business was a sole proprietorship and has been incorporated or has become a partnership. If you check this box, specify in the space provided the type of change made, for example, "from sole proprietorship to partnership."

Purchased going business. Check this box if you purchased an existing business. **Do not** use the former owner's EIN. **Do not** apply for a new EIN if you already have one. Use your own EIN.

Created a trust. Check this box if you created a trust, and enter the type of trust created. For example, indicate if the trust is a nonexempt charitable trust or a split-interest trust.

Note: *Do not check this box if you are applying for a trust EIN when a new pension plan is established. Check "Created a pension plan."*

Exception. Do **not** file this form for certain grantor-type trusts. The trustee does not need an EIN for the trust if the trustee furnishes the name and TIN of the grantor/owner and the address of the trust to all payors. See the Instructions for Form 1041 for more information.

Other (specify). Check this box if you are requesting an EIN for any other reason, and enter the reason.

Line 10. If you are starting a new business, enter the starting date of the business. If the business you acquired is already operating, enter the date you acquired the business. Trusts should enter the date the trust was legally created. Estates should enter the date of death of the decedent whose name appears on line 1 or the date when the estate was legally funded.

Line 11. Enter the last month of your accounting year or tax year. An accounting or tax year is usually 12 consecutive months, either a calendar year or a fiscal year (including a period of 52 or 53 weeks). A calendar year is 12 consecutive months ending on December 31. A fiscal year is either 12 consecutive months ending on the last day of any month other than December or a 52-53 week year. For more information on accounting periods, see **Pub. 538,** Accounting Periods and Methods.

Individuals. Your tax year generally will be a calendar year.

Partnerships. Partnerships generally must adopt one of the following tax years:

● The tax year of the majority of its partners,

● The tax year common to all of its principal partners,

● The tax year that results in the least aggregate deferral of income, or

● In certain cases, some other tax year.

See the Instructions for Form 1065 for more information.

REMIC. REMICs must have a calendar year as their tax year.

Personal service corporations. A personal service corporation generally must adopt a calendar year unless:

● It can establish a business purpose for having a different tax year, or

● It elects under section 444 to have a tax year other than a calendar year.

Trusts. Generally, a trust must adopt a calendar year except for the following:

● Tax-exempt trusts,

● Charitable trusts, and

● Grantor-owned trusts.

Line 12. If the business has or will have employees, enter the date on which the business began or will begin to pay wages. If the business does not plan to have employees, enter N/A.

Withholding agent. Enter the date you began or will begin to pay income to a nonresident alien. This also applies to individuals who are required to file Form 1042 to report alimony paid to a nonresident alien.

Line 13. For a definition of agricultural labor (farmwork), see **Circular A,** Agricultural Employer's Tax Guide (Publication 51).

Line 14. Generally, enter the exact type of business being operated (for example, advertising agency, farm, food or beverage establishment, labor union, real estate agency, steam laundry, rental of coin-operated vending machine, or investment club). Also state if the business will involve the sale or distribution of alcoholic beverages.

Governmental. Enter the type of organization (state, county, school district, municipality, etc.).

Nonprofit organization (other than governmental). Enter whether organized for religious, educational, or humane purposes, and the principal activity (for example, religious organization—hospital, charitable).

Mining and quarrying. Specify the process and the principal product (for example, mining bituminous coal, contract drilling for oil, or quarrying dimension stone).

Contract construction. Specify whether general contracting or special trade contracting. Also, show the type of work normally performed (for example, general contractor for residential buildings or electrical subcontractor).

Food or beverage establishments. Specify the type of establishment and state whether you employ workers who receive tips (for example, lounge—yes).

Trade. Specify the type of sales and the principal line of goods sold (for example, wholesale dairy products, manufacturer's representative for mining machinery, or retail hardware).

Manufacturing. Specify the type of establishment operated (for example, sawmill or vegetable cannery).

Signature. The application must be signed by (a) the individual, if the applicant is an individual, (b) the president, vice president, or other principal officer, if the applicant is a corporation, (c) a responsible and duly authorized member or officer having knowledge of its affairs, if the applicant is a partnership or other unincorporated organization, or (d) the fiduciary, if the applicant is a trust or an estate.

How To Get Forms and Publications

Phone. You can order forms, instructions, and publications by phone 24 hours a day, 7 days a week. Just call 1-800-TAX-FORM (1-800-829-3676). You should receive your order or notification of its status within 10 workdays.

Personal computer. With your personal computer and modem, you can get the forms and information you need using IRS's Internet Web Site at **www.irs.gov** or File Transfer Protocol at **ftp.irs.gov.**

CD-ROM. For small businesses, return preparers, or others who may frequently need tax forms or publications, a CD-ROM containing over 2,000 tax products (including many prior year forms) can be purchased from the National Technical Information Service (NTIS).

To order **Pub. 1796,** Federal Tax Products on CD-ROM, call **1-877-CDFORMS** (1-877-233-6767) toll free or connect to **www.irs.gov/cdorders**

Form SS-8

(Rev. June 1997)

Department of the Treasury
Internal Revenue Service

Determination of Employee Work Status for Purposes of Federal Employment Taxes and Income Tax Withholding

OMB No. 1545-0004

Paperwork Reduction Act Notice

We ask for the information on this form to carry out the Internal Revenue laws of the United States. You are required to give us the information. We need it to ensure that you are complying with these laws and to allow us to figure and collect the right amount of tax.

You are not required to provide the information requested on a form that is subject to the Paperwork Reduction Act unless the form displays a valid OMB control number. Books or records relating to a form or its instructions must be retained as long as their contents may become material in the administration of any Internal Revenue law. Generally, tax returns and return information are confidential, as required by Code section 6103.

The time needed to complete and file this form will vary depending on individual circumstances. The estimated average time is: **Recordkeeping, 34 hr., 55 min.; Learning about the law or the form, 12 min.;** and **Preparing and sending the form to the IRS, 46 min.** If you have comments concerning the accuracy of these time estimates or suggestions for making this form simpler, we would be happy to hear from you. You can write to the Tax Forms Committee, Western Area Distribution Center, Rancho Cordova, CA 95743-0001. **DO NOT send the** tax form to this address. Instead, see **General Information** for where to file.

Purpose

Employers and workers file Form SS-8 to get a determination as to whether a worker is an employee for purposes of Federal employment taxes and income tax withholding.

General Information

Complete this form carefully. If the firm is completing the form, complete it for **ONE** individual who is representative of the class of workers whose status is in question. If you want a written determination for more than one class of workers, complete a separate Form SS-8 for one worker

from each class whose status is typical of that class. A written determination for any worker will apply to other workers of the same class if the facts are not materially different from those of the worker whose status was ruled upon.

Caution: Form SS-8 is not a claim for refund of social security and Medicare taxes or Federal income tax withholding. Also, a determination that an individual is an employee does not necessarily reduce any current or prior tax liability. A worker must file his or her income tax return even if a determination has not been made by the due date of the return.

Where to file.—In the list below, find the state where your legal residence, principal place of business, office, or agency is located. Send Form SS-8 to the address listed for your location.

Location:	Send to:
Alaska, Arizona, Arkansas, California, Colorado, Hawaii, Idaho, Illinois, Iowa, Kansas, Minnesota, Missouri, Montana, Nebraska, Nevada, New Mexico, North Dakota, Oklahoma, Oregon, South Dakota, Texas, Utah, Washington, Wisconsin, Wyoming	Internal Revenue Service SS-8 Determinations P.O. Box 1231, Stop 4106 AUSC Austin, TX 78767
Alabama, Connecticut, Delaware, District of Columbia, Florida, Georgia, Indiana, Kentucky, Louisiana, Maine, Maryland, Massachusetts, Michigan, Mississippi, New Hampshire, New Jersey, New York, North Carolina, Ohio, Pennsylvania, Rhode Island, South Carolina, Tennessee, Vermont, Virginia, West Virginia, All other locations not listed	Internal Revenue Service SS-8 Determinations Two Lakemont Road Newport, VT 05855-1555
American Samoa, Guam, Puerto Rico, U.S. Virgin Islands	Internal Revenue Service Mercantile Plaza 2 Avenue Ponce de Leon San Juan, Puerto Rico 00918

Name of firm (or person) for whom the worker performed services

Name of worker

Address of firm (include street address, apt. or suite no., city, state, and ZIP code)

Address of worker (include street address, apt. or suite no., city, state, and ZIP code)

Trade name

Telephone number (include area code)
( )

Worker's social security number

Telephone number (include area code)
( )

Firm's employer identification number

Check type of firm for which the work relationship is in question:

☐ Individual ☐ Partnership ☐ Corporation ☐ Other (specify) ▶ ....

Important Information Needed To Process Your Request

This form is being completed by: ☐ Firm ☐ Worker

If this form is being completed by the worker, the IRS **must** have your permission to disclose your name to the firm.

Do you object to disclosing your name and the information on this form to the firm? . . . . ☐ Yes ☐ No

If you answer "Yes," the IRS cannot act on your request. **Do not complete the rest of this form unless the IRS asks for it.**

Under section 6110 of the Internal Revenue Code, the information on this form and related file documents will be open to the public if any ruling or determination is made. However, names, addresses, and taxpayer identification numbers will be removed before the information is made public.

Is there any other information you want removed? . . . . ☐ Yes ☐ No

If you check "Yes," we cannot process your request unless you submit a copy of this form and copies of all supporting documents showing, in brackets, the information you want removed. Attach a separate statement showing which specific exemption of section 6110(c) applies to each bracketed part.

Cat. No. 16106T

Form **SS-8** (Rev. 6-97)

This form is designed to cover many work activities, so some of the questions may not apply to you. You must answer ALL items or mark them "Unknown" or "Does not apply." If you need more space, attach another sheet.

Total number of workers in this class. (Attach names and addresses. If more than 10 workers, list only 10.) ▶ _____

This information is about services performed by the worker from _____ to _____
                                                                                 (month, day, year)   (month, day, year)

Is the worker still performing services for the firm? . . . . ☐ Yes ☐ No

● If "No," what was the date of termination? ▶ _____
                                                                  (month, day, year)

1a Describe the firm's business ....

b Describe the work done by the worker ....

....

2a If the work is done under a written agreement between the firm and the worker, attach a copy.

b If the agreement is not in writing, describe the terms and conditions of the work arrangement ....

....

c If the actual working arrangement differs in any way from the agreement, explain the differences and why they occur ....

....

3a Is the worker given training by the firm? . . . . ☐ Yes ☐ No
   ● If "Yes," what kind? ....
   ● How often? ....

b Is the worker given instructions in the way the work is to be done (exclusive of actual training in 3a)? . ☐ Yes ☐ No
   ● If "Yes," give specific examples ....

c Attach samples of any written instructions or procedures.

d Does the firm have the right to change the methods used by the worker or direct that person on how to
do the work? . . . . ☐ Yes ☐ No
   ● Explain your answer ....

....

e Does the operation of the firm's business require that the worker be supervised or controlled in the
performance of the service? . . . . ☐ Yes ☐ No
   ● Explain your answer ....

....

4a The firm engages the worker:
   ☐ To perform and complete a particular job only
   ☐ To work at a job for an indefinite period of time
   ☐ Other (explain) ....

b Is the worker required to follow a routine or a schedule established by the firm? . . . . ☐ Yes ☐ No
   ● If "Yes," what is the routine or schedule? ....

....

c Does the worker report to the firm or its representative?. . . . . ☐ Yes ☐ No
   ● If "Yes," how often? ....
   ● For what purpose? ....
   ● In what manner (in person, in writing, by telephone, etc.)? ....
   ● Attach copies of any report forms used in reporting to the firm.

d Does the worker furnish a time record to the firm? . . . . ☐ Yes ☐ No
   ● If "Yes," attach copies of time records.

5a State the kind and value of tools, equipment, supplies, and materials furnished by:
   ● The firm ....

....

   ● The worker ....

b What expenses are incurred by the worker in the performance of services for the firm? ....

....

c Does the firm reimburse the worker for any expenses? . . . . ☐ Yes ☐ No
   ● If "Yes," specify the reimbursed expenses ....

6a Will the worker perform the services personally? . . . . □ Yes □ No

 b Does the worker have helpers? . . . . □ Yes □ No

    ● If "Yes," who hires the helpers? □ Firm □ Worker

    ● If the helpers are hired by the worker, is the firm's approval necessary? . . . . □ Yes □ No

    ● Who pays the helpers? □ Firm □ Worker

    ● If the worker pays the helpers, does the firm repay the worker? . . . . □ Yes □ No

    ● Are social security and Medicare taxes and Federal income tax withheld from the helpers' pay? . . □ Yes □ No

    ● If "Yes," who reports and pays these taxes? □ Firm □ Worker

    ● Who reports the helpers' earnings to the Internal Revenue Service? □ Firm □ Worker

    ● What services do the helpers perform? ....

7 At what location are the services performed? □ Firm's □ Worker's □ Other (specify) ....

8a Type of pay worker receives:

    □ Salary   □ Commission   □ Hourly wage   □ Piecework   □ Lump sum   □ Other (specify) ....

 b Does the firm guarantee a minimum amount of pay to the worker? . . . . □ Yes □ No

 c Does the firm allow the worker a drawing account or advances against pay? . . . . □ Yes □ No

    ● If "Yes," is the worker paid such advances on a regular basis? . . . . □ Yes □ No

 d How does the worker repay such advances? ....

9a Is the worker eligible for a pension, bonus, paid vacations, sick pay, etc.? . . . . □ Yes □ No

    ● If "Yes," specify ....

 b Does the firm carry worker's compensation insurance on the worker? . . . . □ Yes □ No

 c Does the firm withhold social security and Medicare taxes from amounts paid the worker? . . . . □ Yes □ No

 d Does the firm withhold Federal income tax from amounts paid the worker? . . . . □ Yes □ No

 e How does the firm report the worker's earnings to the Internal Revenue Service?

    □ Form W-2   □ Form 1099-MISC   □ Does not report   □ Other (specify) ....

    ● Attach a copy.

 f Does the firm bond the worker? . . . . □ Yes □ No

10a Approximately how many hours a day does the worker perform services for the firm? ....

 b Does the firm set hours of work for the worker? . . . . □ Yes □ No

    ● If "Yes," what are the worker's set hours? _____ a.m./p.m. to _____ a.m./p.m. (Circle whether a.m. or p.m.)

 c Does the worker perform similar services for others? . . . . □ Yes □ No □ Unknown

    ● If "Yes," are these services performed on a daily basis for other firms? . . . . . □ Yes □ No □ Unknown

    ● Percentage of time spent in performing these services for:

    This firm .... % Other firms .... %   □ Unknown

    ● Does the firm have priority on the worker's time? . . . . □ Yes □ No

    ● If "No," explain ....

 d Is the worker prohibited from competing with the firm either while performing services or during any later period? . . . . □ Yes □ No

11a Can the firm discharge the worker at any time without incurring a liability? . . . . □ Yes □ No

    ● If "No," explain ....

 b Can the worker terminate the services at any time without incurring a liability? . . . . □ Yes □ No

    ● If "No," explain ....

12a Does the worker perform services for the firm under:

    □ The firm's business name   □ The worker's own business name   □ Other (specify) ....

 b Does the worker advertise or maintain a business listing in the telephone directory, a trade journal, etc.? . . . . □ Yes □ No □ Unknown

    ● If "Yes," specify ....

 c Does the worker represent himself or herself to the public as being in business to perform the same or similar services? . . . . □ Yes □ No □ Unknown

    ● If "Yes," how? ....

 d Does the worker have his or her own shop or office? . . . . □ Yes □ No □ Unknown

    ● If "Yes," where? ....

 e Does the firm represent the worker as an employee of the firm to its customers? . . . . □ Yes □ No

    ● If "No," how is the worker represented? ....

 f How did the firm learn of the worker's services? ....

13 Is a license necessary for the work? . . . . □ Yes □ No □ Unknown

    ● If "Yes," what kind of license is required? ....

    ● Who issues the license? ....

    ● Who pays the license fee?

14 Does the worker have a financial investment in a business related to the services performed? . . . . ☐ **Yes**   ☐ **No**   ☐ **Unknown**
- If "Yes," specify and give amount of the investment . . . .

15 Can the worker incur a loss in the performance of the service for the firm? . . . . ☐ **Yes**   ☐ **No**
- If "Yes," how? . . . .

16a Has any other government agency ruled on the status of the firm's workers? . . . . ☐ **Yes**   ☐ **No**
- If "Yes," attach a copy of the ruling.

b Is the same issue being considered by any IRS office in connection with the audit of the worker's tax return or the firm's tax return, or has it been considered recently? . . . . ☐ **Yes**   ☐ **No**
- If "Yes," for which year(s)? . . . .

17 Does the worker assemble or process a product at home or away from the firm's place of business? ☐ **Yes**   ☐ **No**
- If "Yes," who furnishes materials or goods used by the worker? ☐ Firm   ☐ Worker   ☐ Other
- Is the worker furnished a pattern or given instructions to follow in making the product? . . . . . ☐ **Yes**   ☐ **No**
- Is the worker required to return the finished product to the firm or to someone designated by the firm? ☐ **Yes**   ☐ **No**

18 Attach a detailed explanation of any other reason why you believe the worker is an employee or an independent contractor.

Answer items 19a through o only if the worker is a salesperson or provides a service directly to customers.

19a Are leads to prospective customers furnished by the firm? . . . . ☐ **Yes**   ☐ **No**   ☐ **Does not apply**
b Is the worker required to pursue or report on leads? . . . . ☐ **Yes**   ☐ **No**   ☐ **Does not apply**
c Is the worker required to adhere to prices, terms, and conditions of sale established by the firm? . . ☐ **Yes**   ☐ **No**
d Are orders submitted to and subject to approval by the firm? . . . . ☐ **Yes**   ☐ **No**
e Is the worker expected to attend sales meetings? . . . . ☐ **Yes**   ☐ **No**
- If "Yes," is the worker subject to any kind of penalty for failing to attend? . . . . ☐ **Yes**   ☐ **No**
f Does the firm assign a specific territory to the worker? . . . . ☐ **Yes**   ☐ **No**
g Whom does the customer pay?   ☐ Firm   ☐ Worker
- If worker, does the worker remit the total amount to the firm? . . . . ☐ **Yes**   ☐ **No**
h Does the worker sell a consumer product in a home or establishment other than a permanent retail establishment? . . . . ☐ **Yes**   ☐ **No**
i List the products and/or services distributed by the worker, such as meat, vegetables, fruit, bakery products, beverages (other than milk), or laundry or dry cleaning services. If more than one type of product and/or service is distributed, specify the principal one . . . .
j Did the firm or another person assign the route or territory and a list of customers to the worker? . . ☐ **Yes**   ☐ **No**
- If "Yes," enter the name and job title of the person who made the assignment . . . .
k Did the worker pay the firm or person for the privilege of serving customers on the route or in the territory? ☐ **Yes**   ☐ **No**
- If "Yes," how much did the worker pay (not including any amount paid for a truck or racks, etc.)? $ . . . .
- What factors were considered in determining the value of the route or territory? . . . .
l How are new customers obtained by the worker? Explain fully, showing whether the new customers called the firm for service, were solicited by the worker, or both . . . .
m Does the worker sell life insurance? . . . . ☐ **Yes**   ☐ **No**
- If "Yes," is the selling of life insurance or annuity contracts for the firm the worker's entire business activity? . . . . ☐ **Yes**   ☐ **No**
- If "No," list the other business activities and the amount of time spent on them . . . .
n Does the worker sell other types of insurance for the firm? . . . . ☐ **Yes**   ☐ **No**
- If "Yes," state the percentage of the worker's total working time spent in selling other types of insurance . . . . . . %
- At the time the contract was entered into between the firm and the worker, was it their intention that the worker sell life insurance for the firm: ☐ on a full-time basis   ☐ on a part-time basis
- State the manner in which the intention was expressed . . . .
o Is the worker a traveling or city salesperson? . . . . ☐ **Yes**   ☐ **No**
- If "Yes," from whom does the worker principally solicit orders for the firm? . . . .
- If the worker solicits orders from wholesalers, retailers, contractors, or operators of hotels, restaurants, or other similar establishments, specify the percentage of the worker's time spent in the solicitation . . . . %
- Is the merchandise purchased by the customers for resale or for use in their business operations? If used by the customers in their business operations, describe the merchandise and state whether it is equipment installed on their premises or a consumable supply

Under penalties of perjury, I declare that I have examined this request, including accompanying documents, and to the best of my knowledge and belief, the facts presented are true, correct, and complete.

Signature ▶   Title ▶   Date ▶

If the firm is completing this form, an officer or member of the firm must sign it. If the worker is completing this form, the worker must sign it. If the worker wants a written determination about services performed for two or more firms, a separate form must be completed and signed for each firm. Additional copies of this form may be obtained by calling 1-800-TAX-FORM (1-800-829-3676).

Form W-4 (2001)

Purpose. Complete Form W-4 so your employer can withhold the correct Federal income tax from your pay. Because your tax situation may change, you may want to refigure your withholding each year.

Exemption from withholding. If you are exempt, complete only lines 1, 2, 3, 4, and 7, and sign the form to validate it. Your exemption for 2001 expires February 18, 2002.

Note: *You cannot claim exemption from withholding if (1) your income exceeds $750 and includes more than $250 of unearned income (e.g., interest and dividends) and (2) another person can claim you as a dependent on their tax return.*

Basic instructions. If you are not exempt, complete the **Personal Allowances Worksheet** below. The worksheets on page 2 adjust your withholding allowances based on itemized deductions, certain credits, adjustments to

income, or two-earner/two-job situations. Complete all worksheets that apply. They will help you figure the number of withholding allowances you are entitled to claim. **However, you may claim fewer (or zero) allowances.**

Head of household. Generally, you may claim head of household filing status on your tax return only if you are unmarried and pay more than 50% of the costs of keeping up a home for yourself and your dependent(s) or other qualifying individuals. See line E below.

Tax credits. You can take projected tax credits into account in figuring your allowable number of withholding allowances. Credits for child or dependent care expenses and the child tax credit may be claimed using the **Personal Allowances Worksheet** below. See **Pub. 919**, How Do I Adjust My Tax Withholding? for information on converting your other credits into withholding allowances.

Nonwage income. If you have a large amount of nonwage income, such as interest or dividends,

consider making estimated tax payments using **Form 1040-ES,** Estimated Tax for Individuals. Otherwise, you may owe additional tax.

Two earners/two jobs. If you have a working spouse or more than one job, figure the total number of allowances you are entitled to claim on all jobs using worksheets from only one Form W-4. Your withholding usually will be most accurate when all allowances are claimed on the Form W-4 for the highest paying job and zero allowances are claimed on the others.

Check your withholding. After your Form W-4 takes effect, use Pub. 919 to see how the dollar amount you are having withheld compares to your projected total tax for 2001. Get Pub. 919 especially if you used the **Two-Earner/Two-Job Worksheet** on page 2 and your earnings exceed $150,000 (Single) or $200,000 (Married).

Recent name change? If your name on line 1 differs from that shown on your social security card, call 1-800-772-1213 for a new social security card.

Personal Allowances Worksheet (Keep for your records.)

A Enter "1" for **yourself** if no one else can claim you as a dependent . . . . **A** _____

B Enter "1" if:
- You are single and have only one job; or
- You are married, have only one job, and your spouse does not work; or
- Your wages from a second job or your spouse's wages (or the total of both) are $1,000 or less.

    . . **B** _____

C Enter "1" for your **spouse.** But, you may choose to enter -0- if you are married and have either a working spouse or more than one job. (Entering -0- may help you avoid having too little tax withheld.) . . . . **C** _____

D Enter number of **dependents** (other than your spouse or yourself) you will claim on your tax return . . . . **D** _____

E Enter "1" if you will file as **head of household** on your tax return (see conditions under **Head of household** above) . **E** _____

F Enter "1" if you have at least $1,500 of **child or dependent care expenses** for which you plan to claim a credit . . **F** _____

    (**Note:** *Do not include child support payments. See **Pub. 503**, Child and Dependent Care Expenses, for details.*)

G **Child Tax Credit** (including additional child tax credit):
- If your total income will be between $18,000 and $50,000 ($23,000 and $63,000 if married), enter "1" for each eligible child.
- If your total income will be between $50,000 and $80,000 ($63,000 and $115,000 if married), enter "1" if you have two eligible children, enter "2" if you have three or four eligible children, or enter "3" if you have five or more eligible children. **G** _____

H Add lines A through G and enter total here. (**Note:** *This may be different from the number of exemptions you claim on your tax return.*) ▶ **H** _____

For accuracy, complete all worksheets that apply.
- If you plan to **itemize or claim adjustments to income** and want to reduce your withholding, see the **Deductions and Adjustments Worksheet** on page 2.
- If you are **single,** have **more than one job** and your combined earnings from all jobs exceed $35,000, **or** if you are **married** and have a **working spouse or more than one job** and the combined earnings from all jobs exceed $60,000, see the **Two-Earner/Two-Job Worksheet** on page 2 to avoid having too little tax withheld.
- If **neither** of the above situations applies, **stop here** and enter the number from line H on line 5 of Form W-4 below.

- - - - - - - - - - - - - - - - **Cut here and give Form W-4 to your employer. Keep the top part for your records.** - - - - - - - - - - - - - -

Form **W-4**
Department of the Treasury
Internal Revenue Service

Employee's Withholding Allowance Certificate

▶ **For Privacy Act and Paperwork Reduction Act Notice, see page 2.**

OMB No. 1545-0010

2001

1 Type or print your first name and middle initial Last name	2 Your social security number

Home address (number and street or rural route)	3 ☐ Single ☐ Married ☐ Married, but withhold at higher Single rate.

Note: *If married, but legally separated, or spouse is a nonresident alien, check the Single box.*

City or town, state, and ZIP code	4 If your last name differs from that on your social security card, check here. You must call 1-800-772-1213 for a new card. ▶ ☐

5 Total number of allowances you are claiming (from line **H** above **or** from the applicable worksheet on page 2)   **5** _____

6 Additional amount, if any, you want withheld from each paycheck . . . . **6** $ _____

7 I claim exemption from withholding for 2001, and I certify that I meet **both** of the following conditions for exemption:
- Last year I had a right to a refund of **all** Federal income tax withheld because I had **no** tax liability **and**
- This year I expect a refund of **all** Federal income tax withheld because I expect to have **no** tax liability.

If you meet both conditions, write "Exempt" here . . . . ▶ **7** _____

Under penalties of perjury, I certify that I am entitled to the number of withholding allowances claimed on this certificate, or I am entitled to claim exempt status.

Employee's signature
(Form is not valid
unless you sign it.) ▶ _____   Date ▶ _____

8 Employer's name and address (Employer: Complete lines 8 and 10 only if sending to the IRS.)	9 Office code (optional)	10 Employer identification number

Cat. No. 10220Q

Deductions and Adjustments Worksheet

Note: *Use this worksheet only if you plan to itemize deductions, claim certain credits, or claim adjustments to income on your 2001 tax return.*

1   Enter an estimate of your 2001 itemized deductions. These include qualifying home mortgage interest, charitable contributions, state and local taxes, medical expenses in excess of 7.5% of your income, and miscellaneous deductions. (For 2001, you may have to reduce your itemized deductions if your income is over $132,950 ($66,475 if married filing separately). See **Worksheet 3** in Pub. 919 for details.) . . .   **1** $ _____

2   Enter: { $7,600 if married filing jointly or qualifying widow(er) / $6,650 if head of household / $4,550 if single / $3,800 if married filing separately }   . . . .   **2** $ _____

3   **Subtract** line 2 from line 1. If line 2 is greater than line 1, enter -0- . . . . .   **3** $ _____

4   Enter an estimate of your 2001 adjustments to income, including alimony, deductible IRA contributions, and student loan interest   **4** $ _____

5   **Add** lines 3 and 4 and enter the total (Include any amount for credits from **Worksheet 7** in Pub. 919.) .   **5** $ _____

6   Enter an estimate of your 2001 nonwage income (such as dividends or interest) . . . . . .   **6** $ _____

7   **Subtract** line 6 from line 5. Enter the result, but not less than -0- . . . . .   **7** $ _____

8   **Divide** the amount on line 7 by $3,000 and enter the result here. Drop any fraction . . . . . .   **8**   _____

9   Enter the number from the **Personal Allowances Worksheet,** line H, page 1 . . . . . .   **9**   _____

10   **Add** lines 8 and 9 and enter the total here. If you plan to use the **Two-Earner/Two-Job Worksheet,** also enter this total on line 1 below. Otherwise, **stop here** and enter this total on Form W-4, line 5, page 1 .   **10**   _____

Two-Earner/Two-Job Worksheet

Note: *Use this worksheet only if the instructions under line H on page 1 direct you here.*

1   Enter the number from line H, page 1 (or from line 10 above if you used the **Deductions and Adjustments Worksheet**)   **1**   _____

2   Find the number in **Table 1** below that applies to the **lowest** paying job and enter it here . . . . .   **2**   _____

3   If line 1 is **more than or equal to** line 2, subtract line 2 from line 1. Enter the result here (if zero, enter -0-) and on Form W-4, line 5, page 1. **Do not** use the rest of this worksheet . . . .   **3**   _____

Note: *If line 1 is **less than** line 2, enter -0- on Form W-4, line 5, page 1. Complete lines 4–9 below to calculate the additional withholding amount necessary to avoid a year end tax bill.*

4   Enter the number from line 2 of this worksheet . . . .   **4**   _____

5   Enter the number from line 1 of this worksheet . . . .   **5**   _____

6   **Subtract** line 5 from line 4 . . . .   **6**   _____

7   Find the amount in **Table 2** below that applies to the **highest** paying job and enter it here . . . . .   **7** $ _____

8   **Multiply** line 7 by line 6 and enter the result here. This is the additional annual withholding needed . .   **8** $ _____

9   Divide line 8 by the number of pay periods remaining in 2001. For example, divide by 26 if you are paid every two weeks and you complete this form in December 2000. Enter the result here and on Form W-4, line 6, page 1. This is the additional amount to be withheld from each paycheck . . . .   **9** $ _____

Table 1: Two-Earner/Two-Job Worksheet

Married Filing Jointly				All Others			
If wages from LOWEST paying job are—	Enter on line 2 above	If wages from LOWEST paying job are—	Enter on line 2 above	If wages from LOWEST paying job are—	Enter on line 2 above	If wages from LOWEST paying job are—	Enter on line 2 above
$0 - $4,000	0	42,001 - 47,000	8	$0 - $6,000	0	65,001 - 80,000	8
4,001 - 8,000	1	47,001 - 55,000	9	6,001 - 12,000	1	80,001 - 105,000	9
8,001 - 14,000	2	55,001 - 65,000	10	12,001 - 17,000	2	105,001 and over	10
14,001 - 19,000	3	65,001 - 70,000	11	17,001 - 22,000	3		
19,001 - 25,000	4	70,001 - 90,000	12	22,001 - 28,000	4		
25,001 - 32,000	5	90,001 - 105,000	13	28,001 - 40,000	5		
32,001 - 38,000	6	105,001 - 115,000	14	40,001 - 50,000	6		
38,001 - 42,000	7	115,001 and over	15	50,001 - 65,000	7		

Table 2: Two-Earner/Two-Job Worksheet

Married Filing Jointly		All Others	
If wages from HIGHEST paying job are—	Enter on line 7 above	If wages from HIGHEST paying job are—	Enter on line 7 above
$0 - $50,000	$440	$0 - $30,000	$440
50,001 - 100,000	800	30,001 - 60,000	800
100,001 - 130,000	900	60,001 - 120,000	900
130,001 - 250,000	1,000	120,001 - 270,000	1,000
250,001 and over	1,100	270,001 and over	1,100

Privacy Act and Paperwork Reduction Act Notice. We ask for the information on this form to carry out the Internal Revenue laws of the United States. The Internal Revenue Code requires this information under sections 3402(f)(2)(A) and 6109 and their regulations. **Failure to provide a properly completed form will result in your being treated as a single person who claims no withholding allowances; providing fraudulent information may also subject you to penalties.** Routine uses of this information include giving it to the Department of Justice for civil and criminal litigation, to cities, states, and the District of Columbia for use in administering their tax laws, and using it in the National Directory of New Hires.

You are not required to provide the information requested on a form that is subject to the Paperwork Reduction Act unless the form displays a valid OMB control number. Books or records relating to a form or its instructions must be retained as long as their contents may become material in the administration of any Internal Revenue law. Generally, tax returns and return information are confidential, as required by Code section 6103.

The time needed to complete this form will vary depending on individual circumstances. The estimated average time is: **Recordkeeping,** 46 min.; **Learning about the law or the form,** 13 min.; **Preparing the form,** 59 min. If you have comments concerning the accuracy of these time estimates or suggestions for making this form simpler, we would be happy to hear from you. You can write to the Tax Forms Committee, Western Area Distribution Center, Rancho Cordova, CA 95743-0001. **DO NOT** send the tax form to this address. Instead, give it to your employer.

DR-1
iNET R. 08/00

APPLICATION TO COLLECT AND/OR REPORT TAX IN FLORIDA

FLORIDA

DEPARTMENT OF REVENUE

1 Clearwater Service Center
19337 US Highway 19 N Ste 200
Clearwater FL 33764-3149
727-538-7400 (ET)

2 Cocoa Service Center
2428 Clearlake Rd Bldg M
Cocoa FL 32922-5710
321-504-0950 (ET)

3 Coral Springs Service Center
3111 N University Dr Ste 501
Coral Springs FL 33065-5096
954-346-3000 (ET)

4 Daytona Beach Service Center
1821 Business Park Blvd
Daytona Beach FL 32114-1230
904-274-6600 (ET)

5 Fort Myers Service Center
2295 Victoria Ave Ste 270
Fort Myers FL 33901-3871
941-338-2400 (ET)

6 Gainesville Service Center
2610 NW 43rd St Ste 2A
Gainesville FL 32606-7442
352-955-2170 (ET)

7 Hollywood Service Center
6565 Taft St Ste 300
Hollywood FL 33024-3000
954-967-1000 (ET)

8 Jacksonville Service Center
921 N Davis St Ste A250
Jacksonville FL 32209-6829
904-359-6070 (ET)

9 Key West Service Center
3118 Flagler Ave
Key West FL 33040-4698
305-292-6725 (ET)

10 Lake City Service Center
2651 W US Highway 90
Lake City FL 32055-3173
904-758-0420 (ET)

11 Lakeland Service Center
230 S Florida Ave Ste 101
Lakeland FL 33801-4622
863-499-2260 (ET)

12 Leesburg Service Center
734 N 3rd St Ste 117
Leesburg FL 34748-4498
352-360-6660 (ET)

13 Marianna Service Center
4230 Lafayette St Ste D
Marianna FL 32446-8234
850-482-9518 (CT)

14 Miami Service Center
8175 NW 12th St Ste 119
Miami FL 33126-1831
305-470-5001 (ET)

15 Naples Service Center
3200 Bailey Ln Ste 150
Naples FL 34105-8506
941-436-1050 (ET)

16 Orlando Service Center
5420 Diplomat Cir
Orlando FL 32810-5607
407-623-1141 (ET)

17 Panama City Service Center
703 W 15th St
Panama City FL 32401-2238
850-872-4165 (CT)

18 Pensacola Service Center
3670C N L St
Pensacola FL 32505-5217
850-595-5170 (CT)

19 Port Richey Service Center
6709 Ridge Rd Ste 300
Port Richey FL 34668-6842
727-841-4407 (ET)

20 Port Saint Lucie Service Center
900 E Prima Vista Blvd Ste 300
Port Saint Lucie FL 34952-2363
561-871-7620 (ET)

21 Sarasota Service Center
1991 Main St Ste 240
Sarasota FL 34236-5934
941-361-6001 (ET)

22 Tallahassee Service Center
2410 Allen Rd
Tallahassee FL 32312-2603
850-488-9719 (ET)

23 Tampa Service Center
6302 E Martin Luther King Blvd
Ste 100
Tampa FL 33619-1166
813-744-6344 (ET)

24 West Palm Beach Service Center
2468 Metrocentre Blvd
West Palm Beach FL 33407-3199
561-640-2800 (ET)

✳ SALES TAX
✳ USE TAX
✳ SOLID WASTE FEES
✳ GROSS RECEIPTS TAX
(TELECOMMUNICATION, UTILITIES AND DRY CLEANING)
✳ DOCUMENTARY STAMP TAX

Registration Information
5050 W Tennessee St
Tallahassee, FL 32399-0100
850-488-9750

Tax Information Services
1-800-352-3671 (Florida Only)
850-488-6800
TDD: 1-800-367-8331

Internet Site
http://sun6.dms.state.fl.us/dor/
Tax Law Library
http://taxlaw.state.fl.us

FAX on Demand
Forms Retrieval Line
850-922-3676 (anytime)

FLORIDA

DEPARTMENT OF REVENUE

APPLICATION TO COLLECT AND/OR REPORT TAX IN FLORIDA

Information

DR-1
R. 08/00

Who must apply? You may be required to register to collect, accrue and remit the tax or fees listed below if you are engaged in any of the activities listed beneath the tax.

Sales Tax

- Sales, leases or licenses to use certain property or goods (tangible personal property)
- Sales and rentals/admissions, amusement machine receipts, and vending machine receipts for all taxable items
- Repair or alteration of tangible personal property
- Leases or licenses to use commercial real property (includes management companies)
- Rental of transient (six months or less) living or sleeping accommodations (includes management companies)
- Sales or rental of self-propelled, power-drawn, or power-driven farm equipment
- Sales of telecommunication services and electric power or energy
- Sales of prepaid telephone calling cards
- Sales of commercial pest control services, non-residential building cleaning services, commercial/residential burglary and security services, or detective services
- Sales of secondhand goods

Use Tax

- Any taxable purchases, including farm equipment, that were not taxed by the seller at the time of purchase
- Any purchases originally for resale, but later used or consumed by your business or for personal use
- Use of dyed diesel fuel for off-road purposes

Solid Waste Fees

- Sales of new tires for motor vehicles
- Sales of new or remanufactured lead-acid batteries
- Rental or lease of motor vehicles to others

Gross Receipts Tax

- Sales of telecommunication services (i.e., long distance, local and cellular telephone service, paging, pay phones, telex, telegram, teletype services, by-pass providers)
- Sales of electric power or gas
- Sales of two-way cable television services
- Sales of dry-cleaning services (plants or drop-off facilities)

Documentary Stamp Tax

- Entering into written financing agreements (more than five transactions per month)
- Making title loans
- Self-financing dealers (buy here – pay here)
- Banks, mortgage companies, and consumer finance companies
- Promissory notes

222

What if my business has more than one location? Sales Tax: You must complete a separate application for each location. Gross Receipts Tax for Utilities: You have the option of registering all locations under one account number or separately registering each location. Documentary Stamp Tax: You must register each location where books and records are maintained.

What if I am managing commercial rental property for others? If you are registering any number of properties for commercial rental, you must use this application (Form DR-1) for each parcel of property.

What if I am managing living accommodation rental property for others? Agents, representatives, or management companies may register multiple properties for short-term (six months or less) rentals on behalf of individual property owners by using Form DR-1C, *Application for Collective Registration for Rental of Living or Sleeping Accommodations.* Property managers must first obtain a Certificate of Registration in each county where properties are located.

What should I receive from the Department once I register?
1. A Certificate of Registration for the tax(es) for which you registered.
2. Personalized returns for filing, with instructions.
3. For active sales tax dealers, an Annual Resale Certificate will accompany the Certificate of Registration.

What is an Annual Resale Certificate? Beginning February 1, 2000, the Department issues Annual Resale Certificates to active, registered sales tax dealers. These certificates will expire on December 31 of the calendar year for which they are issued. The Annual Resale Certificate allows businesses to make tax-exempt purchases from their suppliers, provided the item is purchased for resale. A copy of a current Annual Resale Certificate must be extended to the supplier; otherwise, tax must be paid on the transaction at the time of purchase. Tax Information Publication (TIP) #99A01-34 explains the "new" resale provisions. The Annual Resale Certificate <u>cannot</u> be used to make tax-exempt purchases or rentals of property or services that are not for resale. **Misuse of the Annual Resale Certificate will subject the user to penalties as provided by law.**

What are my responsibilities?
1. Complete and return this application to the Florida Department of Revenue with the applicable registration fee. IF MAILING, DO NOT SEND CASH. SEND CHECK OR MONEY ORDER.
2. Complete and file tax returns and remit the tax due. A return must be filed even if no tax is due.
3. Notify the Department if your address changes, your business entity or activity changes, you open additional locations, you close your business, etc.
4. Provide your certificate or account number on all returns, remittance or correspondence.

Are seminars offered? Yes, for a schedule of upcoming seminars, visit our Internet site or call the service center nearest you.

Before returning application, remove this page and retain for future reference.

iNET APPLICATION TO COLLECT AND/OR REPORT TAX IN FLORIDA

Please use BLACK or BLUE ink ONLY and type or print clearly.

Indicate tax registration you are seeking.
This application is for (check all that apply):

* The $5 registration fee does not apply if this application is for a business location outside the state of Florida.

✔	Tax Type	Fee Due	Complete Sections
	Sales and Use Tax	$5.00*	A, B, F
	Use Tax Only	No fee	A, B, F
	Solid Waste Fees	No fee	A, B, C, F
	Gross Receipts Tax on Utilities	No fee	A, D, F
	Gross Receipts Tax on Dry Cleaning	$30.00	A, D, F
	Documentary Stamp Tax	No fee	A, E, F

SECTION A — BUSINESS INFORMATION

1. Check the box that applies:

   ☐ New business   ☐ New business location   ☐ Change of county location (from one Florida county to another)   ☐ Change of legal entity (proprietorship to partnership; partnership to corporation, etc.)

   This change is effective (enter date): ☐☐/☐☐/☐☐☐☐   List below your old account or registration number(s) to be canceled.
   month   day   year

   a. If this is a seasonal business (not open year-round), list the first and last months of your season.   First month _____   Last month _____

2. Beginning date of business activity for this location: ☐☐/☐☐/☐☐☐☐
   month   day   year

   Provide the date this business location became or will become liable for Florida tax(es). Do not use your incorporation date unless that is the date your business became liable for the tax. If you have been in business longer than 30 days prior to registering, contact the taxpayer service center nearest you.

   If incorporated, please provide incorporation date: ☐☐/☐☐/☐☐☐☐
   month   day   year

** PLEASE TYPE OR PRINT CLEARLY **

3. **Business Name:** business, trade, or fictitious (d/b/a) name

   Business Telephone Number:

4. **Owner Name:** legal name of individual, principal partner, or corporation

   Owner Telephone Number:

5. **Business Location:** Complete physical address of business or real property. Home-based businesses and flea market/craft show vendors must use their home address. <u>Listing a post office box, private mailbox or rural route number is not permitted.</u>

   Is business located within city limits? ☐ Yes ☐ No

   City/State/ZIP: County:

6. **Mail to the Attention of:**

   Mailing Address:

   City/State/ZIP: County:

   Would you like to receive correspondence via e-mail? ☐ Yes ☐ No   **E-mail address:**

7. If you have a **Consolidated Sales Tax Number** and want to include this business location, please complete the following:

   Consolidated registration name on record with the Florida Department of Revenue.
   If you want to obtain a new consolidated number contact the Department and request Form DR-1CON.

   8 0 ☐☐ ☐☐☐☐☐☐ ☐☐☐

8. Business Entity Identification Number (If an FEIN is not required for your business entity, the Social Security Number of the owner will be accepted.)

   a. Federal Employer Identification Number (FEIN): ☐☐—☐☐☐☐☐☐☐

   b. Social Security Number (SSN) of Owner: ☐☐☐—☐☐—☐☐☐☐

FOR DOR OFFICE USE ONLY

mo	qu	sa	an	se	oc		org code		SUT No.		kind		sic		office code
☐	☐	☐	☐	☐	☐		☐☐		☐☐ ☐☐ ☐☐☐☐☐☐☐		☐ ☐		☐☐☐☐		☐☐

PM/Delivery ☐☐/☐☐/☐☐

Doc Stamp No. ☐☐ ☐☐☐☐☐☐☐ ☐☐☐

Gross Receipts No. ☐☐ ☐☐☐☐☐☐☐ ☐☐☐

9. Identify proprietors or owners, partners, officers, members, or trustees. Include the person whose Social Security Number is listed under Question 8. **Without this information, processing of your application may be delayed.**

Name Title	Social Security Number Driver License Number and State	Home Address City, State, ZIP Code	Telephone Number

10. **Type of Ownership** - Check one box to describe the structure of your business entity.

☐ Sole Proprietorship - an individual or individual and spouse

☐ Partnership - two or more persons or entities that have entered into a voluntary contract

☐ Corporation - legal entity created under the authority of the corporation laws of a state (includes professional service corporation)

☐ Limited Liability Company - legal entity created under the authority of the limited liability company laws of a state (includes professional limited liability company)

☐ Trust - legal entity created by a grantor for the benefit of designated beneficiaries under the laws of a state and valid trust agreement

☐ Other (please specify) _____

11. If a partnership, corporation or limited liability company, provide your fiscal year ending date: ☐☐ / ☐☐
                                                        month   day

12. If incorporated or registered in Florida, provide your corporate document/registration number: _____

If not incorporated or registered in Florida, attach a copy of your Articles of Incorporation as filed with your state's corporate registration authority. For Florida corporation information, call the Florida Department of State, Division of Corporations at 850-488-9000.

13. Business Bank Information – provide the following information about the bank where tax money from this business will be deposited:

_____   ☐ Personal Account   ☐ Business Account
Bank Name

_____
Bank Street Address   City   State   ZIP

14. Is your business location rented? Yes ☐   No ☐   If yes, and you <u>do not operate from your home</u>, provide the following information.

Owner or Landlord's Name _____

Address _____

City/State/ZIP _____

Telephone No. _____

15. Describe your primary (more than 50%) business activity that generates revenue.

_____

_____

16. Does your business activity include (check all that apply):

☐ Sales of property or goods at retail (to consumers)?
☐ Sales of property or goods at wholesale (to registered dealers)?
☐ Sales of secondhand goods?
☐ Rental of commercial real property to individuals or businesses?
☐ Rental of transient living or sleeping accommodations (for six months or less)?
☐ Rental of equipment or other property or goods to individuals or businesses?
☐ Renting/leasing motor vehicles to others?
☐ Repair or alteration of tangible personal property?
☐ Charging admission or membership fees?

☐ Placing and operating coin-operated amusement machines at business locations belonging to others?
☐ Placing and operating vending machines at business locations belonging to others?
☐ Providing any of the following services? (Check all that apply.)
  ☐ Pest control for nonresidential buildings
  ☐ Cleaning services for nonresidential buildings
  ☐ Detective services
  ☐ Protection services
  ☐ Security alarm system monitoring

17. What products do you purchase for resale to your customers, or include in a finished product you manufacture for sale?

_____

_____

SECTION B — SALES TAX ACTIVITY

COIN-OPERATED AMUSEMENT MACHINES

18. Are coin-operated amusement machines being operated at your business location? If yes, answer question 19. .... ☐ Yes ☐ No

19. Do you have a written agreement that requires someone other than yourself to obtain Amusement Machine Certificates for any of the machines at your location? If yes, provide their information below. .... ☐ Yes ☐ No

_____

Name   Address   Telephone No.

NOTE: You must complete an *Application for Amusement Machine Certificate* (Form DR-18) if you answered YES to question 18 <u>and</u> NO to question 19.

CONTRACTORS

20. Are you a contractor who improves real property? If yes, answer questions 21-24. .... ☐ Yes ☐ No
21. a. Do you operate under formal written contracts? .... ☐ Yes ☐ No
   b. If yes, under what type of contracts do you operate?
     ☐ Lump Sum ☐ Cost Plus ☐ Fixed Fee ☐ Other (please explain) _____
22. Do you purchase materials or supplies from vendors located outside of Florida? .... ☐ Yes ☐ No
23. Does your company have a current occupational license in any Florida county? .... ☐ Yes ☐ No
   If yes, please list all counties in which you are licensed and the corresponding license numbers.

_____

24. Do you fabricate/manufacture any building component at a location other than contract sites? .... ☐ Yes ☐ No

MOTOR FUEL

25. Do you sell any type of fuel, or use off-road diesel fuel? If yes, answer questions 26 and 27. .... ☐ Yes ☐ No
26. a. Do you make retail sales of gasoline, diesel fuel, or aviation fuel at posted retail prices? .... ☐ Yes ☐ No
   b. If yes to #26a, does this business exist as a marina? .... ☐ Yes ☐ No
   c. If yes to #26a, provide your Florida Department of Environmental Protection Facility Registration Number for this location. ☐☐☐☐☐☐☐
27. Do you use non-taxed, dyed diesel fuel for non-highway purposes? .... ☐ Yes ☐ No

SECTION C — SOLID WASTE FEES

28. Do you sell tires or batteries, or rent/lease motor vehicles to others? If yes, answer questions 29-31. .... ☐ Yes ☐ No
29. Do you make retail sales of new tires for motorized vehicles (either separately or as a part of a vehicle)? .... ☐ Yes ☐ No
30. Do you make retail sales of new or remanufactured lead-acid batteries sold separately or as a component part of another product such as automobiles, golf carts, boats, etc.? .... ☐ Yes ☐ No
31. Are you in the business of renting or leasing vehicles that transport fewer than nine passengers to individuals or businesses? .... ☐ Yes ☐ No

32. Do you sell telecommunication services, electrical power, or gas? If yes, answer questions a-l and 33, below. .... ☐Yes ☐No
Do you sell:
   a. Electrical power? .... ☐Yes ☐No
   b. Natural or manufactured gas? .... ☐Yes ☐No
   c. Pay phone service? .... ☐Yes ☐No
   d. 2-way cable television service? .... ☐Yes ☐No
   e. Telex, telegram, teletype service? .... ☐Yes ☐No
   f. Cellular service? .... ☐Yes ☐No
   g. Pagers and beepers? .... ☐Yes ☐No
   h. Long distance (inter-exchange service)? .... ☐Yes ☐No
   i. Shared tenant utility service? .... ☐Yes ☐No
   j. Alternative access vendor service? .... ☐Yes ☐No
   k. Telephone service (local exchange)? .... ☐Yes ☐No
   l. Other telecommunication service (by-pass provider, etc.)? .... ☐Yes ☐No
   Describe _____

33. Do you provide billing services to telecommunication service providers? .... ☐Yes ☐No
34. Do you own or operate a dry-cleaning dry drop-off facility or plant in Florida? .... ☐Yes ☐No
    If yes, enclose the $30 dry-cleaning registration fee.
35. Do you produce or import perchloroethylene? .... ☐Yes ☐No
    If yes, you must complete an *Application for Florida License to Produce or Import Taxable Pollutants* (Form DR-166).

SECTION E — DOCUMENTARY STAMP TAX

36. Do you make sales, finalized by written agreements, that do not require recording by the
    Clerk of the Court, <u>but do require documentary stamp tax to be paid</u>? If yes, answer questions 37-39. .... ☐Yes ☐No

37. Do you anticipate five or more transactions subject to documentary stamp tax per month? .... ☐Yes ☐No

38. Do you anticipate your average monthly documentary stamp tax remittance to be less than $80 per month? .... ☐Yes ☐No

39. Is this application being completed to register your <u>first</u> location to collect documentary stamp tax? .... ☐Yes ☐No
    If no, and this application is for additional locations, please list name and address of each additional location.
    (Attach additional sheets if needed.)
    Location Name _____   Address _____

    City, State, ZIP _____   Telephone Number _____

SECTION F — APPLICANT DECLARATION AND SIGNATURE

This application will not be accepted if not signed by the applicant.

Please note that any person (including employees, corporate directors, corporate officers, etc.) who is required to collect, truthfully account for, and pay any taxes and willfully fails to do so shall be liable for penalties under the provisions of §213.29, Florida Statutes (F.S.). All information provided by the applicant is confidential as provided in §213.053, F.S., and is not subject to Florida Public Records Law (§119.07, F.S.).

Under penalties of perjury, I declare that I have read the foregoing application and that the facts stated in it are true.

SIGN
HERE ▷ _____   Title _____

Print Name _____   Date _____

Amount Enclosed: $_____ (See table on top of page 1 for <u>Fee Due</u> with this application.)

NOTE: If the applicant is a sole proprietorship, the proprietor or owner must sign; if a partnership, a partner must sign; if a corporation, an officer of the corporation authorized to sign on behalf of the corporation must sign; if a limited liability company, a member must sign; if a trust, the grantor or a trustee must sign. **The signature of any other person will not be accepted.**

USE THIS CHECKLIST TO ENSURE FAST PROCESSING OF YOUR APPLICATION.

✓ Complete application in its entirety.
✓ Sign and date the application.
✓ Attach check or money order for appropriate registration fee amount.

✓ Mail to: **FLORIDA DEPARTMENT OF REVENUE**
              5050 W TENNESSEE ST
              TALLAHASSEE FL 32399-0100
    ┊ **You may also mail or deliver to any service center listed on front page.**

Employer Registration Report

iNET UCS-1
R. 02/01

FLORIDA
DEPARTMENT
OF REVENUE

□□□□□□□—□
UC Employer Account Number

Please complete front and back in black ink. (Print or type)

1. **Federal Employer Identification Number (FEIN)** □□—□□□□□□□

2. **Legal name of employer** _____
   (Sole proprietor, partners, or corporate name, etc.)

3. **Trade name (d/b/a)** _____ **Telephone No.** (____) _____

4. **Mailing address** _____
   (Street address, City, State, ZIP)

5. **Business location** _____
   (Florida street address, City, State, ZIP)

6. **Legal entity types** (check only one)

   □ Sole proprietor   □ Partnership   □ S corporation
   □ Limited partnership   □ Joint venture   □ Limited liability corp
   □ Corporation   □ Government instrumentality □ Other
   (state incorporated) _____   (city, county, special district, etc.)   (specify) _____

7. **Employer type** (check all that apply)

   □ Regular   □ Domestic (household)
   □ Agricultural   □ Agricultural citrus   □ Agricultural crew chief
   □ Non-profit organization □ Political instrumentality □ Purchased existing business
   (501(c)(3) attached)   (city, county, or municipality)   (complete Form UCS-1S)

8. **Did your business pay federal unemployment tax in another state in the previous or current calendar year?**
   □ Yes   □ No   State(s) _____ Year(s) _____

9. **Date of first employment in Florida** _____
   (This includes full and part-time employees and officers of a corporation. If resuming employment, enter date resumed.)

10. **Do you use, or intend to use, the services of individuals you consider to be self-employed?**
    □ Yes   □ No   If yes, please explain type(s) of services performed. _____
    _____

11. **Do you wish to elect to extend the coverage of the law to your workers who are not covered because they work in exempt employment or because you are not liable for the payment of unemployment tax?**
    □ Yes   □ No   If yes, proper forms will be furnished by this agency. The election would require liability for a period of at least one complete calendar year.

12. **General information**
    A. Information regarding owner, partners, or officers. (Attach a separate sheet if necessary.)

    Full name _____   Title _____
    Home address _____   City, State, ZIP _____
    Home phone number _____ SSN _____

    Full name _____   Title _____
    Home address _____   City, State, ZIP _____
    Home phone number _____ SSN _____

    Full name _____   Title _____
    Home address _____   City, State, ZIP _____
    Home phone number _____ SSN _____

Internet address: www.myflorida.com/dor

B. Payroll maintained by (accountant, bookkeeper, etc.)

Name _____

Address _____

City, State, ZIP _____

Phone # (_____) _____

13. Standard Industrial Classification (SIC) List the location and nature of business conducted in Florida. If you need more space, please attach separate page.

Enter city and county for each work site	Principal products or services (be specific)	Average # of employees
_____	_____	_____
_____	_____	_____
_____	_____	_____
_____	_____	_____

Does the above work site(s) provide support for any other units of the company? ☐ Yes ☐ No

If yes, please indicate whether these services are: ☐ Administrative ☐ Research
☐ Other (specify) _____

14. Did you acquire a business?

☐ Yes ☐ No If you answered yes, you must complete a *Report to Determine Succession* (Form UCS-1S). Please call 1-800-352-3671 to request one.

Note: The *Report to Determine Succession* must be **postmarked within 90 days of the acquisition date to be considered timely.**

15. Enter the number of weeks you had workers in the current year _____

Enter the number of weeks you had workers in the preceding year _____

16. Your Florida gross payroll by calendar quarters (may estimate if not available)

	Quarter ending March 31	Quarter ending June 30	Quarter ending September 30	Quarter ending December 31
Current year _____	$ _____	$ _____	$ _____	$ _____
Prior year _____	$ _____	$ _____	$ _____	$ _____

BE SURE THAT ALL QUESTIONS ARE ANSWERED BEFORE SIGNING

Pursuant to section 443.171(7), Florida Statutes, the information given above is true and correct and is given for the purpose of determining liability under said law and the undersigned is authorized to execute this report on behalf of the employing unit named.

Legal name of employing unit _____

By (print name) _____

Signature _____

Date _____ Title _____

This registration report is due by the end of the month that follows the calendar quarter in which your business commenced operation.

Return address:	Department of Revenue	**For assistance call:**
	P.O. Box 6510	1-800-482-8293
	Tallahassee, FL 32314-6510	

DR-15CS Sales and Use Tax Return — Line-by-Line Instructions

Line A, Sales

"Sales" means the total of all wholesale and retail sales transactions. "Sales" includes, but is not limited to:

- Sales, leases, or licenses to use certain property or goods (tangible personal property)
- Sales and rentals/admissions, amusement machine receipts, and vending machine receipts for all items other than food and beverage
- Leases or licenses to use real property
- Purchases of machines including vending/amusement machines, machine parts, and repairs thereof
- Sales, purchases, and/or rentals of self-propelled, power-drawn, power-driven farm equipment (2.5% rate)
- Sales/purchases of commercial telecommunications services, electric power or energy (7% rate)
- Sales/purchases of prepaid telephone calling cards (6% rate)
- Sales/purchases of dyed diesel fuel for off-road use, including all vessels (6% rate)

Amusement and Vending Machine Sales - Operators of amusement machines and vending machines containing items other than food and beverage should compute their gross sales by dividing the total receipts from the machine(s) by the appropriate divisor for the county tax rate where the machine(s) is located (see table below). Prepaid telephone calling cards sold through vending machines are taxable at 6%. Amusement machine operators must complete Lines 24 (a) and (b) on the back of the return. Operators of vending machines containing food or beverage items, see Line E.

Sales/Surtax Rate	Amusement Divisor	Other Vended Items (Including Prepaid Telephone Calling Cards) Divisor
6.0%	1.040	1.0659
6.5%	1.045	1.0707
6.75%	1.0475	1.0727
7.0%	1.050	1.0749
7.5%	1.055	1.0791

Column 1, Gross Sales

Enter the total amount of gross sales. **Do not include tax collected in this amount.**

Column 2, Exempt Sales

Enter the total amount of tax-exempt sales included in Line A, Column 1. Enter zero, if none. Tax-exempt sales include, but are not limited to, sales for resale, sales of items specifically exempt, and sales to exempt organizations.

Column 3, Taxable Amount

Subtract total exempt sales from gross sales and enter the taxable amount. If you report sales exempt from discretionary sales surtax, complete Lines 15(a) and 15(b) on the back of the return. Report sales subject to discretionary sales surtax on Line 16.

Column 4, Tax Collected

Enter the total amount of tax collected, including discretionary sales surtax. Report the discretionary sales surtax collected on Line 17 on the back of the return.

Line B, Taxable Purchases

Taxable purchases are goods or services you have used or consumed that were not taxed by your suppliers and not purchased for resale (e.g., from catalogs, the Internet, or local or out-of-state vendors), and taxable items originally purchased untaxed for resale but later used or consumed by the business. You must pay use tax on these taxable purchases. The use tax rate is the same as the sales tax rate (6% plus the applicable discretionary sales surtax rate). Use tax must be remitted on the return for the collection period during which the item is used or consumed. Purchases of: 1) self-propelled, power-drawn, or power-driven farm equipment; 2) dyed diesel fuel for off-road use; 3) commercial telecommunications services; and 4) and electric power or energy used that were not taxed at the time of purchase must be included in Line A.

Column 1, Gross Sales Not Applicable

Column 2, Exempt Sales Not Applicable

Column 3, Taxable Amount

Enter the total amount of purchases used or consumed that were not taxed by suppliers and not for resale. If you report purchases exempt from discretionary sales surtax, complete Lines 15(a) and 15(b) on the back of the return. Report purchases subject to discretionary sales surtax on Line 16.

Column 4, Tax Collected

Enter the total amount of use tax owed, including discretionary sales surtax. Report the discretionary sales surtax owed on Line 17 on the back of the return.

Line C, Services

Taxable services include commercial pest control, commercial/residential burglary/security, commercial maintenance/cleaning and detective services.

Column 1, Gross Sales

Enter the total amount of gross sales of services and untaxed services. Do not include tax collected in this amount.

Column 2, Exempt Sales

Enter the total amount of tax-exempt sales of services included in Line C, Column 1. Enter zero, if none.

Column 3, Taxable Amount

Subtract total exempt sales from gross sales and enter the taxable amount. If you report sales of services exempt from discretionary sales surtax, complete Line 15(b) on the back of the return. Report sales of services subject to discretionary sales surtax on Line 16.

Column 4, Tax Collected

Enter the amount of total tax collected, including discretionary sales surtax. Report the discretionary sales surtax collected on Line 17 on the back of the return.

Line D, Transient Rentals

Transient rentals are leases or rentals of short term (6 months or less) living accomodations such as hotels, motels, condominiums, apartments, houses, etc. Declared exempt facilities, which include migrant labor camps, travel trailer parks, mobile home parks, and recreational vehicle parks, are not subject to tax (see Section 212.03, F.S.). If the 11th and 12th digits of your certificate of registration number are 39 or 85, you must report transient rentals on this line. Other rentals are reported on Line A.

Column 1, Gross Sales

Enter the total gross sales of amounts charged for transient rentals only. Do not include tax collected in this amount.

Column 2, Exempt Sales

Enter the total amount of tax-exempt transient rentals included in Line D, Column 1. Enter zero, if none.

Column 3, Taxable Amount

Subtract total exempt transient rentals from total gross transient rentals and enter the taxable amount. If you report transient rentals exempt from discretionary sales surtax, complete Lines 15(a) and 15(b) on the back of the return. Report transient rentals subject to discretionary sales surtax on Line 16.

Column 4, Tax Collected
Enter the amount of total tax collected based on the transient rental rate including discretionary sales surtax. Report the discretionary sales surtax collected on Line 17 on the back of the return.

Line E, Food & Beverage Vending
Operators of food and beverage vending machines should compute their gross sales by dividing the total receipts from the machine(s) by the appropriate food and beverage divisor for the county where the machine(s) is located.

Effective July 1, 1999	
Sales/Surtax Rate	Food and Beverage Divisor
6.0%	1.0645
6.5%	1.0686
6.75%	1.0706
7.0%	1.0726
7.5%	1.0767

Column 1, Gross Sales
Enter the total amount of gross sales computed from food and beverage vending machines receipts. This amount does not include tax collected.

Column 2, Exempt Sales
Enter the total amount of tax-exempt sales included on Line E, Column 1. Enter zero, if none.

Column 3, Taxable Amount
Subtract total exempt sales from gross sales and enter the taxable amount. If you report sales exempt from discretionary sales surtax, complete Line 15(b) on the back of the return. Report vending sales subject to discretionary sales surtax on Line 16.

Column 4, Tax Collected
Enter the total amount of tax collected, including discretionary sales surtax. Report the discretionary sales surtax collected on Line 17 on the back of the return.

Line 5, Total Amount of Tax Collected
Add all the amounts in Column 4, Lines A through E, and enter the total amount of tax collected. If discretionary sales surtax was collected, it must be included in this amount.

Line 6, Less Lawful Deductions
Enter the total amount of all allowable tax deductions. **Do not report sales tax credit memos on this line (see Line 8 instructions).**

Lawful deductions include tax refunded by you to your customers because of returned goods, allowances for damaged merchandise, tax paid by you on purchases of goods intended for use or consumption but resold instead, enterprise zone jobs credits, and any other deductions allowed by law.
- Do not include documentation with your return. Documentation to support lawful deductions may be requested later.
- **If you are claiming enterprise zone jobs credits, first complete Lines 18-20.**

Line 7, Total Tax Due
Subtract Line 6 from Line 5 and enter the amount. If negative, enter zero (0).

Lines 8 and 9, Estimated Tax
If you paid $200,000 or more sales and use tax (excluding any discretionary sales surtax) on returns filed for the period July 1, 1999 through June 30, 2000 (Florida's fiscal year), you must make an estimated sales tax payment every month, **starting with the December 2000 return due January 1, 2001.** Do not pay estimated tax if this is your final return. If you have questions about estimated tax, contact the Department.

Line 8, Less Estimated Tax Paid/DOR Credit Memo(s)
Enter the total amount of estimated tax paid last month and sales tax credit memos issued by the Florida Department of Revenue (DOR). If the DOR credit memo(s) exceeds the total tax due on Line 7, claim the remaining credit memo balance on Line 8 of your next return. If this is your final return, contact the Department to request an *Application for Refund.*

Line 9, Plus Estimated Tax Due Current Month
Enter the total amount of estimated tax due as calculated using one of the three methods as follows.

Three Methods for Computing Estimated Tax
The percentage factor for calculating estimated tax is 60%. Estimated tax liability is based only on Florida sales and use tax due (Form DR-15, Line 7, Total Tax Due minus discretionary sales surtax). **If you forget to enter or incorrectly calculate estimated tax, you cannot amend your return.** Compute your estimated tax liability by one of the following methods:

Method 1
Calculate 60% of your average sales tax liability for those months during the previous calendar year that you reported taxable transactions. If you correctly calculate your estimated tax using this method, you will not be assessed a penalty for underpayment of estimated tax.

Example: When completing your December 2000 return, calculate your average sales tax liability for the 2000 calendar year. To calculate your average, complete the following steps:

Step 1. Review all of your 2000 sales tax returns (including December return).

Step 2. Add together the amounts from Line 7 (minus any discretionary sales surtax) for all 2000 returns.

Step 3. Divide the total of all Line 7 amounts by the number of returns filed with tax due on Line 7. This is your 2000 average sales tax liability.

Step 4. Multiply your 2000 average sales tax liability by 60%.

Step 5. Enter the amount determined in Step 4 on Line 9.

Method 2
Calculate 60% of your sales tax collected during the same month of the previous calendar year.

Example: When completing your December 2000 return, look at your January 2000 return and multiply the amount from Line 7 (minus discretionary sales surtax) by 60%. Enter that amount on Line 9.

Method 3
Calculate 60% of the tax collected for the collection period following this return.

Example: When completing your December 2000 return, your estimated tax liability is 60% of what you will collect (minus discretionary sales surtax) for the January 2001 return. Enter that amount on Line 9.

Line 10, Amount Due
Enter the result of Line 7 minus Line 8 plus Line 9. The amount entered on Line 10 cannot be negative. If this calculation results in a negative amount, contact Taxpayer Services.

Line 11, Less Collection Allowance
If your return and payment are filed on time, enter your collection allowance. The collection allowance is 2.5% (.025) of the first $1,200 of tax due from Line 10, not to exceed $30. If late, enter zero and proceed to Lines 12 and 13.

Line 12, Plus Penalty
Penalty for Late Filing - If your return or payment is late, enter 10% of the amount due from Line 10 for each 30 days, or fraction thereof, that your return or payment is late (see Table of Penalty Charges below). The maximum total penalty is 50% of the amount due. The minimum penalty for monthly filers is $10. For quarterly, semi-annual and annual filers, the minimum penalty is $5. Minimum penalties apply, even if you file a "zero tax due" return.

Penalty for Underpayment of Estimated Tax - If you underpaid your last month's estimated tax on Line 9, a **"specific"** penalty of 10% is due on the underpaid amount. This penalty is added to the late filing penalty (see Table of Penalty Charges).

Table of Penalty Charges			
Days Late	**Rate**	**Days Late**	**Rate**
1-30	10%	61-90	30%
31-60	20%	91-120	40%
		over 120	50%

Line 13, Plus Interest

If your return or payment is late, interest is owed on the tax due (Line 10). Interest rates are established using the formula in Section 213.235 Florida Statutes and updated on January 1 and July 1 each year. To obtain interest rates, visit our Internet site or contact Taxpayer Services.

To compute interest owed, first calculate the prorated daily interest factor by dividing the interest rate for the filing period by 365 days. Next, estimate the number of days your return is late by counting from the LATE AFTER date listed on the front of the return until the date the return will be postmarked by the U.S. Postal Service or hand delivered to the Department. Finally, multiply the amount of tax due by the number of days late and then by the daily interest rate factor.

Interest Calculation Worksheet			
Tax Due	**Days Late**	**Daily Interest**	**Interest Due**
X	X	*varies =	

*Daily interest = the current interest rate ÷ 365

Line 14, Amount Due with Return

If your return and payment are filed on time, subtract Line 11 from Line 10 and enter the amount due. If your return or payment is late, add Lines 12 and 13 to Line 10 and enter the amount. The amount due on Line 14 is the tax you owe, including discretionary sales surtax. Be sure that you have completed all applicable lines on the back of the return.

Electronic Funds Transfer Check Box

If you transmitted your payment electronically, check the box in the bottom left corner of your DR-15 return.

Instructions for Completing Back of Return

Signature

Sign and date your DR-15 return. For corporations, the authorized corporate officer must sign. If someone else prepared the return, the preparer also must sign and date the return in the space provided.

Discretionary Sales Surtax (Lines 15-17)

Discretionary sales surtax must be collected and reported when taxable merchandise or services are sold or delivered to a location within a county imposing a surtax. Out-of-state vendors making sales or deliveries of taxable merchandise or services into Florida must also collect and report surtax. Use the discretionary sales surtax rate imposed by the county where the merchandise or service is delivered. For motor vehicle and mobile home sales, use the surtax rate of the county where the vehicle will be registered. (Refer to Page 4 for county rates.) Only the first $5,000 on a single sale of tangible personal property is subject to surtax. **The entire amount of rentals of real property or services is subject to surtax.** Discretionary sales surtax must be included with tax reported on Lines A through E in Column 4 of your DR-15 return. Do not remit discretionary sales surtax collected to the County Tax Collector's Office.

Line 15(a), Exempt Amount of Items over $5,000

Enter the amount in excess of $5,000 of any single taxable item sold or purchased for more than $5,000. Example: If a single item is sold for $7,000, enter $2,000 (the amount over $5,000) on Line 15(a).

Line 15(b), Other Amounts in Column 3 Not Subject to Surtax

Enter the amount of taxable sales or purchases included in Column 3 not subject to discretionary sales surtax. Do not include amounts shown on Line 15(a).

Line 16, Taxable Sales/Purchases Subject to Surtax

Enter the amount of taxable sales or purchases on which discretionary sales surtax was collected or due. List amounts in the appropriate column, based on the applicable discretionary sales surtax rate.

Line 17, Surtax Amounts Collected

Enter the total amount of discretionary sales surtax collected in the appropriate column. Do not include state sales tax in this amount.

Lines 18-20, Enterprise Zone Jobs Credits

An *Application for the Credit Against Sales Tax for Job Creation* (Form DR-15JZ) must be filed and approved prior to claiming enterprise zone credits. After approval by your local Enterprise Zone Development Agency, claim your sales tax enterprise zone jobs credits by completing the appropriate lines (Lines 18-20). Enter your **Enterprise Zone Number** in the space provided.

Line 18(a), Eligible Employees' Wages x 5% =

For new employees who earn more than $1,500 per month and are not participating in the Welfare Transition Program (WTP), multiply the first $1,500 of their wages by 5% and enter the amount.

Line 18(b), Eligible WTP Participants' Wages x 15% =

For new employees who earn more than $1,500 per month and are participating in the Welfare Transition Program (WTP), multiply the first $1,500 of their wages by 15% and enter the amount.

Line 18(c), Eligible Employees' Wages x 15% =

If 20% or more of your permanent full-time employees are residents of an enterprise zone, multiply eligible employees' (new employees earning not more than $1,500 per month) wages by 15% and enter the amount.

Line 18(d), Eligible Employees' Wages x 10% =

If less than 20% of your permanent full-time employees are residents of an enterprise zone, multiply eligible employees' (new employees earning not more than $1,500 per month) wages by 10% and enter the amount.

Line 19(a), Total Enterprise Zone Jobs Credits

Enter the total of Lines 18(a), 18(b), 18(c), and 18(d).

Line 19(b), Lawful Deductions for Enterprise Zone Jobs Credits Filers Only

Enter the total amount of lawful deductions (applicable to Enterprise Zone filers only). If you have lawful deductions but have no Enterprise Zone Jobs Credits, only complete Line 6 of your return. For more information about deductions, see the Lawful Deductions section of these instructions.

Line 20, Total Enterprise Zone Jobs Credits and Lawful Deductions for Enterprise Zone Filers

Enter the total of Lines 19(a) and 19(b). Also enter this amount on Line 6 on the front of your return.

Line 21, Taxable Sales/Purchases/Rentals of Farm Equipment

Enter the taxable amount of sales, purchases, or rentals of self-propelled, power-drawn, or power-driven farm equipment subject to the 2.5% rate. This amount should also be included in Line A, Column 3.

Line 22, Taxable Sales/Purchases of Commercial Telecommunications/Electric Power or Energy

Enter the taxable amount of sales or purchases of commercial telecommunications services and electric power or energy subject to the 7% rate. If the sale or purchase of commercial telecommunications services or electric power/energy occurred in a county that imposes a discretionary sales surtax, the tax rate would be 7% plus the applicable discretionary sales surtax rate.

Line 23, Taxable Sales/Purchases of Diesel Fuel

Enter the total amount of dyed diesel fuel sales or purchases (subject to sales or use tax) used in self-propelled off-road equipment, including vessels.

Line 24(a), Number of Amusement Machines

Enter the total number of amusement machines operated at your location(s). Do not include vending machines.

Line 24(b), Taxable Sales from Amusement Machines

Enter the amount of taxable sales from amusement machines.

3

DR-15CSN
R. 01/01

Discretionary Sales Surtax Information

These taxes are distributed to local governments throughout the state. **The amount of money distributed is based upon how you complete each tax return.** Dealers should impose the discretionary sales surtax on taxable sales when delivery occurs in a county that imposes surtax. For motor vehicles and mobile home sales, use the surtax rate of the county where the vehicle will be registered. Only the first $5,000 on a single sale of tangible personal property is subject to discretionary sales surtax.

Discretionary Sales Surtax Rates for 2001 (as of December 20, 2000)

COUNTY	TOTAL SURTAX RATE		EFFECTIVE DATE	EXPIRATION DATE	COUNTY	TOTAL SURTAX RATE		EFFECTIVE DATE	EXPIRATION DATE
Alachua	None				Jefferson	1%		Jun 1, 1988	May 2003
Baker	1%		Jan 1, 1994	None	Lafayette	1%		Sep 1, 1991	Aug 2006
Bay	1%	(.5%)	Jan 1, 1995	May 2003	Lake	1%		Jan 1, 1988	Dec 2002
		(.5%)	May 1, 1998	Apr 2008	Lee	None			
Bradford	1%		Mar 1, 1993	None	Leon	1%		Dec 1, 1989	Dec 2019
Brevard	None				Levy	1%		Oct 1, 1992	None
Broward	None				Liberty	1%		Nov 1, 1992	None
Calhoun	1%		Jan 1, 1993	Dec 2008	Madison	1%		Aug 1, 1989	Jul 2004
Charlotte	1%		Apr 1, 1995	Dec 2002	Manatee	None			
Citrus	None				Marion	None			
Clay	1%		Feb 1, 1990	Dec 2019	Martin	1%		Jan 1, 1999	Dec 2001 ◄
Collier	None				Miami-Dade	.5%		Jan 1, 1992	None
Columbia	1%		Aug 1, 1994	None	Monroe	1.5%	(1%)	Nov 1, 1989	Dec 2018
Dade	See Miami-Dade for rates.						(.5%)	Jan 1, 1996	Dec 2005
De Soto	1%		Jan 1, 1988	Dec 2002	Nassau	1%		Mar 1, 1996	None
Dixie	1%		Apr 1, 1990	Mar 2005	Okaloosa	None			
Duval	1%	(.5%)	Jan 1, 1989	None	Okeechobee	1%		Oct 1, 1995	None
		(.5%)	Jan 1, 2001	Dec 2030	Orange	None			
Escambia	1.5%	(1%)	Jun 1, 1992	May 2007	Osceola	1%		Sep 1, 1990	Aug 2025
		(.5%)	Jan 1, 1998	Dec 2002	Palm Bch	None			
Flagler	1%		Dec 1, 1990	Nov 2005	Pasco	None			
Franklin	None				Pinellas	1%		Feb 1, 1990	Jan 2010
Gadsden	1%		Jan 1, 1996	None	Polk	None			
Gilchrist	1%		Oct 1, 1992	None	Putnam	None			
Glades	1%		Feb 1, 1992	Jan 2007	St. Johns	None			
Gulf	.5%		Jul 1, 1997	Jun 2017	St. Lucie	.5%		Jul 1, 1996	Jun 2006
Hamilton	1%		Jul 1, 1990	Jun 2005	Santa Rosa	.5%		Oct 1, 1998	Sep 2008
Hardee	1%		Jan 1, 1998	Dec 2004	Sarasota	1%		Sep 1, 1989	Aug 2004
Hendry	1%		Jan 1, 1988	Dec 2002	Seminole	1%		Oct 1, 1991	Sep 2001 ◄
Hernando	.5%		Jan 1, 1999	Dec 2003	Sumter	1%		Jan 1, 1993	None
Highlands	1%		Nov 1, 1989	Oct 2019	Suwannee	1%		Jan 1, 1988	Dec 2002
Hillsborough	*	(.5%)	Dec 1, 1996	Nov 2026	Taylor	1%		Aug 1, 1989	Dec 2029
		(.25%)	Oct 1, 1997	Sep 2001 ◄	Union	1%		Feb 1, 1993	Dec 2005
		(.5%)	Oct 1, 2001	Sep 2005	Volusia	None			
Holmes	1%		Oct 1, 1995	Sep 2006	Wakulla	1%		Jan 1, 1988	Dec 2002
Indian River	1%		Jun 1, 1989	May 2004	Walton	1%		Feb 1, 1995	None
Jackson	1.5%	(1%)	Jun 1, 1995	May 2010	Washington	1%		Nov 1, 1993	None
		(.5%)	Jul 1, 1996	Jun 2006					

* Through September 30, 2001, the total surtax rate for Hillsborough County is .75 percent. Effective October 1, 2001, the total surtax rate for Hillsborough County is 1 percent.

Internet address: **http://sun6.dms.state.fl.us/dor/**

FLORIDA

DEPARTMENT OF REVENUE

Sales and Use Tax Return

DR-15CS
R. 01/01

iNET

Please complete this return.
Attach your check or money order and mail to:

Florida Department of Revenue
5050 W. Tennessee Street
Tallahassee, FL 32399-0125

TAXPAYER COPY

Sales and Use Tax Return

DR-15 R. 01/01

Florida	1. Gross Sales	2. Exempt Sales	3. Taxable Amount	4. Tax Collected	
A. Sales					20
B. Taxable Purchases					21
C. Services					22
D. Transient Rentals					23
E. Food & Beverage Vending					24

Transient Rental Rate:	Surtax Rate:	Collection Period			
			5.	Total Amount of Tax Collected	25
			6.	**Less Lawful Deductions**	26
			7.	Total Tax Due	27
			8.	**Less Est. Tax Paid/ DOR Memo**	28
Certificate Number	SIC	FEIN/SSN	9.	Plus Est. Tax Due Current Month	29
			10	Amount Due	30
			11.	**Less Collection Allowance**	31
iNET		STOP	12.	Plus Penalty	HD
		After the 20th, see instructions. Lines 11-13	13.	Plus Interest	
			14.	**Amount Due with Return**	

Payment is due on the 1st and LATE
if postmarked or hand delivered after
If late, include penalty and interest. Be sure to sign and date the reverse side.

☐ Electronic Funds Transfer:
Check here if payment was transmitted electronically.

Do Not Write in This Space

Sales and Use Tax Return

DR-15 R. 01/01

Florida	1. Gross Sales	2. Exempt Sales	3. Taxable Amount	4. Tax Collected	
A. Sales					20
B. Taxable Purchases					21
C. Services					22
D. Transient Rentals					23
E. Food & Beverage Vending					24

Transient Rental Rate:	Surtax Rate:	Collection Period			
			5.	Total Amount of Tax Collected	25
			6.	**Less Lawful Deductions**	26
			7.	Total Tax Due	27
			8.	**Less Est. Tax Paid/ DOR Memo**	28
Certificate Number	SIC	FEIN/SSN	9.	Plus Est. Tax Due Current Month	29
			10	Amount Due	30
			11.	**Less Collection Allowance**	31
iNET		STOP	12.	Plus Penalty	HD
		After the 20th, see instructions. Lines 11-13	13.	Plus Interest	
			14.	**Amount Due with Return**	

Payment is due on the 1st and LATE
if postmarked or hand delivered after
If late, include penalty and interest. Be sure to sign and date the reverse side.

☐ Electronic Funds Transfer:
Check here if payment was transmitted electronically.

Do Not Write in This Space

DUE DATE OF RETURN — Your return and payment are **due on the 1st and late after the 20th day of the month** following each collection period. If the 20th falls on a Saturday, Sunday, or state or federal holiday, your return must be postmarked or hand delivered on the first business day following the 20th. **You must file a return even if no tax is due.**

SIGNATURE REQUIREMENT — Sign and date your DR-15 return. For corporations, the authorized corporate officer must sign. If someone else prepared the return, the preparer also must sign and date the return in the space provided.

Fraud Penalties

FRAUDULENT CLAIM OF EXEMPTION; PENALTIES — Section 212.085, Florida Statutes (F.S.), provides that when any person fraudulently, for the purpose of evading tax, issues to a vendor or to any agent of the state a certificate or statement in writing in which he or she claims exemption from sales tax, such person, in addition to being liable for payment of the tax plus a mandatory penalty of 200% of the tax, shall be liable for fine and punishment as provided by law for a conviction of a felony of third degree, as provided in s. 775.082, s. 775.083, or s. 775.084, F.S.

SPECIFIC FRAUD PENALTY — Any person who makes a false or fraudulent return with a willful intent to evade payment of any tax or fee imposed under Ch. 212, F.S., in addition to the other penalties provided by law, will be liable for a specific penalty of 100% of the tax bill or fee and, upon conviction, for fine and punishment as provided in s. 775.082, s. 775.083, or s. 775.084, F.S.

FAILURE TO COLLECT AND PAY OVER TAX OR AN ATTEMPT TO EVADE OR DEFEAT TAX — Any person who is required to collect, truthfully account for, and pay over any tax enumerated in Ch. 201, Ch. 206, or Ch. 212, F.S., and who willfully fails to collect such tax or truthfully account for and pay over such tax or willfully attempts in any manner to evade or defeat such tax or the payment thereof; or any officer or director of a corporation who has administrative control over the collection and payment of such tax and who willfully directs any employee of the corporation to fail to collect or pay over, evade, defeat, or truthfully account for such tax will, in addition to other penalties provided by law, be liable to a penalty equal to twice the total amount of the tax evaded or not accounted for or paid over, as provided in s. 213.29, F.S.

I hereby certify that this return has been examined by me and to the best of my knowledge and belief is a true and complete return.

Signature of Taxpayer   Date   Signature of Preparer   Date

15(a). Exempt Amount of Items Over $5,000 _____

15(b). Other Amounts in Column 3 **NOT** Subject to Surtax _____

Discretionary Sales Surtax

	At .25% Rate	At .5% Rate	At .75% Rate	At 1.0% Rate	At 1.25% Rate	At 1.5% Rate
16. Taxable Sales/Purchases Subject to Surtax						
17. Surtax Amounts Collected						

Enterprise Zone Number _____

18(a). Eligible Employees' Wages x 5% = _____   **18(b).** Eligible WTP Participants' Wages x 15% = _____

18(c). Eligible Employees' Wages x 15% = _____   **18(d).** Eligible Employees' Wages x 10% = _____

19(a). Total of Lines 18(a) through 18(d) _____   **19(b).** Enterprise Zone Lawful Deductions _____

20. Total of Lines 19(a) and 19(b) [Also enter this total on Line 6 on front of coupon] .... **20.** _____

21. Taxable Sales/Purchases/Rentals of **Farm Equipment** — 2.5% Rate (included in Line A) .... **21.** _____

22. Taxable Sales/Purchases of **Commercial Telecommunications/Electric Power or Energy** — 7% Rate (included in Line A) ..... **22.** _____

23. Taxable Sales/Purchases of **Diesel Fuel** — 6% Rate (included in Line A) .... **23.** _____

24(a). Number of **Amusement Machines** _____   **24(b).** Taxable Sales from Amusement Machines (included in Line A) _____

I hereby certify that this return has been examined by me and to the best of my knowledge and belief is a true and complete return.

Signature of Taxpayer   Date   Signature of Preparer   Date

15(a). Exempt Amount of Items Over $5,000 _____

15(b). Other Amounts in Column 3 **NOT** Subject to Surtax _____

Discretionary Sales Surtax

	At .25% Rate	At .5% Rate	At .75% Rate	At 1.0% Rate	At 1.25% Rate	At 1.5% Rate
16. Taxable Sales/Purchases Subject to Surtax						
17. Surtax Amounts Collected						

Enterprise Zone Number _____

18(a). Eligible Employees' Wages x 5% = _____   **18(b).** Eligible WTP Participants' Wages x 15% = _____

18(c). Eligible Employees' Wages x 15% = _____   **18(d).** Eligible Employees' Wages x 10% = _____

19(a). Total of Lines 18(a) through 18(d) _____   **19(b).** Enterprise Zone Lawful Deductions _____

20. Total of Lines 19(a) and 19(b) [Also enter this total on Line 6 on front of coupon] .... **20.** _____

21. Taxable Sales/Purchases/Rentals of **Farm Equipment** — 2.5% Rate (included in Line A) .... **21.** _____

22. Taxable Sales/Purchases of **Commercial Telecommunications/Electric Power or Energy** — 7% Rate (included in Line A) ..... **22.** _____

23. Taxable Sales/Purchases of **Diesel Fuel** — 6% Rate (included in Line A) .... **23.** _____

24(a). Number of **Amusement Machines** _____   **24(b).** Taxable Sales from Amusement Machines (included in Line A) _____

UCT-83
R. 10/00

To Employees-

- **YOUR EMPLOYER**

is registered with the Department of Revenue as a liable employer under the Florida Unemployment Compensation Law and you, as employees, are covered by unemployment insurance. **Unemployment taxes are paid by the employer and, by law cannot be deducted from the employee's wages.**

- You may be eligible to receive unemployment compensation benefits if you meet the following requirements:

  1. You must be totally or partially unemployed through no fault of your own.
  2. You must register for work and file a claim at the Jobs and Benefits Office.
  3. You must have sufficient employment and wages.
  4. You must be ABLE to work and AVAILABLE for work.

- You may file a claim for partial unemployment for any week you work less than full time due to lack of work if your wages during that week are less than your weekly benefit amount.

- You must report all earnings while claiming benefits. Failure to do so is a third degree felony with a maximum penalty of 5 years imprisonment and a $5,000 fine.

- Any claimant who was discharged for misconduct connected with work may be disqualified from 1 to 52 weeks and until the claimant becomes re-employed and has earned at least 17 times the weekly benefit amount.

- Any claimant who voluntarily quits a job without good cause attributable to the employer may be disqualified until the claimant becomes re-employed and has earned at least 17 times the weekly benefit amount.

- If you have any questions regarding unemployment compensation benefits, inquire at the nearest One Stop Career Center or call the Agency for Workforce Innovation at 850-921-3475.

Agency for Workforce Innovation
Office of Workforce Services
1320 Executive Center Drive
Suite 120, Atkins Building
Tallahassee, Florida 32399-0667

This notice must be posted in accordance with Section 443.151(1) of the Florida Unemployment Compensation Law.

Internet: http://sun6.dms.state.fl.us/dor/

Form **8300**

(Rev. August 1997)

Department of the Treasury
Internal Revenue Service

Report of Cash Payments Over $10,000 Received in a Trade or Business

▶ See instructions for definition of cash.

▶ Use this form for transactions occurring after July 31, 1997.

Please type or print.

OMB No. 1545-0892

1 Check appropriate box(es) if: **a** ☐ Amends prior report; **b** ☐ Suspicious transaction.

Part I Identity of Individual From Whom the Cash Was Received

2 If more than one individual is involved, check here and see instructions . . . . ▶ ☐

3 Last name	**4** First name	**5** M.I.	**6** Taxpayer identification number

7 Address (number, street, and apt. or suite no.)	**8** Date of birth . . ▶ M M D D Y Y Y Y (see instructions)

9 City	**10** State	**11** ZIP code	**12** Country (if not U.S.)	**13** Occupation, profession, or business

14 Document used to verify identity: **a** Describe identification ▶ ------------------------

b Issued by ------------------ **c** Number ------------------

Part II Person on Whose Behalf This Transaction Was Conducted

15 If this transaction was conducted on behalf of more than one person, check here and see instructions . . . . . ▶ ☐

16 Individual's last name or Organization's name	**17** First name	**18** M.I.	**19** Taxpayer identification number

20 Doing business as (DBA) name (see instructions)	Employer identification number

21 Address (number, street, and apt. or suite no.)	**22** Occupation, profession, or business

23 City	**24** State	**25** ZIP code	**26** Country (if not U.S.)

27 Alien identification: **a** Describe identification ▶ ------------------------

b Issued by ------------------ **c** Number ------------------

Part III Description of Transaction and Method of Payment

28 Date cash received M M D D Y Y Y Y	**29** Total cash received $ .00	**30** If cash was received in more than one payment, check here . . . ▶ ☐	**31** Total price if different from item 29 $ .00

32 Amount of cash received (in U.S. dollar equivalent) (must equal item 29) (see instructions):

a U.S. currency $ _____ .00 (Amount in $100 bills or higher $ _____ .00)

b Foreign currency $ _____ .00 (Country ▶ _____)

c Cashier's check(s) $ _____ .00   } Issuer's name(s) and serial number(s) of the monetary instrument(s) ▶ ----------

d Money order(s) $ _____ .00

e Bank draft(s) $ _____ .00

f Traveler's check(s) $ _____ .00

33 Type of transaction

a ☐ Personal property purchased   **f** ☐ Debt obligations paid

b ☐ Real property purchased   **g** ☐ Exchange of cash

c ☐ Personal services provided   **h** ☐ Escrow or trust funds

d ☐ Business services provided   **i** ☐ Bail bond

e ☐ Intangible property purchased   **j** ☐ Other (specify) ▶

34 Specific description of property or service shown in 33. (Give serial or registration number, address, docket number, etc.) ▶ ------------------------

Part IV Business That Received Cash

35 Name of business that received cash	**36** Employer identification number

37 Address (number, street, and apt. or suite no.)	Social security number

38 City	**39** State	**40** ZIP code	**41** Nature of your business

42 Under penalties of perjury, I declare that to the best of my knowledge the information I have furnished above is true, correct, and complete.

Signature of authorized official

Title of authorized official

43 Date of signature M M D D Y Y Y Y	**44** Type or print name of contact person	**45** Contact telephone number ( )

For Paperwork Reduction Act Notice, see page 4.

Cat. No. 62133S

Form **8300** (Rev. 8-97)

Multiple Parties
(Complete applicable parts below if box 2 or 15 on page 1 is checked)

Part I   Continued—Complete if box 2 on page 1 is checked

3 Last name	**4** First name	**5** M.I.	**6** Taxpayer identification number

7 Address (number, street, and apt. or suite no.)	**8** Date of birth . . ▶ (see instructions)	M M D D Y Y Y Y

9 City	**10** State	**11** ZIP code	**12** Country (if not U.S.)	**13** Occupation, profession, or business

14 Document used to verify identity: **a** Describe identification ▶ ....
    b Issued by   **c** Number

3 Last name	**4** First name	**5** M.I.	**6** Taxpayer identification number

7 Address (number, street, and apt. or suite no.)	**8** Date of birth . . ▶ (see instructions)	M M D D Y Y Y Y

9 City	**10** State	**11** ZIP code	**12** Country (if not U.S.)	**13** Occupation, profession, or business

14 Document used to verify identity: **a** Describe identification ▶ ....
    b Issued by   **c** Number

Part II   Continued—Complete if box 15 on page 1 is checked

16 Individual's last name or Organization's name	**17** First name	**18** M.I.	**19** Taxpayer identification number

20 Doing business as (DBA) name (see instructions)	Employer identification number

21 Address (number, street, and apt. or suite no.)	**22** Occupation, profession, or business

23 City	**24** State	**25** ZIP code	**26** Country (if not U.S.)

27 Alien identification: **a** Describe identification ▶ ....
    b Issued by   **c** Number

16 Individual's last name or Organization's name	**17** First name	**18** M.I.	**19** Taxpayer identification number

20 Doing business as (DBA) name (see instructions)	Employer identification number

21 Address (number, street, and apt. or suite no.)	**22** Occupation, profession, or business

23 City	**24** State	**25** ZIP code	**26** Country (if not U.S.)

27 Alien identification: **a** Describe identification ▶ ....
    b Issued by   **c** Number

Item You Should Note

Clerks of Federal or State courts must now file Form 8300 if more than $10,000 in cash is received as bail for an individual(s) charged with certain criminal offenses. For these purposes, a clerk includes the clerk's office or any other office, department, division, branch, or unit of the court that is authorized to receive bail. If a person receives bail on behalf of a clerk, the clerk is treated as receiving the bail.

If multiple payments are made in cash to satisfy bail and the initial payment does not exceed $10,000, the initial payment and subsequent payments must be aggregated and the information return must be filed by the 15th day after receipt of the payment that causes the aggregate amount to exceed $10,000 in cash. In such cases, the reporting requirement can be satisfied either by sending a single written statement with an aggregate amount listed or by furnishing a copy of each Form 8300 relating to that payer. Payments made to satisfy separate bail requirements are not required to be aggregated. See Treasury Regulations section 1.6050I-2.

Casinos must file Form 8300 for nongaming activities (restaurants, shops, etc.).

General Instructions

Who must file.—Each person engaged in a trade or business who, in the course of that trade or business, receives more than $10,000 in cash in one transaction or in two or more related transactions, must file Form 8300. Any transactions conducted between a payer (or its agent) and the recipient in a 24-hour period are related transactions. Transactions are considered related even if they occur over a period of more than 24 hours if the recipient knows, or has reason to know, that each transaction is one of a series of connected transactions.

Keep a copy of each Form 8300 for 5 years from the date you file it.

Voluntary use of Form 8300.—Form 8300 may be filed voluntarily for any suspicious transaction (see **Definitions**), even if the total amount does not exceed $10,000.

Exceptions.—Cash is not required to be reported if it is received:

● By a financial institution required to file **Form 4789**, Currency Transaction Report.

● By a casino required to file (or exempt from filing) **Form 8362**, Currency Transaction Report by Casinos, if the cash is received as part of its gaming business.

● By an agent who receives the cash from a principal, if the agent uses all of the cash within 15 days in a second transaction that is reportable on Form 8300 or on Form 4789, and discloses all the information necessary to complete Part II of Form 8300 or Form 4789 to the recipient of the cash in the second transaction.

● In a transaction occurring entirely outside the United States. See **Pub. 1544**, Reporting Cash Payments Over $10,000 (Received in a Trade or Business),

regarding transactions occurring in Puerto Rico, the Virgin Islands, and territories and possessions of the United States.

● In a transaction that is not in the course of a person's trade or business.

When to file.—File Form 8300 by the 15th day after the date the cash was received. If that date falls on a Saturday, Sunday, or legal holiday, file the form on the next business day.

Where to file.—File the form with the Internal Revenue Service, Detroit Computing Center, P.O. Box 32621, Detroit, MI 48232, or hand carry it to your local IRS office.

Statement to be provided.—You must give a written statement to each person named on a required Form 8300 on or before January 31 of the year following the calendar year in which the cash is received. The statement must show the name, telephone number, and address of the information contact for the business, the aggregate amount of reportable cash received, and that the information was furnished to the IRS. Keep a copy of the statement for your records.

Multiple payments.—If you receive more than one cash payment for a single transaction or for related transactions, you must report the multiple payments any time you receive a total amount that exceeds $10,000 within any 12-month period. Submit the report within 15 days of the date you receive the payment that causes the total amount to exceed $10,000. If more than one report is required within 15 days, you may file a combined report. File the combined report no later than the date the earliest report, if filed separately, would have to be filed.

Taxpayer identification number (TIN).—You must furnish the correct TIN of the person or persons from whom you receive the cash and, if applicable, the person or persons on whose behalf the transaction is being conducted. **You may be subject to penalties for an incorrect or missing TIN.**

The TIN for an individual (including a sole proprietorship) is the individual's social security number (SSN). For certain resident aliens who are not eligible to get an SSN and nonresident aliens who are required to file tax returns, it is an IRS Individual Taxpayer Identification Number (ITIN). For other persons, including corporations, partnerships, and estates, it is the employer identification number.

If you have requested but are not able to get a TIN for one or more of the parties to a transaction within 15 days following the transaction, file the report and attach a statement explaining why the TIN is not included.

Exception: You are not required to provide the TIN of a person who is a nonresident alien individual or a foreign organization **if** that person does not have income effectively connected with the conduct of a U.S. trade or business **and** does not have an office or place of business, or fiscal or paying agent, in the United States. See Pub. 1544 for more information.

Penalties.—You may be subject to penalties if you fail to file a correct and complete Form 8300 on time and you cannot show that the failure was due to reasonable cause. You may also be subject to penalties if you fail to furnish timely a correct and complete statement to each person named in a required report. A minimum penalty of $25,000 may be imposed if the failure is due to an intentional disregard of the cash reporting requirements.

Penalties may also be imposed for causing, or attempting to cause, a trade or business to fail to file a required report; for causing, or attempting to cause, a trade or business to file a required report containing a material omission or misstatement of fact; or for structuring, or attempting to structure, transactions to avoid the reporting requirements. These violations may also be subject to criminal prosecution which, upon conviction, may result in imprisonment of up to 5 years or fines of up to $250,000 for individuals and $500,000 for corporations or both.

Definitions

Cash.—The term "cash" means the following:

● U.S. and foreign coin and currency received in any transaction.

● A cashier's check, money order, bank draft, or traveler's check having a face amount of $10,000 or less that is received in a **designated reporting transaction** (defined below), or that is received in any transaction in which the recipient knows that the instrument is being used in an attempt to avoid the reporting of the transaction under section 6050I.

Note: Cash does not include a check drawn on the payer's own account, such as a personal check, regardless of the amount.

Designated reporting transaction.—A retail sale (or the receipt of funds by a broker or other intermediary in connection with a retail sale) of a consumer durable, a collectible, or a travel or entertainment activity.

Retail sale.—Any sale (whether or not the sale is for resale or for any other purpose) made in the course of a trade or business if that trade or business principally consists of making sales to ultimate consumers.

Consumer durable.—An item of tangible personal property of a type that, under ordinary usage, can reasonably be expected to remain useful for at least 1 year, and that has a sales price of more than $10,000.

Collectible.—Any work of art, rug, antique, metal, gem, stamp, coin, etc.

Travel or entertainment activity.—An item of travel or entertainment that pertains to a single trip or event if the combined sales price of the item and all other items relating to the same trip or event that are sold in the same transaction (or related transactions) exceeds $10,000.

Exceptions.—A cashier's check, money order, bank draft, or traveler's check is not considered received in a designated reporting transaction if it constitutes the proceeds of a bank loan or if it is received as a payment on certain promissory notes, installment sales contracts, or down payment plans. See Pub. 1544 for more information.

Person.—An individual, corporation, partnership, trust, estate, association, or company.

Recipient.—The person receiving the cash. Each branch or other unit of a person's trade or business is considered a separate recipient unless the branch receiving the cash (or a central office linking the branches), knows or has reason to know the identity of payers making cash payments to other branches.

Transaction.—Includes the purchase of property or services, the payment of debt, the exchange of a negotiable instrument for cash, and the receipt of cash to be held in escrow or trust. A single transaction may not be broken into multiple transactions to avoid reporting.

Suspicious transaction.—A transaction in which it appears that a person is attempting to cause Form 8300 not to be filed, or to file a false or incomplete form. The term also includes any transaction in which there is an indication of possible illegal activity.

Specific Instructions

You must complete all parts. However, you may skip Part II if the individual named in Part I is conducting the transaction on his or her behalf only.

Item 1.—If you are amending a prior report, check box 1a. Complete the appropriate items with the correct or amended information only. Complete all of Part IV. Staple a copy of the original report to the amended report.

To voluntarily report a suspicious transaction (see **Definitions**), check box 1b. You may also telephone your local IRS Criminal Investigation Division or call 1-800-800-2877.

Part I

Item 2.—If two or more individuals conducted the transaction you are reporting, check the box and complete Part I for any one of the individuals. Provide the same information for the other individual(s) on the back of the form. If more than three individuals are involved, provide the same information on additional sheets of paper and attach them to this form.

Item 6.—Enter the taxpayer identification number (TIN) of the individual named. See **Taxpayer identification number (TIN)** under **General Instructions** for more information.

Item 8.—Enter eight numerals for the date of birth of the individual named. For example, if the individual's birth date is July 6, 1960, enter 07 06 1960.

Item 13.—Fully describe the nature of the occupation, profession, or business (for example, "plumber," "attorney," or "automobile dealer"). Do not use general or

nondescriptive terms such as "businessman" or "self-employed."

Item 14.—You must verify the name and address of the named individual(s). Verification must be made by examination of a document normally accepted as a means of identification when cashing checks (for example, a driver's license, passport, alien registration card, or other official document). In item 14a, enter the type of document examined. In item 14b, identify the issuer of the document. In item 14c, enter the document's number. For example, if the individual has a Utah driver's license, enter "driver's license" in item 14a, "Utah" in item 14b, and the number appearing on the license in item 14c.

Part II

Item 15.—If the transaction is being conducted on behalf of more than one person (including husband and wife or parent and child), check the box and complete Part II for any one of the persons. Provide the same information for the other person(s) on the back of the form. If more than three persons are involved, provide the same information on additional sheets of paper and attach them to this form.

Items 16 through 19.—If the person on whose behalf the transaction is being conducted is an individual, complete items 16, 17, and 18. Enter his or her TIN in item 19. If the individual is a sole proprietor and has an employer identification number (EIN), you must enter both the SSN and EIN in item 19. If the person is an organization, put its name as shown on required tax filings in item 16 and its EIN in item 19.

Item 20.—If a sole proprietor or organization named in items 16 through 18 is doing business under a name other than that entered in item 16 (e.g., a "trade" or "doing business as (DBA)" name), enter it here.

Item 27.—If the person is **NOT** required to furnish a TIN (see **Taxpayer identification number (TIN)** under **General Instructions**), complete this item. Enter a description of the type of official document issued to that person in item 27a (for example, "passport"), the country that issued the document in item 27b, and the document's number in item 27c.

Part III

Item 28.—Enter the date you received the cash. If you received the cash in more than one payment, enter the date you received the payment that caused the combined amount to exceed $10,000. See **Multiple payments** under **General Instructions** for more information.

Item 30.—Check this box if the amount shown in item 29 was received in more than one payment (for example, as installment payments or payments on related transactions).

Item 31.—Enter the total price of the property, services, amount of cash exchanged, etc. (for example, the total cost

of a vehicle purchased, cost of catering service, exchange of currency) if different from the amount shown in item 29.

Item 32.—Enter the dollar amount of each form of cash received. Show foreign currency amounts in U.S. dollar equivalent at a fair market rate of exchange available to the public. **The sum of the amounts must equal item 29.** For cashier's check, money order, bank draft, or traveler's check, provide the name of the issuer and the serial number of each instrument. Names of all issuers and all serial numbers involved must be provided. If necessary, provide this information on additional sheets of paper and attach them to this form.

Item 33.—Check the appropriate box(es) that describe the transaction. If the transaction is not specified in boxes a–i, check box j and briefly describe the transaction (for example, car lease, boat lease, house lease, aircraft rental).

Part IV

Item 36.—If you are a sole proprietorship, you must enter your SSN. If your business also has an EIN, you must provide the EIN as well. All other business entities must enter an EIN.

Item 41.—Fully describe the nature of your business, for example, "attorney," "jewelry dealer." Do not use general or nondescriptive terms such as "business" or "store."

Item 42.—This form must be signed by an individual who has been authorized to do so for the business that received the cash.

Paperwork Reduction Act Notice

The requested information is useful in criminal, tax, and regulatory investigations, for instance, by directing the Federal Government's attention to unusual or questionable transactions. Trades or businesses are required to provide the information under 26 U.S.C. 6050I.

You are not required to provide the information requested on a form that is subject to the Paperwork Reduction Act unless the form displays a valid OMB control number. Books or records relating to a form or its instructions must be retained as long as their contents may become material in the administration of any Internal Revenue law. Generally, tax returns and return information are confidential, as required by Code section 6103.

The time needed to complete this form will vary depending on individual circumstances. The estimated average time is 21 minutes. If you have comments concerning the accuracy of this time estimate or suggestions for making this form simpler, you can write to the Tax Forms Committee, Western Area Distribution Center, Rancho Cordova, CA 95743-0001. DO NOT send this form to this office. Instead, see **Where To File** on page 3.

Form **8850**
(Rev. November 1998)
Department of the Treasury
Internal Revenue Service

Pre-Screening Notice and Certification Request for the Work Opportunity and Welfare-to-Work Credits

▶ See separate instructions.

OMB No. 1545-1500

Job applicant: Fill in the lines below and check any boxes that apply. Complete only this side.

Your name _____   Social security number ▶ _____

Street address where you live _____

City or town, state, and ZIP code _____

Telephone no. (_____) _____ - _____

If you are under age 25, enter your date of birth (month, day, year) _____ / _____ / _____

Work Opportunity Credit

1 ☐ Check here if you received a conditional certification from the state employment security agency (SESA) or a participating local agency for the work opportunity credit.

2 ☐ Check here if **any** of the following statements apply to you.

- I am a member of a family that has received assistance from Aid to Families with Dependent Children (AFDC) or its successor program, Temporary Assistance for Needy Families (TANF), for any 9 months during the last 18 months.

- I am a veteran and a member of a family that received food stamps for at least a 3-month period within the last 15 months.

- I was referred here by a rehabilitation agency approved by the state or the Department of Veterans Affairs.

- I am at least age 18 but **not** over age 24 and I am a member of a family that:
  a Received food stamps for the last 6 months, OR
  b Received food stamps for at least 3 of the last 5 months, BUT is no longer eligible to receive them.

- Within the past year, I was convicted of a felony or released from prison for a felony AND during the last 6 months I was a member of a low-income family.

- I received supplemental security income (SSI) benefits for any month ending within the last 60 days.

Welfare-to-Work Credit

3 ☐ Check here if you received a conditional certification from the SESA or a participating local agency for the welfare-to-work credit.

4 ☐ Check here if you are a member of a family that:
- Received AFDC or TANF payments for at least the last 18 months, OR
- Received AFDC or TANF payments for any 18 months beginning after August 5, 1997, OR
- Stopped being eligible for AFDC or TANF payments after August 5, 1997, because Federal or state law limited the maximum time those payments could be made.

All Applicants

Under penalties of perjury, I declare that I gave the above information to the employer on or before the day I was offered a job, and it is, to the best of my knowledge, true, correct, and complete.

Job applicant's signature ▶ _____   Date _____ / _____ / _____

For Privacy Act and Paperwork Reduction Act Notice, see page 2.   Cat. No. 22851L   Form **8850** (Rev. 11-98)

For Employer's Use Only

Employer's name _____ Telephone no. ( ) - _____ EIN ▶ _____

Street address _____

City or town, state, and ZIP code _____

Person to contact, if different from above _____ Telephone no. ( ) - _____

Street address _____

City or town, state, and ZIP code _____

If, based on the individual's age and home address, he or she is a member of group 4 or 6 (as described under **Members of Targeted Groups** in the separate instructions), enter that group number (4 or 6) . . . . ▶ _____

DATE APPLICANT: Gave information / /   Was offered job / /   Was hired / /   Started job / /

Under penalties of perjury, I declare that I completed this form on or before the day a job was offered to the applicant and that the information I have furnished is, to the best of my knowledge, true, correct, and complete. Based on the information the job applicant furnished on page 1, I believe the individual is a member of a targeted group or a long-term family assistance recipient. I hereby request a certification that the individual is a member of a targeted group or a long-term family assistance recipient.

Employer's signature ▶ _____   Title _____   Date / /

Privacy Act and Paperwork Reduction Act Notice

Section references are to the Internal Revenue Code.

Section 51(d)(12) permits a prospective employer to request the applicant to complete this form and give it to the prospective employer. The information will be used by the employer to complete the employer's Federal tax return. Completion of this form is voluntary and may assist members of targeted groups and long-term family assistance recipients in securing employment. Routine uses of this form include giving it to the state employment security agency (SESA), which will contact appropriate sources to confirm that the applicant is a member of a targeted group or a long-term family

assistance recipient. This form may also be given to the Internal Revenue Service for administration of the Internal Revenue laws, to the Department of Justice for civil and criminal litigation, to the Department of Labor for oversight of the certifications performed by the SESA, and to cities, states, and the District of Columbia for use in administering their tax laws.

You are not required to provide the information requested on a form that is subject to the Paperwork Reduction Act unless the form displays a valid OMB control number. Books or records relating to a form or its instructions must be retained as long as their contents may become material in the administration of any Internal Revenue law. Generally, tax returns and return information are confidential, as required by section 6103.

The time needed to complete and file this form will vary depending on individual circumstances. The estimated average time is:

Recordkeeping . . . . 2 hr., 47 min.
Learning about the law or the form . . . . 28 min.
Preparing and sending this form to the SESA . . . . 36 min.

If you have comments concerning the accuracy of these time estimates or suggestions for making this form simpler, we would be happy to hear from you. You can write to the Tax Forms Committee, Western Area Distribution Center, Rancho Cordova, CA 95743-0001.

DO NOT send this form to this address. Instead, see **When and Where To File** in the separate instructions.

Instructions for Form 8850

Department of the Treasury
Internal Revenue Service

(Revised November 1998)

Pre-Screening Notice and Certification Request for the Work Opportunity and Welfare-to-Work Credits

Section references are to the Internal Revenue Code unless otherwise noted.

General Instructions

A Change To Note

The Tax and Trade Relief Extension Act of 1998 extended the work opportunity credit and the welfare-to-work credit to cover individuals who begin work for the employer before July 1, 1999.

Purpose of Form

Employers use Form 8850 to pre-screen and to make a written request to a state employment security agency (SESA) to certify an individual as:

- A member of a targeted group for purposes of qualifying for the work opportunity credit, or
- A long-term family assistance recipient for purposes of qualifying for the welfare-to-work credit.

Submitting Form 8850 to the SESA is but one step in the employer qualifying for the work opportunity credit or the welfare-to-work credit. The SESA must certify the job applicant is a member of a targeted group or is a long-term family assistance recipient. After starting work, the employee must meet the minimum number-of-hours-worked requirement for the work opportunity credit or the minimum number-of-hours, number-of-days requirement for the welfare-to-work credit. The employer may elect to take the applicable credit by filing **Form 5884**, Work Opportunity Credit, or **Form 8861**, Welfare-to-Work Credit.

Who Should Complete and Sign the Form

The job applicant gives information to the employer on or before the day a job offer is made. This information is entered on Form 8850. Based on the applicant's information, the employer determines whether or not he or she believes the applicant is a member of a targeted group (as defined under **Members of Targeted Groups** below) or a long-term family assistance recipient (as defined under **Welfare-to-Work Job Applicants** on page 2). If the employer believes the applicant is a member of a targeted group or a long-term family assistance recipient, the employer completes the rest of the form no later than the day the job offer is made. Both the job applicant and the employer must sign Form 8850 no later than the date for submitting the form to the SESA.

Instructions for Employer

When and Where To File

Do not file Form 8850 with the Internal Revenue Service. Instead, send it to the work opportunity tax credit (WOTC) coordinator for your SESA no later than the 21st day after the job applicant begins work for you.

To get the name, address, and phone and fax numbers of the WOTC coordinator for your SESA, visit the Department of Labor, Employment and Training Administration (ETA) web site at **www.ttrc.doleta.gov/common/directories**, or call **202-219-9092** (not a toll-free number).

Additional Requirements for Certification

In addition to filing Form 8850, you must complete and send to your state's WOTC coordinator **either:**

- **ETA Form 9062,** Conditional Certification Form, if the job applicant received this form from a participating agency (e.g., the Jobs Corps), **or**
- **ETA Form 9061,** Individual Characteristics Form, if the job applicant did not receive a conditional certification.

Using the Department of Labor's fax on demand service, you can get a directory of WOTC coordinators and ETA Form 9061 by calling **703-365-0768** (not a toll-free number) from the telephone connected to your fax machine and following the prompts. You can also get ETA Form 9061 from your local public employment service office, or you can download it from the ETA web site at **www.doleta.gov**.

Recordkeeping

Keep copies of Forms 8850, along with any transmittal letters that you submit to your SESA, as long as they may be needed for the administration of the Internal Revenue Code provisions relating to the work opportunity credit and the welfare-to-work credit. Records that support these credits usually must be kept for 3 years from the date any income tax return claiming the credits is due or filed, whichever is later.

Members of Targeted Groups

A job applicant may be certified as a member of a targeted group if he or she is:

1. A member of a family receiving assistance under a state plan approved under part A of title IV of the Social Security Act relating to Aid to Families with Dependent Children (AFDC) or its successor program, Temporary Assistance for Needy Families (TANF). The assistance must be received for any 9 months during the 18-month period that ends on the hiring date.

2. A veteran who is a member of a family receiving assistance under the Food Stamp program for generally at least a 3-month period during the 15-month period ending on the hiring date. See section 51(d)(3).

To be considered a **veteran**, the applicant must:
- Have served on active duty (not including training) in the Armed Forces of the United States for more than 180 days OR have been discharged for a service-connected disability, AND
- Not have a period of active duty (not including training) of more than 90 days that ended during the 60-day period ending on the hiring date.

3. An ex-felon who:
- Has been convicted of a felony under any Federal or state law,
- Is hired not more than 1 year after the conviction or release from prison for that felony, AND
- Is a member of a family that had income on an annual basis of 70% or less of the Bureau of Labor Statistics lower living standard during the 6 months preceding the earlier of the month the income determination occurs or the month in which the hiring date occurs.

Cat. No. 24833J

4. An individual who is at least age 18 but not yet age 25 on the hiring date and lives in an empowerment zone or enterprise community.

The Secretary of Housing and Urban Development (HUD) designated parts of the following cities as urban empowerment zones:

- Atlanta, GA (9.29 square miles)
- Baltimore, MD (6.8 square miles)
- Philadelphia, PA/Camden, NJ (4.4 square miles)
- Chicago, IL (14.33 square miles)
- Detroit, MI (18.3 square miles)
- New York City, NY (the Bronx and Manhattan) (7.6 square miles)

The Secretary of Agriculture (USDA) designated the following rural empowerment zones:

- The Kentucky Highlands (part of Wayne and all of Clinton and Jackson counties)
- Mid-Delta, Mississippi (parts of Bolivar, Holmes, Humphreys, Leflore, Sunflower, and Washington counties)
- Rio Grande Valley, Texas (parts of Cameron, Hidalgo, Starr, and Willacy counties)

Under section 1400, parts of Washington, DC, are treated as an empowerment zone. For more details, see Notice 98-57, 1998-47 I.R.B. 9.

There are 64 urban and 30 rural enterprise communities located in 35 states. There are no empowerment zones or enterprise communities in Puerto Rico, Guam, or any U.S. possession.

You may call HUD at **1-800-998-9999** for information on the six urban empowerment zones and Washington, DC. You may call the USDA at **1-800-645-4712** about the rural empowerment zones. On the Internet, you can visit the EZ/EC Home Page at **www.ezec.gov**. Your SESA has information on where the enterprise communities are located. Also, many enterprise communities have their own web sites.

5. An individual who has a physical or mental disability resulting in a substantial handicap to employment and who was referred to the employer upon completion of (or while receiving) rehabilitation services under a state plan of employment or a program approved by the Department of Veterans Affairs.

6. An individual who:

- Performs services for the employer between May 1 and September 15,
- Is age 16 but not yet age 18 on the hiring date (or if later, on May 1),
- Has never worked for the employer before, AND
- Lives in an empowerment zone or enterprise community.

7. An individual who:

- Is at least age 18 but not yet age 25 AND
- Is a member of a family that–

  a. Has received food stamps for the 6-month period ending on the hiring date OR

  b. Is no longer eligible for such assistance under section 6(o) of the Food Stamp Act of 1977 and the family received food stamps for at least 3 months of the 5-month period ending on the hiring date.

8. An individual who is receiving supplemental security income benefits under title XVI of the Social Security Act (including benefits of the type described in section 1616 of the Social Security Act or section 212 of Public Law 93-66) for any month ending within the 60-day period ending on the hiring date.

Welfare-to-Work Job Applicants

An individual may be certified as a long-term family assistance recipient if he or she is a member of a family that:

- Has received assistance payments from AFDC or TANF for at least 18 consecutive months ending on the hiring date, OR
- Receives assistance payments from AFDC or TANF for any 18 months (whether or not consecutive) beginning after August 5, 1997, OR
- After August 5, 1997, stops being eligible for assistance payments because Federal or state law limits the maximum period such assistance is payable, and the individual is hired not more than 2 years after such eligibility for assistance ends.

INDEX

SPHINX® PUBLISHING'S NATIONAL TITLES
Valid in All 50 States

LEGAL SURVIVAL IN BUSINESS

How to Form a Delaware Corporation from Any State	$24.95
How to Form a Limited Liability Company	$22.95
How to Form a Nevada Corporation from Any State	$24.95
How to Form a Nonprofit Corporation	$24.95
How to Form Your Own Corporation (3E)	$24.95
How to Form Your Own Partnership	$22.95
How to Register Your Own Copyright (3E)	$21.95
How to Register Your Own Trademark (3E)	$21.95
Most Valuable Business Legal Forms You'll Ever Need (2E)	$19.95
Most Valuable Corporate Forms You'll Ever Need (2E)	$24.95

LEGAL SURVIVAL IN COURT

Debtors' Rights (3E)	$14.95
Grandparents' Rights (3E)	$24.95
Help Your Lawyer Win Your Case (2E)	$14.95
Jurors' Rights (2E)	$12.95
Legal Research Made Easy (2E)	$14.95
Winning Your Personal Injury Claim (2E)	$24.95

LEGAL SURVIVAL IN REAL ESTATE

How to Buy a Condominium or Townhome	$19.95
How to Negotiate Real Estate Contracts (3E)	$18.95
How to Negotiate Real Estate Leases (3E)	$18.95

LEGAL SURVIVAL IN PERSONAL AFFAIRS

Como Hacer su Propio Testamento	$16.95
Guia de Inmigracion a Estados Unidos (2E)	$24.95
Como Solicitar su Propio Divorcio	$24.95
How to File Your Own Bankruptcy (4E)	$19.95
How to File Your Own Divorce (4E)	$24.95
How to Make Your Own Will (2E)	$16.95
How to Write Your Own Living Will (2E)	$16.95
How to Write Your Own Premarital Agreement (2E)	$21.95
How to Win Your Unemployment Compensation Claim	$19.95
Living Trusts and Simple Ways to Avoid Probate (2E)	$22.95
Most Valuable Personal Legal Forms You'll Ever Need	$19.95
Neighbor v. Neighbor (2E)	$16.95
The Nanny and Domestic Help Legal Kit	$22.95
The Power of Attorney Handbook (3E)	$19.95
Repair Your Own Credit and Deal with Debt	$18.95
Social Security Benefits Handbook (2E)	$16.95
Unmarried Parents' Rights	$19.95
U.S.A. Immigration Guide (3E)	$19.95
Your Right to Child Custody, Visitation and Support	$22.95

Legal Survival Guides are directly available from Sourcebooks, Inc., or from your local bookstores.
Prices are subject to change without notice.

For credit card orders call 1–800–432–7444, write P.O. Box 4410, Naperville, IL 60567-4410
or fax 630-961-2168

SPHINX® PUBLISHING ORDER FORM

Qty	ISBN	Title	Retail	Ext.
		SPHINX PUBLISHING NATIONAL TITLES		
	1-57248-148-X	Como Hacer su Propio Testamento	$16.95	
	1-57248-147-1	Como Solicitar su Propio Divorcio	$24.95	
	1-57071-342-1	Debtors' Rights (3E)	$14.95	
	1-57248-139-0	Grandparents' Rights (3E)	$24.95	
	1-57248-087-4	Guia de Inmigracion a Estados Unidos (2E)	$24.95	
	1-57248-103-X	Help Your Lawyer Win Your Case (2E)	$14.95	
	1-57071-164-X	How to Buy a Condominium or Townhome	$19.95	
	1-57071-223-9	How to File Your Own Bankruptcy (4E)	$19.95	
	1-57248-132-3	How to File Your Own Divorce (4E)	$24.95	
	1-57248-100-5	How to Form a DE Corporation from Any State	$24.95	
	1-57248-083-1	How to Form a Limited Liability Company	$22.95	
	1-57248-101-3	How to Form a NV Corporation from Any State	$24.95	
	1-57248-099-8	How to Form a Nonprofit Corporation	$24.95	
	1-57248-133-1	How to Form Your Own Corporation (3E)	$24.95	
	1-57071-343-X	How to Form Your Own Partnership	$22.95	
	1-57248-119-6	How to Make Your Own Will (2E)	$16.95	
	1-57071-331-6	How to Negotiate Real Estate Contracts (3E)	$18.95	
	1-57071-332-4	How to Negotiate Real Estate Leases (3E)	$18.95	
	1-57248-124-2	How to Register Your Own Copyright (3E)	$21.95	
	1-57248-104-8	How to Register Your Own Trademark (3E)	$21.95	
	1-57071-349-9	How to Win Your Unemployment Compensation Claim	$19.95	
	1-57248-118-8	How to Write Your Own Living Will (2E)	$16.95	
	1-57071-344-8	How to Write Your Own Premarital Agreement (2E)	$21.95	
	1-57071-333-2	Jurors' Rights (2E)	$12.95	
	1-57071-400-2	Legal Research Made Easy (2E)	$14.95	
	1-57071-336-7	Living Trusts and Simple Ways to Avoid Probate (2E)	$22.95	
	1-57071-345-6	Most Valuable Bus. Legal Forms You'll Ever Need (2E)	$19.95	
	1-57071-346-4	Most Valuable Corporate Forms You'll Ever Need (2E)	$24.95	
	1-57248-130-7	Most Valuable Personal Legal Forms You'll Ever Need	$19.95	
	1-57248-098-X	The Nanny and Domestic Help Legal Kit	$22.95	
	1-57248-089-0	Neighbor v. Neighbor (2E)	$16.95	
	1-57071-348-0	The Power of Attorney Handbook (3E)	$19.95	
	1-57071-337-5	Social Security Benefits Handbook (2E)	$16.95	
	1-57071-399-5	Unmarried Parents' Rights	$19.95	
	1-57071-354-5	U.S.A. Immigration Guide (3E)	$19.95	
	1-57248-138-2	Winning Your Personal Injury Claim (2E)	$24.95	
	1-57248-097-1	Your Right to Child Custody, Visitation and Support	$22.95	
		CALIFORNIA TITLES		
	1-57248-150-1	CA Power of Attorney Handbook (2E)	$18.95	
	1-57248-151-X	How to File for Divorce in CA (3E)	$26.95	
	1-57071-356-1	How to Make a CA Will	$16.95	
	1-57248-145-5	How to Probate and Settle an Estate in California	$26.95	
	1-57248-146-3	How to Start a Business in CA	$18.95	
	1-57071-358-8	How to Win in Small Claims Court in CA	$16.95	
	1-57071-359-6	Landlords' Rights and Duties in CA	$21.95	
		FLORIDA TITLES		
	1-57071-363-4	Florida Power of Attorney Handbook (2E)	$16.95	
	1-57248-093-9	How to File for Divorce in FL (6E)	$24.95	
	1-57071-380-4	How to Form a Corporation in FL (4E)	$24.95	
	1-57248-086-6	How to Form a Limited Liability Co. in FL	$22.95	
	1-57071-401-0	How to Form a Partnership in FL	$22.95	
	1-57248-113-7	How to Make a FL Will (6E)	$16.95	
	1-57248-088-2	How to Modify Your FL Divorce Judgment (4E)	$24.95	

Form Continued on Following Page   **SUBTOTAL**

SPHINX® PUBLISHING ORDER FORM

Qty	ISBN	Title	Retail	Ext.
_____	1-57248-081-5	How to Start a Business in FL (5E)	$16.95	_____
_____	1-57071-362-6	How to Win in Small Claims Court in FL (6E)	$16.95	_____
_____	1-57248-123-4	Landlords' Rights and Duties in FL (8E)	$21.95	_____
GEORGIA TITLES				
_____	1-57248-137-4	How to File for Divorce in GA (4E)	$21.95	_____
_____	1-57248-075-0	How to Make a GA Will (3E)	$16.95	_____
_____	1-57248-140-4	How to Start a Business in Georgia (2E)	$16.95	_____
ILLINOIS TITLES				
_____	1-57071-405-3	How to File for Divorce in IL (2E)	$21.95	_____
_____	1-57071-415-0	How to Make an IL Will (2E)	$16.95	_____
_____	1-57071-416-9	How to Start a Business in IL (2E)	$16.95	_____
_____	1-57248-078-5	Landlords' Rights & Duties in IL	$21.95	_____
MASSACHUSETTS TITLES				
_____	1-57248-128-5	How to File for Divorce in MA (3E)	$24.95	_____
_____	1-57248-115-3	How to Form a Corporation in MA	$24.95	_____
_____	1-57248-108-0	How to Make a MA Will (2E)	$16.95	_____
_____	1-57248-106-4	How to Start a Business in MA (2E)	$16.95	_____
_____	1-57248-107-2	Landlords' Rights and Duties in MA (2E)	$21.95	_____
MICHIGAN TITLES				
_____	1-57071-409-6	How to File for Divorce in MI (2E)	$21.95	_____
_____	1-57248-077-7	How to Make a MI Will (2E)	$16.95	_____
_____	1-57071-407-X	How to Start a Business in MI (2E)	$16.95	_____
MINNESOTA TITLES				
_____	1-57248-142-0	How to File for Divorce in MN	$21.95	_____
NEW YORK TITLES				
_____	1-57248-141-2	How to File for Divorce in NY (2E)	$26.95	_____
_____	1-57248-105-6	How to Form a Corporation in NY	$24.95	_____
_____	1-57248-095-5	How to Make a NY Will (2E)	$16.95	_____
_____	1-57071-185-2	How to Start a Business in NY	$16.95	_____
_____	1-57071-187-9	How to Win in Small Claims Court in NY	$16.95	_____
_____	1-57071-186-0	Landlords' Rights and Duties in NY	$21.95	_____

Qty	ISBN	Title	Retail	Ext.
_____	1-57071-188-7	New York Power of Attorney Handbook	$19.95	_____
_____	1-57248-122-6	Tenants' Rights in NY	$21..95	_____
NORTH CAROLINA TITLES				
_____	1-57071-326-X	How to File for Divorce in NC (2E)	$22.95	_____
_____	1-57248-129-3	How to Make a NC Will (3E)	$16.95	_____
_____	1-57248-096-3	How to Start a Business in NC (2E)	$16.95	_____
_____	1-57248-091-2	Landlords' Rights & Duties in NC	$21.95	_____
OHIO TITLES				
_____	1-57248-102-1	How to File for Divorce in OH	$24.95	_____
PENNSYLVANIA TITLES				
_____	1-57248-127-7	How to File for Divorce in PA (2E)	$24.95	_____
_____	1-57248-094-7	How to Make a PA Will (2E)	$16.95	_____
_____	1-57248-112-9	How to Start a Business in PA (2E)	$18.95	_____
_____	1-57071-179-8	Landlords' Rights and Duties in PA	$19.95	_____
TEXAS TITLES				
_____	1-57071-330-8	How to File for Divorce in TX (2E)	$21.95	_____
_____	1-57248-114-5	How to Form a Corporation in TX (2E)	$24.95	_____
_____	1-57071-417-7	How to Make a TX Will (2E)	$16.95	_____
_____	1-57071-418-5	How to Probate an Estate in TX (2E)	$22.95	_____
_____	1-57071-365-0	How to Start a Business in TX (2E)	$16.95	_____
_____	1-57248-111-0	How to Win in Small Claims Court in TX (2E)	$16.95	_____
_____	1-57248-110-2	Landlords' Rights and Duties in TX (2E)	$21.95	_____

SUBTOTAL THIS PAGE _____

SUBTOTAL PREVIOUS PAGE _____

Shipping — $5.00 for 1st book, $1.00 each additional _____

Illinois residents add 6.75% sales tax _____

Connecticut residents add 6.00% sales tax _____

TOTAL _____

To order, call Sourcebooks at 1-800-432-7444 or FAX (630) 961-2168 (Bookstores, libraries, wholesalers—please call for discount)

Prices are subject to change without notice.